PRODUCTIVITY
Prospects for Growth

PRODUCTIVITY
Prospects for Growth

Edited by
Jerome M. Rosow

Van Nostrand Reinhold / Work in America Institute Series

VNR
VAN NOSTRAND REINHOLD COMPANY
NEW YORK CINCINNATI ATLANTA DALLAS SAN FRANCISCO
LONDON TORONTO MELBOURNE

Van Nostrand Reinhold Company Regional Offices:
New York Cincinnati Atlanta Dallas San Francisco

Van Nostrand Reinhold Company International Offices:
London Toronto Melbourne

Library of Congress Catalog Card Number: 80-22096
ISBN: 0-442-29326-7

Manufactured in the United States of America

Published by Van Nostrand Reinhold Company
135 West 50th Street, New York, N.Y. 10020

Published simultaneously in Canada by Van Nostrand Reinhold Ltd.

15 14 13 12 11 10 9 8 7 6 5 4 3 2 1

Library of Congress Cataloging in Publication Data

Main entry under title:

Productivity: prospects for growth

(Van Nostrand Reinhold/Work in America Institute series)
Includes index.
1. Industrial productivity—United States—Addresses, essays, lectures. I. Rosow, Jerome M. II. Series.
HC110.I52P76 338'.06'0973 80-22096
ISBN 0-442-29326-7

Van Nostrand Reinhold/Work in America Institute series

Practical Management for Productivity, by *John R. Hinrichs*
Work in America: The Decade Ahead, edited by *Clark Kerr* and *Jerome M. Rosow*
Young Programs for Older Workers, by *Beverly Jacobson*
Productivity: Prospects for Growth, edited by *Jerome M. Rosow*

VNR/WORK IN AMERICA INSTITUTE SERIES

The VNR/Work in America Institute Series is designed to provide practical insight into new and better ways to advance productivity and the quality of working life. The objective is to create heightened awareness of the opportunities for an enriched work life that can exist in innovative organizations, and to reveal the benefits of linking people and production in a common goal, through clearer understanding of the key factors contributing to worker output and job satisfaction.

The Series will provide guidance on a number of concerns that influence work performance, not only in today's work environment, but also in the even more complex world of work that lies ahead. Titles in the World of Work Series will focus on five fundamental issues affecting the work community: (1) *The quality of working life,* exploring opportunity, recognition, participation, and rewards for employees to optimize their involvement in and contribution to the work organization; (2) *Productivity,* focusing on the human factors in the productivity equation, to increase both individual and organizational output through more effective use of human resources; (3) *Education and the world of work,* discussing ways to improve the match between the entry-level worker and the job, by building bridges from education to the world of work; (4) *Employee-management cooperation,* recognizing that employees contribute important know-how and ingenuity to increase output, reduce waste, maintain product quality, and improve morale; and (5) *National labor force policy,* examining policies of the United States and other industrialized nations as they affect productivity and the quality of working life.

Preface

Productivity: Prospects for Growth represents an original effort by the Work in America Institute to examine the prospects for U.S. productivity growth from the perspective of a variety of experts. All fifteen chapters, commissioned under a grant from the Ford Foundation, were written especially for this book. Each author speaks from his own experience—and most are optimistic and positive in their analyses and proposals for the future.

As editor of this volume I am deeply indebted to a number of my associates. Dr. Matthew Radom served as liaison with each of the contributing authors in his characteristically effective way. Robert Zager prepared the initial version of the introduction with insight and clarity. Bea Walfish edited each contribution and worked closely with me to produce the final version. Frances Harte's assistance through all stages of production was invaluable.

This represents the fourth volume in the Van Nostrand Reinhold/ Work in America series. We believe it is timely, original, and pertinent to the needs of our society in a period characterized by hesitation and doubt in seeking solutions to the productivity problem.

—Jerome M. Rosow

Contents

Introduction

by Jerome M. Rosow
President, Work in America Institute, Inc.

Productivity has become the buzzword of our times. Few agree upon the definition of productivity, but everyone is certain of one thing—the more productivity the better. Shocked and confused by the declining rate of productivity growth, and now by the actual decline of U.S. productivity, the nation is searching for answers—and action. Action, however, first requires an understanding of the issues. This brings us clearly to the purpose of this volume of contributed papers, each of which is targeted toward a portion of the productivity problem. Taken as a whole, this book analyzes the reasons for the decline, postulates solutions, and provides some original ideas for new policies and programs to improve productivity in the 1980s.

First and foremost, the authors of this book agree that productivity is a complex concept, and reflects a variety of factors acting together to increase the value of output faster than the cost of input. The public debate too often has become mired in the issue of the relative importance of each factor—and often in an oversimplified attempt to fix upon a single dominant one. In comparing the roles played by the traditional threesome—money, management, and personnel—money usually heads the list. Thus, capital investment and technology, both highly significant elements in sustaining productivity at enterprise, industry, or national level, have attracted the lion's share of attention.

The contributors to this volume accept the importance of capital factors, yet they differ as to the most effective means of increasing the flow of investment in a manner consistent with other national needs and goals. Capital investment, technology, and research and development receive careful analysis throughout the book. The authors are attentive to their importance—but they are not single-minded or narrowly directed to one-track solutions.

Management is a more subtle issue. It has always been implicit in the productivity equation, especially at the enterprise level. In this book, however—particularly throughout part II—it receives close attention. Without benefit of consultation among themselves, many of the authors point to the need for leadership and the opportunity for chief executives to meet the productivity issue head-on and to succeed. This is an inner-directed concept, one which accepts the competitive system and has confidence in the power of leadership to achieve change within the enterprise itself.

Personnel—or the human factor in the productivity challenge—is the principal focus of part III. A work force that is more highly educated and more diverse than ever before offers organizations a rich pool of talent. At the same time, however, these workers tend to have higher expectations for, among other things, the opportunity to use their skills and to develop their individual abilities on the job. Because these new breed workers are no longer willing to follow orders blindly, they are more difficult to manage but, managed wisely, they have much to offer organizations in terms of initiative and resourcefulness. This book points to an increasing awareness of the significance of the human factor to productivity and to the need for using it well.

Finally, the real and lasting answer to achieving a satisfactory rate of productivity growth lies in the ability to bring all of these factors into harmonious interaction. Capital investment, with its innovations, new technology, and long-term commitment to research and development, is generated by a free and profitable economy with reasonably balanced growth. But a profitable economy cannot depend on government action alone; it leans heavily as well on sound management that is committed to productivity and to the improvement of quality as an element in productivity growth. In the same sense, the human talent within every organization holds the potential for ever-increasing contributions to the efficiency of the enterprise. But as the authors stress again and again, the participation of employees must be increased, a sense of fairness maintained, and a balance of interests assured.

These chapters present a feast of ideas. The contributors do not pretend to offer one easy answer to the productivity question, but each has some thoughtful and provocative ideas. Not all will suit every reader's taste, of course. In the final analysis, the reader alone must select, must critique, and—most important of all—must apply the appropriate solutions to his or her particular situation.

Trends and Prospects

The first part of the book, "Trends and Prospects," considers the prospects for U.S. productivity growth in terms of economic history (Fabricant); sectoral-level analysis with special attention to the impact of the high price of energy (Jorgenson); national and industry-wide productivity measurements (Mark); the impact of international trade (Samuel); and, finally, the effect of unions on productivity (Oswald).

Dr. Solomon Fabricant's opening chapter is a comprehensive sweep of the history of American productivity with an eye to both the present and the future. In a broad but insightful look at the complexities of the productivity-growth issue, Fabricant defines critical external factors, including savings, quality of labor, the efficient use of capital and labor, and incentives to work. The competing objectives at the national level are placed in perspective to clarify the issues. Finally, Fabricant goes beyond the data and their inferences to propose a series of far-ranging policies to stimulate productivity growth in the decade ahead. He concludes on an optimistic, albeit cautious, note for the future.

Whereas the President's Economic Report (1980) came up empty with regard to the effect of energy prices on productivity, Dr. Dale Jorgenson has devised an original sectoral analysis to assess the effects of capital, labor, energy, and material inputs plus the level of technology on the price of outputs, and concludes that the single most important cause of declining productivity growth since 1973 is the staggering rise in the price of energy.

Jorgenson's econometric model is elaborated and analyzed across 35 industries that constitute the producing sector of the United States. His model specifically associates slower growth in productivity with higher energy prices in 29 of these 35 industries.

Jorgenson offers a dismal prognosis for the American economy.

He forecasts further declines in productivity growth for a wide range of U.S. industries and for the U.S. economy as a whole and projects a further slowdown in U.S. economic growth if there are no reductions in the cost of inputs. His recommended remedy is a change in tax policy: proposed cuts in taxes on income from capital to reduce the price of capital input, and reduced payroll taxes to lower the price of labor input. Jorgenson's cogent analysis of the dampening effect of energy costs would, it seems, lead one to consider ways and means of restraining further price inflation, by reducing imports, increasing domestic production, developing alternate forms of energy, and restraining consumption, rather than limiting one's options to the tax route alone. Still, Jorgenson has done a major job in placing the onus on energy prices, which remain inextricable from the issue of economic growth with efficiency.

Jerome Mark, who as assistant commissioner of productivity and technology in the U.S. Department of Labor is in charge of national productivity statistics, is clearly the nation's expert on productivity measurement. A careful reading of Mark's chapter, which addresses the various measurement concepts and techniques, is a basic requirement to understanding measurement achievements, problems, and improvements currently under way.

In characteristically objective fashion, Mark examines the combined input measurements of leading private researchers, including John Kendrick, Edward Denison, Dale Jorgenson, and Frank Gollop. Stated in practical terms, Mark is not an idealist who expects productivity measurement to achieve statistical infallibility. Rather, he takes a practical view of the question of precision in relation to purpose and use.

Howard Samuel heads the AFL/CIO Industrial Union Department and recently served as U.S. deputy undersecretary of labor for international labor affairs. Essentially, Samuel argues that international trade does not necessarily increase productivity. In fact, he posits that certain types of international trade can be harmful to the United States, specifically: (1) disruptive fair trade, (2) unfair trade based on labor exploitation, and (3) unfair trade based upon violation of international agreements.

Samuel favors restriction of imports in "sunset" industries to allow time for adjustment by workers, companies, and communities. The best policy would be an "adequate degree" of import restraint rather than unduly severe restraint, a proposal that is both moderate and gradual. He opposes giving advantages to foreign industries that thrive on child labor, forced labor, or manifestly dangerous labor conditions. In sum, he conceives of unfair trade practices as counterproductive for the United States and fears the expansion of such practices in the 1980s. Finally, Samuel denies that slow productivity growth in the United States is responsible for our declining international competitiveness or the fall in the dollar's value. Instead, he points to our less vigorous innovation in recent years, for example, in consumer electronics, machine tools, and automobiles.

Rudy Oswald devotes his chapter to the thesis that union workers are much more productive than nonunion workers. He points to studies of specific unionized industries, such as construction and cement, which indicate that output per employee-hour rose with unionization.

On the other hand, Oswald attributes much of the slowdown in productivity growth to an understatement of output for nonmanufacturing firms—especially in construction and in finance, real estate, and other services. Searching for the true causes of a slower rate of productivity growth in the United States, Oswald points to slow economic growth, frequent recessions, and the failure to fight inflation through a direct attack on the prices of energy, food, housing, and medical care.

Corporate Decisions

Part II of this book—"Corporate Decisions"—focuses on the individual enterprise. This section includes six contributions by national personalities who have had extensive experience with the issues of productivity and national economic growth. Within a specific area, each author examines the prospects for growth at the level of the enterprise and against the backdrop of national economic conditions.

The chapters written by John Donnelly, John Diebold, Thomas Donahue, and Robert Ranftl direct attention to the significance of the human factor in technological and efficiency issues. All support improved R&D and technological innovation, while at the same time remaining tuned in to the significance of supervision and personnel policies that are sensitive to people as well as to technology. The chapter by Reginald Jones lays the responsibility directly upon the chief executive as does the chapter by Donnelly, each from a different perspective.

Donnelly writes as chief executive of an innovative, highly productive company. He speaks from long experience and from the vantage point of a company that has had continued financial success in a highly competitive industry. Donnelly attributes unsatisfactory U.S. productivity performance to five factors: (1) government regulation; (2) taxes, inflation, and other disincentives to investment; (3) high energy costs; (4)) lack of innovation; and (5) employee indifference. He views employee indifference as the factor most amenable to change by the CEO, and the conquest of indifference as the key to dealing with the other four factors.

Donnelly Mirrors has adapted the Scanlon Plan to its operations and stresses the three factors identified as crucial by Scanlon Plan expert Carl Frost, namely: identity, participation, and equity. Donnelly describes the meaning of each of these factors and the ABCs of how to make them work. His chapter, right on target, will be of particular interest to top executives seeking practical approaches to a productivity initiative with long-term value. Donnelly Mirrors now supplies about one-third of the auto mirrors for Japanese imports—no mean achievement in the quality/price competition. He suggests that such results are the product of the management system, and not of technology alone. With the increasing need for innovative and effective executive leadership as the key to productivity *within* an enterprise, the Donnelly contribution is timely, practical, and worthy of attention.

Alfred Neal's chapter, "Capital Investment and Tax Policy," asserts the overwhelming importance of capital investment in productivity growth. Neal agrees with the Jorgenson thesis on the negative impact of oil price inflation on capital investment and, hence, on productivity since 1973. Both high inflation and unsound tax policies cause the rapid erosion of capital investment, says Neal. He criticizes outmoded cost recovery allowances stemming from tax laws and the voluntary practices of business in undercosting inventory and depreciation, practices which lead, in time, to the overstatement of profits, excessive income taxes, excessive dividends paid out of capital, and starvation of internal funds for investment. In his analysis, Neal reviews most tax-reform proposals but concludes that they do not go to the undercosting of capital.

Reginald Jones, chairman of the General Electric Company, addresses the challenging question of "How Do We Revitalize Our Technology Infrastructure?" in chapter 8. He believes that U.S. industrial policy has been headed in the wrong direction. Jones identifies the United States as the home of high technology and sees technological advantage as basic to high productivity. In fact, a study commissioned by General Electric found that high-technology industries have productivity growth rates *double* those of low-technology industries.

Inflation blocks investment in innovation and production, says Jones, because it raises the "hurdle" rate and forces companies to look for quick, low-risk payouts.

Jones advocates a set of new policies:

- Adopt a national strategy to do more of what we do best—namely, the highest technology.
- Stop protecting noncompetitive "sunset" industries (in contrast with Samuel's views in chapter 4).
- Stop discouraging the growth of multinationals, which are among the leading exponents of high technology.
- End the excesses in the regulation of industry and technology.

He notes that it will be up to business leaders to spearhead the campaign to communicate the need for these new policies. They must also develop a comprehensive technological strategy, tightly integrated with their business strategy. And, finally, they must put corporate money into long-term innovation through R&D. Certainly this is a viewpoint firmly committed to both leadership and long-term strategy.

In chapter 9, "Increasing Office Productivity through Information Technology," John Diebold, an early pioneer in office automation, takes a hard look at the 1980s and predicts a virtual transformation of office work through automation. He considers the driving forces to be the need for higher productivity, domestic and foreign competition, and changing values in needs and attitudes. Diebold defines office automation as "the utilization of computer-based systems to enhance effectiveness and productivity of personnel working in an operational or administrative office"; office automation, he emphasizes, is not to be confused with data processing or word processing, which are more limited concepts.

White-collar workers now comprise over 50 percent of the work force, but their productivity has declined in recent years, while their costs have increased. Advances in computer technology and the tremendous decline in the cost of computer hardware at last make office automation economically attractive. Diebold points out, however, that "office employees are not usually technically oriented and they are rarely technically trained. Thus they have little interest in how a system works." Since they rarely adjust their own behavioral patterns to fit systems whose purpose it is to make their jobs easier, he says, "it seems probable that office automatic systems will not succeed until a *human-centered design approach*, focused on real or perceived needs, has been adopted."

"The business organizations that are most successful in the decades to come," says Diebold, "will also be those that have discovered that office automation is to their administrative activities what automation has been to the factory—a giant step into a new era of efficiency and profitability that has benefited employee, consumer, and business owner alike."

Tom Donahue, secretary-treasurer of the AFL-CIO, sets out neither to bury nor to praise new technology in chapter 10, "Labor Looks at New Technology." All of us have heard plenty about what new technology does *for* people, he says; labor's concern is what the new technology does *to* people.

Donahue lists some of the harmful effects of technology with which the labor movement must be concerned in order to guard its members, including: (1) the elimination of jobs, changes of job content, changes of skill requirements, and changes of work flow; (2) changes in the location of industries; (3) carcinogens, health hazards, stress; and (4) the underuse of employee qualifications.

As the American economy becomes service-based, technological change in the service area will accelerate. On a positive note, Donahue says, "The time is now to develop a strategy for dealing with technological change in a creative manner that minimizes injury and maximizes the accommodation of technology to people and people to technology while providing the benefits of technological advances to a better world for all people. The creative tool which the trade unions bring to this process is collective bargaining. . . . If employers are willing to sit down with the unions representing their employees, then they will find a partner. . . . The labor movement does not oppose technology but . . . unions oppose throwing people on a scrap heap."

In chapter 11 Robert Ranftl, director of engineering design management for Hughes Aircraft, focuses on research and development as the source of technological advance, which in turn underlies productivity improvement. He examines the management and operation of an R&D effort and its impact on the enterprise.

The Hughes Aircraft productivity study of 1973, on which many of Ranftl's conclusions are based, set out to identify useful techniques for optimizing productivity in technology-based organizations. It investigated not only R&D, but also the interaction between R&D and marketing, finance, procurement, manufacturing, information systems, support systems, and services. Fifty-nine organizations, 28 consultants, and 3500 R&D managers took part in the survey.

The key finding of the study was that "productivity improvement in virtually all organizations is 'there for the asking.' "

Ranftl notes five paths to improving the operational productivity of an R&D department: (1) investment in a long-term R&D strategy and plan, with adequate staffing, plant, hardware, and outside aids; (2) organization of the department in an effective grouping of functions—a squat pyramid, with adequate service and support activities and titles based on need; (3) careful staffing, with frequent infusions of new blood, especially of those who are fresh in the technology; (4) planning by those who will do the work, in order to insure involvement and commitment; and (5) control by the setting of realistic targets and schedules.

Human Factors

This part of the book is devoted to four views of the human factor in the productivity equation, those of Jerome Rosow, Wayne Horvitz, Stephen Fuller, and Douglas Fraser. All four authors, writing from differing vantage points and with diverse institutional experiences, join in a common theme, both humanistic and optimistic. The human factor is represented as a deep, rich vein running below the surface of work organizations—a vein which should be discovered and utilized to the mutual advantage of workers and managers.

Rosow defines the negative and positive factors affecting productivity growth in human terms and then describes a variety of targets of opportunity. In a sense, this is an agenda for American management. Horvitz delves deeply into the American experience with labor-management committees and documents its history with diverse and highly successful examples in different industries, companies, and entire communities. This is industrial democracy at its best, offering almost unlimited potential but also requiring a genuine bilateral approach and a commitment to change by cooperation. As the nation's highest official working to achieve labor peace, Horvitz has the hard experience and practical wisdom to support his challenge.

The General Motors revolution in work style is defined by Stephen Fuller in a clear and vivid report. In many ways this chapter epitomizes the art of the possible. Fuller translates theory to practice, and philosophy to an everyday way of life in the factories and offices of General Motors. Because Fuller writes as a representative of the *Fortune* No. 1 manufacturing corporation and as an executive who has been deeply involved in its noble experiment in quality of work life, this chapter should be given serious consideration. "Engine Charlie" Wilson, former CEO of General Motors caused a mild sensation some years ago by stating, "What's good for General Motors is good for the country." That controversial slogan was certainly too all-embracing—and is open to many interpretations. However, within the specific terms of its highly successful ten-year-old active partnership with the UAW, one could certainly claim that what is good for General Motors *is* good for American industry.

Finally, UAW President Douglas Fraser presents a comprehensive view of productivity in economic, historical, and social terms. He sees and appreciates the needs and goals of American industry, but he speaks clearly of the needs of workers and the protective programs that must become the quid pro quo of open and long-term labor cooperation. Job security, he believes, is the key to cooperative responses by workers and their leaders.

The future agenda for Fraser, who is a leading labor statesman and spokesperson, is simply that labor cannot be expected to bear either all or the major share of the burden of cost and pain which is often the by-product of technology. He also defends his new (and yet-to-be-evaluated) role as a director of the Chrysler Corporation, which may have precedent-setting implications.

In conclusion, Douglas Fraser offers a legislative program to underline and support a national effort to improve productivity. Donahue's chapter earlier in the book speaks to the same issues from the AFL/CIO viewpoint, and many of his ideas are reinforced and paralleled by those of Fraser.

Finally, the Fraser and Fuller chapters should be seen as possible harbingers of the future of labor-management cooperation in improving productivity. In the summer of 1980 both Ford and Chrysler embraced the identical goal of increasing worker involvement to advance both product quality and productivity in their organizations to meet the Japanese challenge head-on. In a separate development, AT&T and the Communications Workers of America established a national committee for labor-management cooperation in a contract covering one million employees. And earlier in the same year the steel industry negotiated the first industry-wide three-year commitment to the evolving principle of "participation teams." Thus the nation entered the eighties with three major industries engaged in some form of worker participation.

A look back at the long road General Motors has had to travel, moving from philosophy to practice in the office and on the shop floor, has obviously not discouraged others from following suit. Although encouraging employee participation will require a determined, unwavering effort, they have undoubtedly discovered that improving productivity must involve people. And they are going to give it a try.

PRODUCTIVITY
Prospects for Growth

I.
TRENDS AND PROSPECTS

1.
The Productivity Issue: An Overview

Solomon Fabricant
Professor Emeritus of Economics, New York University
Former Director of Research, National Bureau of Economic Research, Inc.

INTRODUCTION

For as many as seven years now—since the business-cycle peak of 1973—the nation's output of goods and services has risen little more rapidly, on net balance, than the aggregate number of hours worked by the employed labor force. Averaged over the cycle since 1973, then, output per worker-hour has moved up very slowly. To a generation grown accustomed to more favorable news on this widely quoted measure of productivity—and along with it, to the inclusion of a comfortable "improvement factor" in wage and fringe-benefit bargains—the recent record must be as disappointing as it is surprising.

Yet some anxiety about productivity should have been felt even before the experience of recent years. Signs of retardation in our productivity growth, though modest compared with the recent slowdown, could have been noticed by a discerning eye before 1973. And through most of the postwar years it was evident that productivity in other industrial countries was advancing more rapidly than in the United States.

Were the nation's productivity performance of minor importance, this retardation and our lag relative to other countries would not be cause for much concern. But it is not minor. An upward trend in the nation's output per hour is the basic source of improvement in real compensation per worker-hour. Not less important, rising productivity is a vital element in the economic and political strength the United States must have to maintain its position in the world community. Further, the nation counts on rising productivity to help meet its ever-advancing standards of health, safety, and a habitable physical environment, as well as other social objectives. And rising productivity helps also, if only a little, to ease upward pressures on the general price level—not a trivial benefit in an age of inflation. Productivity deserves the attention it has been receiving.

People have been discovering that the productivity problem is not easy to deal with. They are beginning—but only beginning—to understand that the rate of productivity growth is determined not by a single dominant cause, but rather by a host of many causes; that these causes interact with one another in subtle ways; that about most of these causes, and even about productivity itself, quantitative information is rough, if not altogether lacking; that this dearth of information, and widespread ignorance of the information that is available, allows sharply conflicting views on the importance of particular causes.

As a result, we have some distance to go to realize that a policy to improve productivity requires action on many fronts and at all levels. Certainly what has happened to productivity, and what can be done about it, is not the sole responsibility of the private or of the public sector and should not be placed, as is too often the tendency, on government, business management, or the workers. Nor should we merely point at OPEC or complain about the niggardliness of nature.

We need also to recognize better than we have in the past that to push up the rate of productivity growth may entail costs in terms of other national objectives, and conversely, that vigorously pursuing these objectives may be costly in terms of productivity growth.

This is the situation that needs to be appreciated if the prospects for better productivity performance in the years ahead are to be enhanced without excessive cost. Unless the problem is understood, we will not commit ourselves earnestly enough to the large-scale, patient, and persistent process of education, research, and improvement in organization, institutional arrangements, and policy—private and public, domestic and foreign—that is required.

PRODUCTIVITY TRENDS

To explain the recent retardation in the trend of productivity, and beyond that, the primary trend from which it is a deviation, will involve some speculation. That is implied by the lack of full agreement on the causes of productivity change. But even the productivity trends set down in table 1.1 are inevitably surrounded with some uncertainty. The "facts" to be explained must themselves be qualified—and not only because measuring aggregate output in a world in which qualitative as well as quantitative change is universal necessarily involves arguable assumptions.

Very likely, the headings in table 1.1 will already have raised some questions in the minds of close readers. They will have noticed that the estimates do not quite cover the entire economy, since they omit some of the activities most difficult to measure acceptably, namely, those classified in the national accounts under government, households, and the foreign sector.[1] They will have realized, also, that the average rates of growth shown provide only one of several possible indications of the trends. Among other limitations, these are simply measured from peak to peak, thereby ignoring the fluctuations between the peaks. They may have wondered, also, whether the estimates going back into the nineteenth century, included in order to provide perspective on the more recent developments, can be as accurate as those covering the later years. These doubts point to some very real questions about productivity measurements and the need to answer them better than is now possible. Still, the table provides a broad view sufficiently close to the mark for our purposes.

To be noted first is, of course, the very low average rate of productivity growth between the business-cycle peak of 1973 and the latest year available, 1979, which also could turn out to be a cyclical peak, or close to one. The rate of 0.6 percent per annum over the six-year period was lower than the trend rate, measured peak to peak, during any other post-World War II period. Even the *total* increase of 3.7 percent over the six years (the 0.6 percent compounded) was not much above the *annual* increase of 3.2 percent experienced early in the postwar period—the "productivity guidepost" for noninflationary wage increase set up under the Kennedy Administration. No less striking, the recent productivity trend rate

Table 1.1. Labor Productivity, 1890–1979
Private Domestic Business Sector[a]
Average Annual Rates of Change in Output per Worker-Hour
Between Business-Cycle Peak Years (percentages)

Between Successive Business-Cycle Peaks					
1890–92	4.0	1913–18	1.4	1948–53	3.6
1892–95	0.9	1918–20	2.7	1953–57	2.4
1895–99	1.9	1920–23	3.9	1957–60	2.4
1899–1903	1.7	1923–26	2.3	1960–69	3.1
1903–07	2.3	1926–29	2.0	1969–73	2.3
1907–10	0.1	1929–37	1.1	1973–79[b]	0.6
1910–13	2.4	1937–44	3.4		
		1944–48	1.5		
Averaged over Longer Periods					
1890–1913	1.8	1913–48	2.2	1948–79	2.5

[a]Private domestic economy, for 1890–1948.

[b]The year 1979 is assumed to be a business-cycle peak year.

Sources: For 1890–1929, derived from estimates of John W. Kendrick, *Productivity Trends in the United States* (Princeton: Princeton University Press, for the National Bureau of Economic Research, 1961), table A-XXII; for 1929–1948, John W. Kendrick, *Postwar Productivity Trends in the United States, 1948–1969* (New York: National Bureau of Economic Research, 1973), table A-19; and for 1948–1979, U.S. Department of Labor, Bureau of Labor Statistics, quarterly releases on *Productivity and Costs*. The business-cycle peak years are those identified by the National Bureau of Economic Research.

was lower than any other in the entire 90-year record, with the exception only of the period including the severe recession of 1907. Even during the Deep Depression between 1892 and 1895 and the Great Depression between 1929 and 1937, productivity rose more rapidly than in the past six years.

The table provides, second, some evidence of the retardation in the postwar rate of productivity growth before 1973 that was mentioned earlier. The retardation revealed is moderate, compared with the sharp drop-off after 1973. But the evidence is sensitive to the choice of the periods compared. A somewhat different choice would greatly strengthen the suggestion of retardation before 1973 and heighten its degree (see tables 1.2 and 1.4).

But, third, this postwar retardation looks different viewed against the longer historical background provided in the table. Some of the wide variation in the productivity trend rates shown by table 1.1

reflects the imperfections in the underlying data and the limitations of the simple trend measure previously mentioned. But after allowing for these, the wide variation must indicate a considerable degree of variability in the factors that determine the rate of productivity growth. Even the longer-term rates, which are less affected by erratic changes, have varied rather considerably. In the light of this historical record, little confidence could be put in a simple projection of the current low rate—or of any trend, low or high, current or long-term—without more persuasive evidence than is now commonly offered in support of such projections. Certainly, the fact that the rate of productivity growth during the postwar period taken as a whole is higher than the rate of the preceding period, and that this rate in turn is higher than the one preceding it, provides no secure basis for expecting the generation ahead to experience a still higher rate.

Perhaps the surest conclusion to be drawn from the table, both about the past and what is implied for the future, concerns the persistence of forces making for productivity growth. Every one of the peak-to-peak trends in the 90-year record, without exception, was upward.

An examination of the trends among individual industries reinforces the impression of strong and persistent forces making for productivity growth. For while industries have varied greatly in rate of productivity growth, hardly any of their longer-term trends have been anything but upward. Indeed, we would be led to suspect that industries with negative rates of productivity growth, and even the few with positive but low rates, have experienced large product-quality improvements not captured by the output data.

Within industries, also, we would expect to find few establishments, if any, experiencing a long-term decline in productivity, to judge from the rather scarce information available. Even old plants usually undergo some modernization that improves productivity before they become entirely obsolete and are closed down and replaced by new plants.

PRODUCTIVITY AND RELATED CONCEPTS

The fact that productivity growth has been widespread among individual industries and probably among most individual establishments, as well as persistent over time in the economy as a whole, begins to reveal something about the factors that underlie productivity growth. But additional information is needed in order to be more specific about the factors, and to say something about their relative importance.

As will be seen in the tables that follow, the rate of growth in output per worker-hour is accounted for by the sum of the contributions of a number of component sources.

Output per worker-hour measures the fruitfulness of an hour of labor. But the labor is not naked, so to speak—not human labor, at any rate. It is supported by the services of the tangible and intangible capital always found—in large or small amount, of superior or inferior quality—associated with human labor. Output per worker-hour reflects, second, the diligence, skill, knowledge, and quality of organization and management with which labor and capital are applied in the process of production.

The effect on productivity of the inputs associated with worker-hours is measured by their weighted total per worker-hour. This total may be subdivided, as it is in table 1.2, among the three kinds of input shown there; or it may be subdivided still further, as in table 1.4.[2] (The absence of intangible capital from table 1.2 will be explained later.) The number of subclasses will be determined by the available information and by the significance of the distinctions among the several kinds of inputs.

The efficiency with which labor and capital inputs are used in production is measured by the ratio of output to the weighted combination or aggregation of all inputs, including hours of labor as well as the services of tangible and intangible capital. This ratio may be called "output per unit of labor and capital combined," as it is in the table, or "total factor productivity," as economists often do. Subclassification is possible here also, as in table 1.4.

It is not easy to distinguish between the input of capital and the efficiency with which labor and capital are used. Are not knowledge, skill, and organization, for example, also forms of capital—the results of investment—and are not their contributions therefore classified as well or better under inputs than under efficiency? The distinction is actually drawn largely on practical grounds, whether the contribution can be satisfactorily measured. In effect, inputs are the services of those resources for which property records are conventionally kept—plant and equipment, for example—or for which sufficiently adequate values can be imputed by a reasonable process of estimation, such as education.[3]

The weights mentioned rest on the presumption that, in a reasonably competitive economy, the relative market values of the services of different kinds of labor and capital are proportionate to their quality. (This is also the presumption that underlies the use of market-value weights in aggregating diverse types of outputs.) Most economists believe it to be a reasonable presumption, on the whole, despite the reservations they feel to be necessary because market imperfections distort relative values.[4] Thus, labor input, measured by the sum of worker-hours weighted by hourly rates in some "base" period, will rise more or less than the simple sum of unweighted worker-hours as changes occur in the composition of the labor supply. These changes in composition can result from formal education, on-the-job training, shifts in the age–sex mix of workers, and changes in such other aspects of labor quality as are reflected in hourly compensation rates and taken into account—individually or in combination—in calculating the weighted worker-hours. A change in the ratio of weighted to unweighted hours provides, then, a measure of change in the average quality of labor. This is the measure shown in tables 1.2 and 1.3.

Based on the same reasoning, the rental price or imputed value of the services of a given capital asset, relative to the value of the asset itself, is presumed to reflect the quality of the services of this capital.[5] The ratio of the weighted measure of capital input to the simple sum of the dollar values of the assets involved changes with shifts in the distribution of assets among more or less remunerative uses, per dollar of assets. The ratio, then, provides an index of capital quality.

As already noted, some inputs, particularly those reflecting investment in technology and certain other types of intangible capital, cannot be measured satisfactorily. For this reason, they are omitted from the list of inputs included in the denominator of the total factor productivity ratio. This concept of productivity is then better identified as "multifactor productivity," as the Panel to Review Productivity Statistics has recently recommended,[6] and this is the term that will be used in this chapter. To the extent that multifactor productivity falls short of measuring total-factor productivity, it is an imperfect measure of efficiency. Change in multifactor productivity will reflect also any substitution that may occur between the inputs omitted and the inputs covered; measured multifactor productivity will therefore overstate or understate the change in efficiency.

PRODUCTIVITY FACTORS

To avoid burdening the reader, just one of the sets of estimates of the sources of productivity growth listed in table 1.3[7] is given in some detail in table 1.2.

Accepting the estimates in table 1.2 at their face value, four conclusions may be drawn. First, all four sources of change in labor productivity appear to be of sufficient importance to warrant further thought and analysis. Certainly, none may be neglected when asking what has determined labor productivity growth in the past and what may be expected to determine it in the future. Second, the contribution of each has varied in importance over the three periods shown. But, third, the major source in all three periods has been, by far, the rate of change in the efficiency with which labor and tangible

Table 1.2. Sources of Change in Labor Productivity, Private Business Sector, 1948–78

Average Annual Contribution to Rate of Growth of Output per Worker-Hour between Selected Years (percentages)

	1948–65	1965–73	1973–78
Labor Productivity			
Output per worker-hour worked	3.37	2.46	1.29
Sources of Change in Labor Productivity			
Labor quality	0.27	0.26	0.03
Tangible capital			
Quantity per worker-hour	0.76	0.75	0.21
Quality	0.18	0.27	0.08
Output per unit of labor and tangible capital	2.16	1.18	0.97

Source: Adapted, with some changes in terminology and classification, from estimates in J. R. Norsworthy, M. J. Harper, and K. Kunze, "The Slowdown in Productivity Growth: Analysis of Some Contributing Factors," *Brookings Papers on Economic Activity*, vol. 2 (Washington, D.C.: The Brookings Institution, 1979), p. 414.

capital are used in production. Fourth, the rate of labor productivity growth was lower during 1973–78 than during the two preceding periods shown because all four sources were lower.

But should the estimates in table 1.2 be accepted at their face value? Comparison between these estimates and the others in table 1.3 may stir up some doubts. It would be unfair to compare the estimates without stressing that they relate to somewhat different areas of the economy. The scope of the estimates that include household capital is considerably broader than that of the three estimates excluding households entirely; and the private-business

Table 1.3. Comparison of Four Estimates of Sources of Change in Labor Productivity

Average Annual Contribution to Rates of Growth of Output per Worker-Hour, 1948–73 (percentages)

	Private Business Sector (Norsworthy et al.)	Nonresidential Business Sector (Denison)	Domestic Business Sector (Kendrick)	Private Domestic Sector, including Household Capital (Christensen and Jorgenson)
Labor Productivity				
Output per worker-hour	3.1	3.0	3.1	3.2
Sources of Change in Labor Productivity				
Labor quality	0.3	0.5	0.9	0.5
Tangible capital				
Quantity per worker-hour	0.8	0.4	0.7	1.0
Quality	0.2	—	0.3	0.4
Output per unit of labor and tangible capital	1.8	2.0	1.2	1.3

Source: For the estimates by Norsworthy et al., see the source of table 2. The other estimates have been adapted, also with some changes in terminology and classification, from calculations in E. F. Denison, *Accounting for Slower Economic Growth* (Washington, D.C.: Brookings, 1979); J. W. Kendrick, "Productivity Trends and the Recent Slowdown: Historical Perspective, Causal Factors, and Policy Options," in William Fellner, project director, *Contemporary Economic Problems 1979* (Washington, D.C.: American Enterprise Institute for Public Policy Research, 1979), pp. 33-34; and L. R. Christensen and D. W. Jorgenson, "U. S. Input, Output, Saving and Wealth, 1929–1977," Harvard Institute of Economic Research, Harvard University, n.d. It should be noted that the authors may not entirely agree with the changes in classification and terminology made here; also, that the two decimal points given in three of the sources have been rounded down to one.

sector is somewhat broader than the nonresidential business sector. That is one reason why the Christensen–Jorgenson estimates of the contribution of tangible capital, both in quantity and quality, are larger than the other estimates. The differences in scope also serve to explain some of the slight differences among the estimates of increase in labor productivity itself. And there are other reasons: In the estimate by Norsworthy and his collaborators, a rather rough estimate of hours actually worked is substituted for hours paid, something not done by the others. Denison's estimate of capital's contribution is much lower than any of the others, first because he made no explicit calculation of change in the quality of capital (which pushes its contribution into the estimate for output per unit of labor and tangible capital),[8] and second, because he treated tangible capital net of capital consumption, which cuts sharply into the weight assigned to change in the quantity of tangible capital per hour. The estimate of labor quality by Norsworthy et al., is much lower than any of the others, because it is based on a much more detailed calculation and results in a more effective allowance for interrelationships among the various sources of difference in hourly rates of compensation. Finally, because output per unit of labor and tangible capital, the measure of multifactor productivity, is what is left over after accounting for labor and tangible capital inputs, and the authors differ in what they include in these inputs and in how they estimate them, the respective residuals also differ, and rather considerably.

While the estimates may be expected to differ without actually being in conflict, there is, in fact, a good deal of conflict among them, as the respective authors are fully aware. Yet the broad conclusions drawn from the estimates in table 1.2 would, I believe, stand up, on the whole, had any of the other estimates been selected for the initial presentation. Conclusions going beyond these, however, would be suspect—open, at least, to the doubts initially raised by the comparisons in table 1.3. Economists have much to do to improve and reconcile their estimates, if they are to come to closer agreement on the quantitative dimensions of the sources of productivity growth.

But even if there were closer agreement on the labor and tangible capital inputs, and therefore also on the residual, it is rather certain that the latter would continue to bulk large among the sources of change in labor productivity.

What can be said in quantitative terms about the individual contributions of the factors grouped together under the heading of multifactor productivity? Not much, I am afraid, that reflects anything but one's best judgment or guess. It is worthwhile, however, to see how far Edward Denison, the leading practitioner of growth accounting, has felt able to go in distinguishing among these factors and putting his judgments on their separate contributions into numbers.[9]

First, some of the detailed estimates—the contributions of "economies of scale," for example—are more adventurous than are others, as Denison is careful to emphasize. That there have been contributions by the factors specified and that they have probably been significant, few economists would deny. But even fewer have been bold enough to estimate their magnitude.

Second, as economists generally do, I have referred to multifactor productivity as "the residual"—what is left over after accounting for measurable inputs. When, however, any of the factors collected under the heading of multifactor productivity are separately identified and measured, as some are in Denison's tables, the residual must refer to something less than multifactor productivity. This is the item in table 1.4 labeled "advances in knowledge, and not elsewhere classified." It is the dominant component of change in multifactor productivity. The major part of this final residual is often presumed to be technological advance. But there are also organizational, managerial, and social innovations, as Denison makes clear, and these can hardly be dismissed as negligible. Further, even if advance in the input yielded by the *total* stock of knowledge constitutes a major component of the residual, which may be the case, the residual is big enough to leave a substantial balance over to the credit of the "not elsewhere classified (n.e.c.)" factors. Among these may conceivably be the trends in labor-management relations and in labor and management attitudes toward discipline to which reference is often made these days.

Third, much the greater part of the decline in multifactor productivity—and also in labor productivity—between 1973 and 1976, the last year for which the estimates are available (and this can probably

Table 1.4. Sources of Growth in Multifactor Productivity Nonresidential Business Sector

Average Annual Contribution, 1948–73 and 1973–76 (percentages)

	1948–73	1973–76
Multifactor Productivity		
Output per unit of labor and tangible capital	1.97	−0.87
Sources of Change in Multifactor Productivity		
Improved resource allocation	0.37	−0.01
Farm	0.26	0.02
Nonfarm self-employment	0.11	−0.03
Legal and human environment	−0.04	−0.44
Pollution abatement	−0.02	−0.23
Worker safety and health	−0.01	−0.12
Dishonesty and crime	−0.01	−0.09
Economies of scale	0.41	0.24
Irregular factors	−0.18	0.09
Weather in farming	0.00	−0.02
Labor disputes	0.00	−0.01
Intensity of demand	−0.18	0.12
Advances in knowledge and not elsewhere classified	1.41	−0.75

Source: E. F. Denison, *Accounting for Slower Economic Growth* (Washington, D.C.: The Brookings Institution, 1979), table 7–3.

be said also of the slowdown between 1973 and 1979) is not convincingly identified. It has to be ascribed by Denison to the final residual. Yet it hardly seems possible to suppose that a drop in the contribution of advances in knowledge is the dominant factor in the decline from an average of +1.41 percentage points during 1948–73 to an average of −.75 during 1973–76.[10] Here too, it appears, the explanation must be found among the sources "not elsewhere classified," including the rate at which old and new knowledge is put to use.

Still another caveat about the estimates in tables 1.2 to 1.4 is necessary. The simple decomposition, or "growth accounting," that yields these estimates implicitly assumes—except for some *ad hoc* allowances—that the several separate components of labor productivity are independent of one another. This is not so, however, as the comment on labor quality should have suggested. Doubling the number of shovels per worker will not double the contribution of shovels, for the value in production of the additional shovels will be less than that of the existing stock of shovels. Nor, if new technologies must be "embodied" in machinery and in highly trained workers to be useful (as is very often the case), will the contribution of technology to productivity growth depend only on what is happening to technology: it will depend also on the rates of change in tangible capital, improvement of labor quality, and "turnover" of labor and capital. Further, beyond these interrelationships, there are undoubtedly, among the factors, more complicated relations of cause and effect spread over time. The rate of investment in tangible capital and in education, for example, is sooner or later influenced by the opportunities opened up when there is a spurt in technological advances of wide applicability. And technology can, in turn, be influenced by the rate of investment. To deal adequately with these interrelationships would require the use of a model, involving production and other "functions," that is far more complicated than that assumed in growth accounting, and also one that would demand more and better statistical data than are now available.

UNDERLYING SOURCES OF PRODUCTIVITY GROWTH

Quantitative analyses of the factors making for productivity growth are naturally focused on those that immediately impinge on productivity. These are more or less plainly evident and amenable to some sort of measurement or quantitative judgment. However, underlying the proximate factors and determining their direction, magnitude, and weight, are the basic factors. These give rise to the saving and investment that increase tangible capital, influence the composition and allocation of capital among alternative uses, determine the quality of labor, and condition the efficiency with which labor and tangible capital are used in production. It is on knowledge of these factors that projections of the proximate factors should rest.

Because the explanations of productivity changes that economists offer depend so much on qualitative judgment, their explanations are bound to differ widely. The differences are not so much in the casts listed in their *dramatis personae*, however, as in the assignment of leading and supporting roles. Rather than attempt to review the various explanations, I shall limit myself to the points I believe to be salient.[11]

Certainly, one of the points to be emphasized concerns incentives—the incentives that impel people everywhere to strive constantly to advance their standards of living, within the bounds imposed by institutional and legal arrangements.

I say people "everywhere" because back of every source of productivity listed in the preceding tables, are the activities of all people, not only of those narrowly identified as "entrepreneurs." The productivity of the American economy is the end result of decisions by millions of persons. They are not equally important, but they are all significantly involved, as owners and managers of business enterprises, or as workers and members of labor unions; as producers or as consumers; as garret inventors or as laboratory scientists; as voters or as government officials; even as philanthropists, for the motives of few people are entirely selfish. If students of economic development are correct in stressing the importance of attitudes, it is the attitudes of all people that form the foundation of the nation's productivity.

These efforts are not isolated or unrelated to one another. They interact and their effects spread through the markets for labor and capital. Thus, when savings make tangible capital plentiful in relation to labor, and the services of labor become more expensive than the services of tangible capital, managers in all industries find it profitable to increase the volume of tangible capital per worker. Because many technological developments must be embodied in equipment or other tangible capital and operated by trained people, inducements for families to save and educate themselves and for management to employ more tangible capital per worker and better-educated workers are maintained and strengthened. When new technologies are potentially versatile enough to be used in different industries, sooner or later the profit motive and competitive pressures see to it that they are widely diffused.

Indeed, what happens or could happen to technology, scale of operations, tangible capital per worker, or any other factor affecting productivity in any industry depends on what is happening or could happen in the rest of the economy. Just as it is wrong to say that change in labor productivity reflects the quality or effort of labor alone, when so much else can be playing a part, so it is wrong to assign to an industry all the credit or blame for what happens to its productivity.

Similarly, the productivity of any country depends, in part, on what is happening beyond its borders. The hike by OPEC in the price of petroleum in many significant ways affected and will continue to affect productivity in all U.S. industries, including those not directly using petroleum or its immediate products. And there are also the effects of immigration on the quality of labor, of imported technology and other knowledge on efficiency, and of international trade on the scale of operations.

Nor should it be forgotten that while the forces that make for increase in labor productivity operate broadly across the entire economy, it is a matter of chance how strongly they operate in any single industry or sector, or in industry at large. Technological research or exploration for natural resources can be undertaken, for example, but just what results will emerge is uncertain. Indeed, every source of growth, proximate or basic, contains a random element.

And to a degree, also, how strongly the forces of productivity growth operate depends on the factors that stimulate or impede these forces—stimulants and impediments that are more powerful at some times than at others. An analysis of these factors follows.

CONDITIONS OF PRODUCTIVITY GROWTH

Of the many factors that condition productivity growth, particular attention is paid here to those that have some bearing on the productivity-growth slowdown. I group them under three heads: the "taste" for objectives other than productivity growth; restrictions on the freedom to pursue the objective of productivity growth; and limitations that dull the inducement to pursue this objective.[12]

The nation has, we all know, other goals besides the expansion of output per worker-hour. Besides higher average real income or leisure time, there is also a more even distribution of income and of employment opportunities and a higher and stabler level of income and employment. And besides the economic goals there are the so-called noneconomic goals, including a satisfactory physical and social environment, national defense, and political freedom.

Productivity growth, then, is not the only or overriding national objective. In fact, in recent years there has been a greater emphasis on national goals that compete with productivity growth. This shift has not necessarily been a mistake, but it is a question whether, in pursuing the other objectives, the nation has moved too far, too fast, and shown too little understanding of the costs entailed in pursuing them. According to Denison's estimates (table 1.4), for example, the retarding effect on labor productivity of the diversion of capital funds and labor to improving the environment and meeting higher health and safety standards on and off the job has been significant. But this is only the cost side of the calculation; it is not yet the "bottom line," which must take account also of the benefits.

There are also the goals of individual workers that tend to compete with the advance of productivity. The resistance to technological changes that disturb and threaten to undermine the security of workers in their jobs is an ancient story. What has cropped up more recently, and to which reference is often made in explanations of the productivity slowdown, is the so-called deterioration of workers' attitudes toward their jobs and the emphasis workers now place on a favorable work environment. These changes also may be viewed as a shift toward objectives that compete with the drive for real income that rising productivity can bring. And here, too, there is a difficult question about the trade-offs between the objectives.

In considering these trade-offs, it is important to understand that investment in the competing programs can have a favorable effect on labor quality and thus serve to offset some of the retarding effects on productivity caused by a slower rate of increase in what is narrowly viewed as "productive" plant and equipment. Further, solution of pollution problems, by that very fact, can and often does mean more effective use of the raw materials and the waste end products that now constitute the pollutants. Investment in the reduction of pollution can be profitable—or less costly than commonly supposed—to business as well as to society at large, and productivity need not necessarily be reduced or reduced significantly. Finally, improvement in the quality of the environment and reduction in illness and accidents yield benefits that are not now included in our conventional measures of national output. If these benefits were covered, output per worker-hour—not now, perhaps, but later, after a lag—might tell a different story. How different—that is a question. In any case, we should not let ourselves be misled, before we know the answer, by imperfections in our statistical measurements.

The second obstacle to productivity growth consists of restrictions on the freedom to pursue activities that lead to productivity growth. In the view of some observers, curbs on economic freedom have grown in recent years. They point to monopolistic practices in private markets not always effectively restrained by government and sometimes actually encouraged and supported by it. These practices restrict freedom of entry, hamper price competition, and impede adaptation to technological and other change. But some curbs to competition have in recent years been removed or diminished by legislative or administrative action and also by the growth of foreign competition and the development of a wider range of substitutes for many materials, products, or services. The picture is mixed; whether the recent net drift has, in fact, been toward imperfect competition in private industry, or away from it, is unclear.

The trend with regard to governmental regulations has more clearly been upward both in number and complexity. These regulations always have, or are said to have, virtuous objectives. But the issue here is not the relative value of the objectives, but how to reach the objectives—in the case of pollution control, for example, whether to regulate or to tax effluents. Regulation entails costs to governmental authorities as well as to those regulated; recent estimates suggest these have grown and are now substantial. The question here is whether these costs are greater than the costs of alternative and equally effective enforcement procedures.

Even regulations that have stayed put, so to speak, may have had their effects amplified in recent years by changes in the economy. A striking example is the enormously greater impact on the financial system and the flow of funds, as a result of inflation, of the multitude of regulations that have long been in existence.

There are, third, the limitations that dull incentives to work, save and invest, and seek greater efficiency in the use of labor and capital. These incentives may be blunted by tax rates and other provisions written into the tax codes, another old complaint. What is new and may help to explain the productivity slowdown is the reference now being made to the "hidden" income tax imposed by inflation.

Another relevant factor is the tendency of the Social Security system to reduce the rate of personal savings or keep it from rising as average real income rises. The system is now over 40 years old, and increases in Social Security coverage since the early 1950s have been relatively modest. However, the accumulated "Social Security wealth" of individuals appears to have grown much more rapidly than gross national product (GNP) or personal income over the postwar period and at a higher rate in recent than in earlier decades.[13]

Some of the factors already mentioned, and others as well, have contributed to increased uncertainty and risk in recent years. They have thereby tended to slow up capital investment and the development of new processes and new products. Thus, the flood of laws and regulations aimed at national goals other than growth not only divert resources to better protect the physical environment and the safety and health of workers, but also divert the time of managers who must learn what the regulations mean, how and when the regulations may be expected to change, and how to adjust to them now and in the future.

Tending in the same direction are the jumps in the price of petroleum in 1973 and later. In this case, also, investment of funds and of time has had, and will have, to be devoted to learning how to adjust to the radically new set of relative cost prices and to actually making the adjustment. This task has not been made easier for businessmen, who have to worry about the complicated and often poorly drafted energy policies that have and will continue to come out of Washington. The high and unsteady rate of inflation over the past 15 years, in which the rather erratic governmental efforts to deal with inflation have played a major role, has also increased risk and created uncertainty. And a fourth factor, especially important in basic scientific research, has been the violent fluctuation in the federal government's support of R&D and of the professional training that accompanies it. This could hardly have failed to lower the efficiency with which research and postgraduate training are planned and carried out.

Finally, there are the institutional arrangements that tend to dampen incentives to economize in some of our most rapidly growing and now very large industries. These include hospitals and other health and nonprofit institutions supported in whole or in part by governmental funds. And outside the private sector, government itself, inclusive of state and local government, has also been growing more rapidly in terms of employment than the private-business sector; and it is in government, no less than in the health industries, that incentives to cut costs and improve productivity tend to be weak.

How important these factors and others that could be mentioned have really been in dampening incentives to raise productivity is a matter of controversy. But it hardly seems likely that the effects have been negligible.

POLICY TO STIMULATE PRODUCTIVITY GROWTH

From this discussion of productivity growth and the obstacles that may account for its slowdown, implications for policy to speed up productivity growth have begun to emerge. These implications relate not only to public policy, but also to private policy. And we should remember that in raising productivity the principal role is played by private enterprise and the supporting role by government. This relationship defines the character of public policy.

A major reason why we must look primarily to private enterprise for productivity increase is the enormous diversity of this world. Production units are classified by industry, but, in fact, these groupings are homogeneous only to a very limited extent in respect of the factors that determine productivity. Inputs of labor, capital, and materials vary considerably among establishments within an industry and even among divisions within establishments, in kind, quantity, quality, price, markets in which obtained, and contractual arrangements with suppliers. Outputs vary in similar respects. And the relationships between inputs and outputs vary because the sizes of establishments and enterprises vary, managements vary, technologies vary. As a result, managers of the establishments and enterprises will, as a rule, know more about the detailed conditions within which they do their business, and more about what they can as well as wish to do, than can any outsider, in government or elsewhere.

Further, this is a world of incessant change in all these respects. Close and constant attention must be paid to these changes and adaptation made as changes become evident—and even *before* they become evident—within the limits imposed by existing commitments and current pressures and in the light of expectations regarding the future. Here, too, those close to the situation are, as a rule, more familiar with, better prepared, and readier to deal with the details of what is happening and to consider and explore opportunities that open up or are promised by the changes in sight than are outsiders.

What I have said about managers can be said, with some obvious qualifications, about the workers, investors, and consumers who play a role in the joint process of raising productivity.

This is not to say that managers and the others involved know or can know everything about their respective circumstances; or that they always seek, and react promptly and effectively to, information useful in their activities; or that governmental bureaus—as well as nonprofit institutions, including labor unions, consumer organizations, and schools—have no significant part to play in supplementing or correcting the flood of information constantly being generated and disseminated in the marketplace; or finally, that a good case cannot be made for governmental protection of consumers and workers in certain situations. In short, I do not mean to imply that the role of the private sector in raising productivity is acted out to anything like perfection.

Those in charge of business enterprises, for example, would be better prepared to discover and seize opportunities to raise productivity if productivity accounting were more widely practiced. Manuals setting forth the principles and methods of productivity accounting are now of fairly early vintage.[14] Yet I have the impression—I hope I am wrong—that no great proportion of business enterprises, even among the larger companies, undertakes any systematic and regular productivity accounting and analysis.

There is another point that needs to be stressed. Productivity in any firm, in the sense of output per worker-hour, can always be improved. But the payoff from productivity improvement will not always match the costs of attaining it. In making this calculation, however, indirect as well as direct, and long-term as well as short-term, costs and benefits need to be taken into account. Also, changes in conditions may shift the balance between the costs and the benefits, and traditional views will, in that case, become obsolete. This is not always clearly recognized.

Perhaps the movement to improve the quality of working life provides an apt illustration. Improvement in one or another of the many dimensions of working life has always been an objective of workers. With income, knowledge, and standards higher, and tastes different, quality of working life is now a far more important objective. Opinions on what may at any particular time be accepted as the "legitimate aspirations" of workers will always differ, but surely what is legitimate today, or close to being legitimate, was less so a generation or two ago. This must be more widely recognized by managers than it now appears to be. For example, changes in labor-management relations, which the business community felt were undesirable and fought in the past, may have indirect or longer-run benefits—and with changes in conditions, even more direct and immediate benefits—that may make these changes worthwhile. Improvements in the quality of working life which managers once believed hinder productivity may, in fact, enhance it. Information to decide whether this is so is not always at hand; it should then be sought out. When what is needed is movement along untrodden paths, support of research may be indicated.

While in the future, as in the past, it may be expected that productivity gains will depend primarily on the efforts of individuals and businesses, the strength and success of these efforts will be greatly influenced by public policy, if the reasoning set forth earlier has any merit.

Our discussion has also hinted at the principles by which choice of public policy should be guided.

With exceptions, appropriate or otherwise, made to approach national goals other than economic efficiency, the handicap of government in dealing with details outside its own immediate sphere of operations has generally been recognized, at least in the free world, in drawing up the agenda and pursuing the policies of government. It follows that sound governmental policy for improving productivity in the private sector should, as a rule, be in terms of enhancing the *general* environment within which *all* industries operate. The number, size, and variety of private industries is too great, and the limitations on the scale and flexibility of governmental bureaus and the knowledge of government officials too severe, to do otherwise.

To enhance the general environment within which all industries operate means to foster an environment in which the private decisions of savers and investors, producers and consumers, workers and employers, wherever they are, can be made more freely, more confidently, and more rationally than they can now be made.

Government should provide or support the facilities, knowledge, and information that are of general benefit to the public, but of only limited benefit to private suppliers. For example, government should continue to support health and education, primarily to reach other national goals, but also to raise national productivity.

In pursuing this objective, it is essential to recognize and admit the unpleasant fact that our understanding of productivity is severely limited. The facts about the level and rate of change in productivity, not only in government itself,[15] but also in many industries in the private sector, are far from clear. The experts know less than the public believes they know about productivity. It may be sufficient, here, to recall the attempt by the Council of Economic Advisers (CEA) in the 1979 *Economic Report of the President* to determine and explain the trend of national productivity in recent years. The council's statement had to end with a frank confession of ignorance.

Because too little is yet known about the connection between any given policy and its results, it is desirable that policy be kept flexible. At the same time, however, shifts in policy should not be so erratic as to create uncertainty and thereby discourage private plans and actions for raising productivity. Limitations on our knowledge also suggest the importance of research, not only on technology as it is usually defined, but on organizational, managerial, and motivational questions, as well as on other economic, social, and political problems. Suggested, as well, is the importance of experimenting with new ideas on a modest scale. This requires holding open the possibility of retreat, which in turn requires that commitments to keep unsuccessful experiments alive be avoided. It follows, also, that every experiment should provide for prompt and reliable feedback of information on the costs and benefits of the experimental policy, information to be weighed not only by those who may have developed a vested interest in the programs but by persons who can be more objective.

Because there is no dominant source of productivity growth to be singled out, pursuit of a policy to raise productivity must proceed on a wide front. And if this is true, the reader will not expect a list of specific programs, nor would it be possible to give one. Consider, for example, the fact that a major source of productivity growth is increased capital investment. Any policy to reduce the risk and uncertainty that confronts investors and to increase the rate of return they may expect, is, then, an option for improving productivity. But obviously it is not so much *an* option as it is a large *family* of options. There are many ways to stimulate capital formation. Each way would surely entail direct costs and have unintended effects that would need to be weighed, if the best way is to be chosen. What, to illustrate, can be done to deal with the depressant effect on the rate of national saving of the Social Security system as it is now organized and operated, without destroying its ability to meet the objective for which it was established?

It would be foolish, in an overview of the productivity problem, to try to go into any detail on this sort of question. For, besides policies to encourage more capital formation, consideration would have to be given also to policies to strengthen the process of training and education; to support and encourage the development of new basic knowledge and technologies and the diffusion and adaptation of the old and the new more swiftly; to assist in improving business (and nonprofit) organization and management; to remove obstacles to competition and lessen discrimination against minorities; and to strengthen the international exchange of goods and services.

The list of policies to improve productivity is long. Many also are the forms that implementation of these policies could take in the tax codes, regulations, and government support of research, statistics, and education. This raises a question about the choice among the implements of policy. Should the implements take the form of general rules and regulations or be tailored to the specific details of particular situations? In the case of regulation, for example, where highly specific "do's and don'ts" now fill the Federal Register, a policy shift toward more general rules and penalties—user charges, in the case of environmental services, to recall that example—would reduce the governmental burden. And the benefits could be greater, for producers and consumers would be encouraged to seek out the most economical means appropriate to their particular technical, economic, and environmental circumstances—circumstances that vary and the details of which they are in the best position to know.

Finally, because productivity is so important to the well-being of the people, steadier and closer attention should be paid to it, not only by the federal government but by the state and local governments, and not only by government but by business and labor and citizens more generally. There is need for a permanent federal agency charged with the responsibility, and armed with the resources, to place and keep the idea and importance of productivity prominently in the public view, to explain its meaning and determinants, and to act as a clearinghouse in the continuing and wide-ranging task of improving it. The National Council on Productivity is hardly equipped to carry this responsibility. In any case, it has done very little, so far. Perhaps proposals for a productivity agency in the Department of Commerce may lead to something more effective.

PRODUCTIVITY PROSPECTS

What I have said elsewhere about the prospects for growth of the nation's output may be said also, with appropriate changes, about the prospects for the growth of productivity, the major component of output growth. [16]

We can be reasonably confident on the basis of past experience and our understanding of the factors involved that, after averaging current and any later cyclical fluctuations, the nation's labor productivity will continue to grow. What we cannot be confident about is the speed at which productivity growth will proceed.

That speed will depend in part on certain developments in the economy that have already taken place and their effects, of which we know something, although not everything. The postwar rise and then decline in the birth rate will obviously greatly influence but not entirely determine the "quality" of the labor force in the years ahead. The jump in the world price of petroleum in 1973, and since then, will for years cause users of petroleum to seek means to conserve energy.

The future rate of productivity growth will depend in part also on developments over which we have—or could have—considerable control, such as the rate of capital formation and of investment in education and R&D. But we must choose to exercise this control, and this would mean accepting costs and settling controversies over the best way to exercise control.

The rate of productivity growth will depend also on developments over which we have little control. Economic and political changes outside the United States are the major examples. We can only try harder to obtain cooperation from other countries.

The rate of productivity growth will depend, finally, on all the developments that go under the heading of "luck," over which we have virtually no control. Even here, however, we can try to be better prepared than in the past to offset any dampening tendencies such changes may have on our productivity growth.

It is for these reasons that projections of output, input, and productivity are—or should be—accompanied by "conditions" or assumptions about policy and other causal factors, and are—or should be—offered in the form of two or more alternatives. But even conditional statements involve a strong element of judgment. They are *selected* as the most probable, and therefore as the most deserving of consideration, from what is inevitably a very wide range of possibilities. The fact that a projection is based on a trend does not preclude the need to choose. For example, one could project to 1990 the average rate of productivity growth during 1948–73 or 1947–79 or 1969–79 or even only 1973–79. Further, one could assume a constant rate of growth, or one could allow for a degree of retardation, as is suggested by the data covering the postwar period. The results would differ considerably. Whatever the projections selected, they would always be subject to revision as events unfolded and judgments about the effects of past and prospective developments were reconsidered.

Projections, it should be evident, are not the unambiguous forecasts that people usually ask for. Only if, out of the variety of possible futures projected, one is selected as *the* most likely is a forecast made. A judgment is still required on the conditions on which the selected projection depends and on the extent to which it depends on them. Involved also, however, is a judgment that it is *these* conditions that will most likely materialize. A political judgment, as well as an economic judgment, is implied, and this is not one that economists are especially well equipped to make.

With this warning in mind, readers will be prepared to view the sample of projections assembled in table 1.5 with the caution required. Their skepticism will not be lessened if they compare the BLS projection for 1977–80 (published in 1978) with the −0.2 percent per annum already experienced between 1977 and 1979 and with what may reasonably be expected for 1979–80 with the economy in a "growth recession," if not yet in a "classical recession." And they will understand, I trust, why I have not included a projection, or set of projections, of my own.

Table 1.5. Labor Productivity

Projected Average Annual Rates of Growth*
(percentage rates)

	Bureau of Labor Statistics, private sector	
	Base	High Employment
1977–80	2.8	2.9
1980–85	1.7	2.2
1985–90	1.0	1.4
	Council of Economic Advisers, total economy, potential	
1979–82	1	
1982–85	1.5–2	
	Kendrick, domestic business economy	
1980–90	2.1	
	Data Resources, nonfarm business sector	
	Long-term	Cyclical Alternative
1978–85	1.5	} 1.4
1985–90	1.9	
	Coen and Hickman, total economy, potential	
1978–83	1.7	
1983–92	1.8	

* The projections for the total economy should be raised by about 0.2 percetage points, as indicated earlier, to be comparable with the projections for the private or business sectors; or the latter should be reduced by that amount to be comparable with the former.

Sources: N.C. Saunders, "The U.S. Economy to 1990: Two Projections for Growth," *Monthly Labor Review*, December 1978.

Council of Economic Advisers, *Economic Report of the President* (Washington, D.C.: U.S. Government Printing Office, 1980).

Kendrick. See table 1.3 in this chapter.

Data Resources, *U.S. Long-Term Review* (Lexington, Mass.: Data Resources, Inc., 1979).

R.M. Coen, and B.G. Hickman, "Investment and Growth in an Econometric Model of the United States." Paper presented at the annual meeting of the American Economic Association, December 29, 1979.

There is much that could be said, without excessive speculation—and has been said by the makers of the projections—about some of the expectations summarized in these projections: the expectations about the future age–sex mix and its probable effect on labor quality, the gain in efficiency resulting from future reductions in average hours worked, continued investment in education, the decline in the rate of shift of workers from farm and nonfarm self-employment to more advantageous occupations, and a few others. Even then, only a few factors would have been weighed—not of controlling importance even taken together—about which something fairly definite could be said. For the great bulk of the rest—the prospects for tangible capital formation and the factors affecting multifactor productivity—we would find ourselves far deeper in the realm of speculation. At the end we would be left, at best, with a rather wide distribution of probabilities and a rather long list of conditions attached to each. Whether labor productivity will grow less rapidly in the future, measured from 1979 or from the next peak in the business cycle, than it did on the average between 1948 and 1973, and more rapidly than it has since 1973, as all the projections assembled in the table indicate, would remain a question.

It is better simply to say that this is the possibility that needs to be emphasized. The slow rate of productivity growth in recent years puts us on notice that things have not gone as well as we would like and that we may be disappointed also in the future unless positive support is given to factors favorable to higher productivity; or unless we accept the fact that a slower rate of growth in productivity is the price of progress toward other national goals—if that is, indeed, the dominant reason for the slowdown. But even if it is the dominant reason, it is surely not the only reason. What happens to productivity in the years ahead depends not only on the choices we make among our national and personal objectives; it depends also on the policies we pursue and the means we select to reach these objectives.

Even if the "most likely" future rate of productivity growth falls within the range of about 1.5 to 2.0 percent per annum, accepting the projections collected in table 1.5 as defining what is "most likely" (and ignoring the differences among the periods covered by the projections), a glance back at the historical rates in table 1.1 would remind us that the distribution of probable future rates could be wide. It is certainly easy to imagine futures that are not even as favorable as 1.5 percent per annum when the more extreme possibilities are considered. We could speculate on the hazards confronting the continued supply, at reasonable prices or at any price, of critical materials that must be imported, such as chromium, cobalt, and petroleum. We could wonder about a drift to much more, rather than less, protectionism, which would seriously heighten obstacles to the changes in the industrial, occupational, and regional structures of production that are required for growth. We could consider the consequences of an even stronger resistance than now exists to the production of atomic energy. But here, too, the possibilities are endless.

We can also imagine better futures. A heightened awareness of the social costs of a slower rate of growth in productivity, a clearer understanding that many factors are involved, and appropriate action to deal with these factors could increase the probability of doing as well in the future as in the past three decades. To the extent that some decline in the rate of productivity growth accompanies advances along other dimensions of economic and social welfare, a wider understanding of that fact might at least spur the search for a more economical trade-off.

With this we return to a question raised earlier: to what extent more rapid productivity growth need be, or in fact is, at the cost of a slower approach to, or some retreat from, other national objectives. This is not a settled issue, as I indicated. Some economists believe, for example, that less regulation and more economic freedom favor increased productivity, as Adam Smith argued long ago, and that with higher productivity we can better succeed in approaching other goals. Other economists would reverse the order but end up with much the same conclusion. They believe that reduction of racial discrimination eventually makes for higher productivity, as well as a more even income distribution, and that investment to improve the environment and to meet higher health and safety standards on the job must sooner or later favorably affect productivity and serve to offset some or all of the retarding effects on output caused by a slower rate of increase in "productive" plant and equipment.

CONCLUSION

When the *Economic Report of the President* appeared in February 1975, one of its appendix tables revealed an extraordinary combination of facts. The output of the private business economy had fallen during the recession under way, as it had in all previous recessions. But no accompanying decline had occurred, as in earlier recessions, in the number of worker-hours employed. This number had, in fact, risen slightly. As a result, output per worker-hour was substantially lower in 1974 than in 1973, the only year-to-year decline recorded in the table, which covered the entire postwar period. Yet nothing was said about productivity in the Council of Economic Advisers' discussion of economic developments during 1974. The only comment that seemed to be elicited was indirect: it concerned the accuracy of the output measure.

There are still some questions about the accuracy of the output (and labor input) measures and the derived productivity measure, but the decline in productivity between 1973 and 1974, its slow average growth from 1974 to 1978, and a second decline between 1978 and 1979, are not now what is in serious question. The question is, what are the causes of the slowdown in productivity and what can be done to improve the situation.

No *Economic Report* since 1975 has failed to take notice of the productivity problem and its difficulties. The Council of Economic Advisers, in the 1979 *Economic Report*, found it hard to distinguish the long-term rate of advance in productivity from the changes reflecting "nonrecurrent" or episodic events of recent years; the CEA in the 1980 *Economic Report* begins its section on "potential GNP" with the statement that "the uncertainties surrounding the causes and extent of the decline in trend productivity make the assessment of the rate of growth of the economy's productive potential most difficult."

However, there is more to the problem than its statistical and economic aspects. There are also the political problems of dealing with the productivity slowdown. These I have hardly mentioned. They also are very difficult. Even national objectives on which all agree are valued differently by different people; each section of the community has its own private objectives; and efforts to rationalize institutions and governmental organization seldom fail to encounter serious obstacles.

Perhaps this elaboration of the productivity problem may seem to have put too much stress on the difficulties and the gaps and uncertainties in our knowledge, the "empty portion of the bottle." If so, let me say, in redress, that had I been writing a history of productivity measurement, analysis, and policy, I would have had some progress to report. But my job was to look forward. I can only hope that at this final point of my text, the reader will not be muttering:

> Oh, rather give me commentators plain,
> Who with no deep researches vex the brain.[17]

NOTES

1. In these sectors are reported about 15 percent or 20 percent of the nation's employment and gross national product, as these are conventionally calculated. The estimates that have been made for productivity growth in the economy as a whole have run, in recent years, about 0.2 percentage points below those given in table 1.1 for the private domestic sector.
2. The quantity of labor, in terms of worker-hours, is taken into account in the denominator of the labor productivity and capital-per-hour ratios. This involves certain assumptions about the relation between quantity of labor and quantity of output, and between number of workers and hours per worker, which are bones of contention among economists. In a more sophisticated analysis, these assumptions would be avoided, but the necessary statistics are hard to come by.

   When output is measured by real total value of product, as it usually is in analyzing the productivity of individual industries or firms, the real cost of materials, fuel, components, services, and supplies purchased from other industries or firms constitutes another input, and therefore a possible source of change in labor productivity. The last component listed in table 1.2 would then be "output per unit of labor, tangible capital, and purchased goods and services."
3. What is "satisfactory" or "sufficiently adequate" depends on the quantity and quality of available information, which has improved over the years (input estimates now common were unheard of years ago). What is satisfactory depends also on the knowledge, ingenuity, and daring of those who undertake to do productivity analyses, which also have changed over time, and on their standards of accuracy. Variation in these respects accounts for some of the differences among the estimates in table 1.3.

   What is satisfactory to those who use the measures will depend, of course, on *their* standards and purposes—and sophistication.
4. These stem from monopoly and discrimination, and also from lags in adjustment to the incessant changes that occur in demand and supply.
5. Estimation of rental prices involves complexities and issues which cannot be discussed here. Especially controversial is, first, the meaning and measurement of depreciation and obsolescence, particularly with regard to their bearing on the distinction between changes in the quantity and quality of capital that result from technological advance; and second, the treatment of depreciation and

obsolescence in calculating the rental price. On the second point, when a rental price net of capital consumption is used, the measured importance of capital as a source of increase in labor productivity is lower than when a gross rental price is used. The difference can be considerable, as is suggested by the estimates in table 1.3.

6. Panel to Review Productivity Statistics, National Research Council, *Measurement and Interpretation of Productivity* (Washington, D.C.: National Academy of Sciences, 1979).
7. Only one of the sets of estimates in table 1.3 is available through 1978. Of the other two, one is available through 1977, and the other, only through 1976. None of the four estimates in table 1.3 is yet available through 1979.

   It should be noted that the several compilations are not entirely independent of one another. A great deal of the underlying data is common to all, and a certain amount of borrowing of detailed estimates has taken place.
8. By making separate estimates for four classes of assets (see table 1.4), Denison is to that extent implicitly taking account of change in the quality of capital.
9. Denison's efforts deserve a fuller discussion than can be given here, but the constraints of space permit only a few brief comments. For more complete information, the reader should refer to Denison's important book, *Accounting for Slower Economic Growth: The U.S. in the 1970s* (Washington, D.C.: The Brookings Institution, 1979).

   J. W. Kendrick's estimates (given only in summary in table 1.3) are also available in detail. He goes much further than Denison in some directions; and except where he borrows from Denison, his estimates are rather different. An evaluation will be possible when Kendrick's estimates are published in final form, with the necessary supporting evidence.
10. Zvi Griliches recently posed a question of interest in this connection. Could the slowdown in the growth of real R&D expenditures, which began in the mid-1960s but covers only investment in technology, explain the slowdown in productivity growth, wholly or in part? His answer was "Probably not." (See his paper on "R&D and the Productivity Slowdown," presented before the American Economic Association in December 1979.) The word "probably" hints at the difficulties encountered in efforts to answer the question.
11. A critical review of various explanations of the slowdown appears in Denison's *Accounting for Slower Economic Growth*, op. cit., particularly chapter 9.
12. Here and in the next section I draw on a paper prepared for the National Science Foundation (see "The Economics of Productivity: Some Options for Improvement," in Volume II of the Foundation's *The Five-Year Outlook: Problems, Opportunities, and Constraints in Science and Technology* [Washington, D.C.: National Science Foundation, 1980]).
13. Estimates of Social Security wealth are necessarily somewhat hypothetical. However, the estimates made on different assumptions all show a rise, and at a somewhat accelerated pace, relative to gross national product (GNP). See M. Feldstein, "Social Security, Induced Retirement, and Aggregate Capital Accumulation," *Journal of Political Economy*, September-October 1974, and R. J. Barro, *The Impact of Social Security on Private Savings: Evidence from the U.S.*

Time Series, Studies in Social Security and Retirement Policy (Washington, D.C.: American Enterprise Institute, 1978).

14. See the pioneer work by Hiram S. Davis, *Productivity Accounting* (Philadelphia: University of Pennsylvania Press, 1955); also, J. W. Kendrick and D. Creamer, "Measuring Company Productivity," *Studies in Business Economics, No. 74* (New York: The Conference Board, 1961), revised in *No. 89* (1965).
15. Since I have scolded managers for their laggard recognition and acceptance of productivity accounting, I should also take to task government officials for an even longer lag. We do not have an acceptable measure of national productivity because measures of productivity in government are primitive at best. The measure of output (GNP) reported in the national accounts as originating in government is based entirely on payments to government workers, with no allowance for the services of capital. This is mainly because balance sheets—or any adequate records—showing capital assets are kept by very few governmental units. This serious deficiency is hardly conducive to efficient management of the large capital resources held by government.
16. See my monograph, *The Economic Growth of the United States: Perspective and Prospective*, in the series on *Canada-U.S. Prospects* (Montreal: C. D. Howe Research Institute, 1979; and Washington, D.C.: National Planning Association, 1979).
17. The couplet is from one of George Crabbe's poems.

2.
Energy Prices and Productivity Growth

Dale W. Jorgenson
Professor of Economics, Harvard University

INTRODUCTION

The growth of the U.S. economy in the postwar period has been very rapid by historical standards. The rate of economic growth reached its maximum during the period 1960 to 1966. Growth rates have slowed substantially since 1966 and declined further since 1973. A major source of uncertainty in projections concerning the future of the U.S. economy is whether patterns of growth will better conform to the rapid growth of the early 1960s, the more moderate growth of the late 1960s and early 1970s, or the disappointing growth since 1973.

Our first objective here is to identify more precisely the sources of uncertainty about future U.S. economic growth. For this purpose we decompose the growth of output during the postwar period into contributions of capital input, labor input, and productivity growth. For the period 1948 to 1976 we find that all three sources of economic growth are significant and must be considered in analyzing future growth potential. For the postwar period capital input has made the most important contribution to the growth of output, productivity growth has been next most important, and labor input has been least important.

Focusing on the period 1973 to 1976, we find that the fall in the rate of economic growth has been due to a dramatic decline in productivity growth. Declines in the contributions of capital and labor input are much less significant in explaining the slowdown.

We conclude that the future growth of productivity is the main source of uncertainty in projections of future U.S. economic growth.

Our second objective is to analyze the slowdown in productivity growth for the U.S. economy as a whole in greater detail. For this purpose we decompose productivity growth during the postwar period into components that can be identified with productivity growth at the sectoral level and with reallocations of output, capital input, and labor input among sectors. For the period 1948 to 1976, we find that these reallocations are insignificant relative to sectoral productivity growth. The combined effect of all three reallocations is slightly negative, but sufficiently small in magnitude to be negligible as a source of aggregate productivity growth.

Again focusing on the period 1973 to 1976, it is possible that the economic dislocations that accompanied the severe economic contraction of 1974 and 1975 could have resulted in shifts of output and inputs among sectors that contributed to the slowdown of productivity growth at the aggregate level. Alternatively, the sources of the slowdown might be found in slowing productivity growth at the level of individual industrial sectors. We find that the contribution of reallocations of output and inputs among sectors was positive rather than negative during the period 1973–1976 and relatively small. Declines in productivity growth for the individual industrial sectors of the U.S. economy must bear the full burden of explaining the slowdown in productivity growth for the economy as a whole.

The decomposition of the growth of output among contributions of capital input, labor input, and productivity growth is helpful in isolating the sources of uncertainty in future growth projections. The further decomposition of productivity growth among reallocations of output, capital input, and labor input among sectors and growth in productivity at the sectoral level provides additional detail. The uncertainty in future growth projections can be resolved only by providing an explanation for the fall in productivity growth at the sectoral level. For this purpose an econometric model of sectoral productivity growth is required.

Our third objective is to present the results of an econometric analysis of the determinants of productivity growth at the sectoral level. Our econometric model determines the growth of sectoral productivity as a function of relative prices of sectoral inputs. For each sector we divide inputs among capital, labor, energy, and materials inputs. We allow for the fact that the value of sectoral output includes the value of intermediate inputs—energy and materials—as well as the value of primary factors of production—capital and labor. Differences in relative prices for inputs are associated with differences in productivity growth for each sector.

After fitting our econometric model of productivity growth to data for individual industrial sectors, we find that productivity growth decreases with an increase in the price of capital input for a very large proportion of U.S. industries. Similarly, productivity growth falls with higher prices of labor input for a large proportion of industries. Higher energy prices tend to slow the growth of productivity for a large proportion of industries. By contrast we find that an increase in the price of materials input is associated with increases in productivity growth for almost all industries.

Since 1973 the relative prices of capital, labor, energy, and materials inputs have been altered radically as a consequence of the increase in the price of energy relative to other productive inputs. Higher world petroleum prices following the Arab oil embargo of late 1973 and 1974 have resulted in sharp increases in prices for all forms of energy in the U.S. economy—oil, natural gas, coal, and electricity generated from fossil fuels and other sources. Although the U.S. economy has been partly shielded from the impact of higher world petroleum prices through a system of price controls, all industrial sectors have experienced large increases in the price of energy relative to other inputs.

Our econometric model reveals that slower productivity growth at the sectoral level is associated with higher prices of energy relative to other inputs. Our first conclusion is that the slowdown of sectoral productivity growth after 1973 is a consequence of the sharp increase in the price of energy relative to other productive inputs that began with the run-up of world petroleum prices in late 1973 and early 1974. The fall in sectoral productivity growth after 1973 is responsible in turn for the decline in productivity growth for the U.S. economy as a whole. Slower productivity growth is the primary source of the slowdown in U.S. economic growth since 1973.

Our final objective is to consider the prospects for future U.S. economic growth. Exports of petroleum from Iran dropped sharply during 1979, following the revolution in that country in late 1978. During 1979 world petroleum prices jumped 130 to 140 percent, resulting in large and rapid price increases for petroleum products in the United States. During 1979 the prices of petroleum products began to move to world levels as a consequence of the decontrol of domestic prices by the U.S. government over the period 1979 to 1981. Prices of natural gas will also be allowed to rise through decontrol by 1985 or, at the latest, by 1987. Prices of energy confronted by individual industries within the United States have already increased relative to other productive inputs and can be expected to increase further.

Based on the performance of the United States economy since 1973, we can anticipate a further slowdown in the rate of economic growth, a decline in the growth of productivity for the economy as a whole, and declines in sectoral productivity growth for a wide range of industries. These dismal conclusions suggest that a return to the rapid growth of the early 1960s is highly unlikely, that even the slower growth of the late 1960s and early 1970s will be difficult to attain, and that the performance of the U.S. economy during the 1980s could be worse than during the period from 1973 to the present. We conclude the chapter with a discussion of policy measures to ameliorate the negative effects of higher energy prices on future U.S. economic growth.

THE GROWTH SLOWDOWN

In this section we begin our analysis of the slowdown in U.S. economic growth by decomposing the growth of output for the economy as a whole into the contributions of capital input, labor input, and productivity growth.[1] The results are given in table 2.1 for the postwar period 1948–1976 and for the following seven subperiods: 1948–1953, 1953–1957, 1957–1960, 1960–1966, 1966–1969, 1969–1973, and 1973–1976.[2] Except for the period from 1973 to 1976, each of the subperiods covers economic activity from one cyclical peak to the next. The last period covers economic activity from the cyclical peak in 1973 to 1976, a year of recovery from the sharp downturn in economic activity in 1974 and 1975.

We first present rates of growth for output, capital input, labor input, and productivity for the U.S. economy. For the postwar period as a whole, output grew at 3.50 percent per year, capital input grew at 4.01 percent, and labor grew at 1.28 percent. The

Table 2.1. Growth of Output and Inputs for the U.S. Economy, 1948–1976
(Percentage Growth)

	1948–1976	1948–1953	1953–1957	1957–1960	1960–1966	1966–1969	1969–1973	1973–1976
Growth Rates								
Output	3.50	4.57	3.13	2.79	4.83	3.24	3.24	0.89
Capital input	4.01	5.07	3.93	2.74	3.76	5.06	3.96	3.12
Labor input	1.28	1.60	0.23	0.99	1.99	1.85	1.16	0.58
Productivity	1.14	1.66	1.46	1.13	2.11	0.04	0.95	−0.70
Contributions								
Capital input	1.61	1.94	1.54	1.09	1.56	2.11	1.61	1.26
Labor input	0.75	0.97	0.13	0.57	1.16	1.08	0.68	0.33

growth of productivity averaged 1.14 percent per year. The rate of economic growth reached its maximum at 4.83 percent during the period 1960–1966 and grew at only 0.89 percent during the recession and partial recovery of 1973–1976. The growth of capital input was more even, exceeding 5 percent in 1948–1953 and 1966–1969 and falling to 3.12 percent in 1973–1976. The growth of labor input reached its maximum in the period 1960–1966 at 1.99 percent and fell to 0.58 percent in 1973–1976, which was above the minimum of 0.23 percent in the period 1953–1957.

We can express the rate of growth of output for the U.S. economy as a whole as the sum of a weighted average of the rates of growth of capital and labor inputs and the growth of productivity. The weights associated with capital and labor inputs are average shares of these inputs in the value of output. The contribution of each input is the product of the average share of this input and the corresponding input growth rate. We present contributions of capital and labor inputs to U.S. economic growth for the period 1948–1976 and for seven subperiods in table 2.1. Considering productivity growth, we find that the maximum occurred from 1960 to 1966 at 2.11 percent per year. During the period 1966–1969 productivity growth was almost negligible at 0.04 percent. Productivity growth recovered to 0.95 percent during the period 1969–1973 and fell to a negative 0.70 percent during 1973–1976.

Since the value shares of capital and labor inputs are very stable over the period 1948–1976, the movements of the contributions of these inputs to the growth of output largely parallel those of the growth rates of the inputs themselves. For the postwar period as a whole, the contribution of capital input of 1.61 percent is the most important source of output growth. Productivity growth is next most important at 1.14 percent, while the contribution of labor input is the third most important at 0.75 percent. All three sources of growth are significant and must be considered in an analysis of the slowdown of economic growth during the period 1973–1976. However, capital input is clearly the most important contributor to the rapid growth of the U.S. economy during the postwar period.[3]

Focusing on the period 1973 to 1976, we find that the contribution of capital input fell to 1.26 percent for a drop of 0.35 percent from the postwar average; the contribution of labor input fell to 0.33 percent for a drop of 0.42 percent; and the productivity growth at a negative 0.70 percent dropped 1.84 percent. We conclude that the fall in the rate of U.S. economic growth during the period 1973–1976 was largely due to the fall in productivity growth. Declines in the contributions of capital and labor inputs are much less significant in explaining the slowdown. A detailed explanation of the fall in productivity growth is needed to account for the slowdown in U.S. economic growth.

To analyze the sharp decline in productivity growth for the U.S. economy as a whole during the period 1973 to 1976 in greater detail, we employ data on productivity growth for individual industrial sectors. For this purpose it is important to distinguish between productivity growth at the aggregate level and productivity growth at the sectoral level. At the aggregate level the appropriate concept of output is value added, defined as the sum of the values of capital and labor inputs for all sectors of the economy. At the sectoral level the appropriate concept of output includes the value of primary factors of production at the sectoral level—capital and labor inputs—and the value of intermediate inputs—energy and materials inputs. In aggregating over sectors to obtain output for the U.S. economy as a whole, the production and consumption of intermediate goods cancel out, so that values of energy and materials inputs do not appear at the aggregate level.

We can express productivity growth for the U.S. economy as a whole as the sum of four components. The first component is a weighted sum of productivity growth rates for individual industrial sectors. The weights are ratios of the value of output in each sector to value added in that sector. The sum of these weights over all sectors exceeds unity, since productivity growth in each sector contributes to the growth of output in that sector and to the growth of output in other sectors through deliveries of intermediate inputs to those sectors. The remaining components of aggregate productivity growth represent the contributions of reallocations of value added, capital input, and labor input among sectors to productivity growth for the economy as a whole.[4]

The role of reallocations of output, capital input, and labor input among sectors is easily understood. For example, if capital input moves from a sector with a relatively low rate of return to a sector with a high rate of return, the quantity of capital input for the economy as a whole is unchanged, but the level of output is increased, so that productivity has improved. Similarly, if labor input moves from a sector with low wages to a sector with high wages, labor input is unchanged, but productivity has improved. Productivity growth for the economy as a whole is a combination of improvements in productivity at the sectoral level and reallocations of output, capital input, and labor input among sectors. Data on reallocations of output, capital input, and labor input for the postwar period 1948 to 1976 and for seven subperiods are given in table 2.2.[5]

For the postwar period as a whole, productivity growth at the aggregate level is dominated by the contribution of sectoral productivity growth of 1.24 percent per year. The contributions of reallocations of output, capital input, and labor input are a negative 0.16 percent, a positive 0.08 percent, and a negative 0.02 percent. Adding these contributions together, we find that the combined effect of the three reallocations is a negative 0.10 percent, which is negligible by

Table 2.2. Productivity Growth for the U.S. Economy, 1948–1976 (Percentage Growth)

	1948–1976	1948–1953	1953–1957	1957–1960	1960–1966	1966–1969	1969–1973	1973–1976
Sectoral productivity growth	1.24	2.19	1.77	1.45	2.17	0.25	0.48	1.13
Reallocation of value added	−0.16	−0.75	−0.30	−0.10	−0.16	−0.25	0.30	0.46
Reallocation of capital input	0.08	0.22	0.08	−0.01	0.02	0.01	0.10	0.08
Reallocation of labor input	−0.02	−0.0	−0.08	−0.21	0.08	0.04	0.06	−0.11

comparison with the effect of productivity growth at the sectoral level. Productivity growth at the aggregate level provides an accurate picture of average productivity growth for individual industries; this picture is not distorted in an important way by the effect of reallocations of output and inputs among sectors.

Again focusing on the period 1973–1976, we find that the contribution of sectoral productivity growth to productivity growth for the economy as a whole fell to a negative 1.13 percent for a drop of 2.37 percent from the postwar average. By contrast the contribution of reallocations of output rose to 0.46 percent for a gain of 0.62 percent from the postwar average. The contribution of the reallocation of capital input was unchanged at 0.08 percent, while the contribution of labor input fell to a negative 0.11 percent for a drop of 0.09 percent from the postwar average. The combined contribution of all three reallocations rose 0.53 percent, partially offsetting the precipitous decline in productivity growth at the sectoral level. We conclude that declines in productivity growth for the individual industrial sectors of the U.S. economy are more than sufficient to explain the decline in productivity growth for the economy as a whole.

To summarize our findings on the slowdown of U.S. economic growth during the period 1973–1976, we find that the drop in the growth of output of 2.61 percent per year from the postwar average is the sum of a decline in the contribution of labor input of 0.42 percent per year, a sharp dip in sectoral rates of productivity growth of 2.37 percent, a rise in the role of reallocations of output among sectors of 0.62 percent per year, no change in the reallocations of capital input, and a decline in the contribution of reallocations of labor input of 0.09 percent per year. Whatever the causes of the slowdown, they are to be found in the collapse of productivity growth at the sectoral level rather than in a slowdown in the growth of capital and labor inputs at the aggregate level or in the reallocations of output, capital input, or labor input among sectors.

The decomposition of economic growth into the contributions of capital input, labor input, and productivity growth is helpful in pinpointing the causes of the slowdown. The further decomposition of productivity growth for the economy as a whole into contributions of sectoral productivity growth and reallocations of output, capital input, and labor input is useful in providing additional detail.

However, our measure of sectoral productivity growth is simply the unexplained residual between growth of sectoral output and the contributions of sectoral capital, labor, energy, and materials inputs. The problem remains of providing an explanation for the fall in productivity growth at the sectoral level.

SECTORAL PRODUCTIVITY GROWTH

We have now succeeded in identifying the decline in productivity growth at the level of individual industrial sectors within the U.S. economy as the main culprit in the slowdown of U.S. economic growth that took place after 1973. To provide an explanation for the slowdown, we must go behind the measurements to identify the determinants of productivity growth at the sectoral level. For this purpose we require an econometric model of sectoral productivity growth. In this section we present a summary of the results of applying such an econometric model to detailed data on sectoral output and capital, labor, energy, and materials inputs for 35 individual industries in the United States.

Our complete econometric model is based on sectoral price functions for each of the 35 industries included in our study.[6] Each price function gives the price of the output of the corresponding industrial sector as a function of the prices of capital, labor, energy, and materials inputs and time, where time represents the level of technology in the sector.[7] Obviously, an increase in the price of one of the inputs, holding the prices of the other inputs and the level of technology constant, will necessitate an increase in the price of output. Similarly, if productivity in a sector improves and the prices of all inputs into the sector remain the same, the price of output must fall. Price functions summarize these and other relationships among the prices of output, capital, labor, energy, and materials inputs, and the level of technology.

Although the sectoral price functions provide a complete model of production patterns for each sector, it is useful to express this model in an alternative and equivalent form. We can express the shares of each of the four inputs—capital, labor, energy, and materials—in the value of output as functions of the prices of these inputs and time, again representing the level of technology.[8] We can add to these four equations for the value shares an equation that expresses productivity growth as a function of the prices of the four inputs and time.[9] In fact, the negative of the rate of productivity growth is a function of the four input prices and time. This equation is our econometric model of sectoral productivity growth.[10]

Like any econometric model, the relationships determining the value shares of capital, labor, energy, and materials inputs and the negative of the rate of productivity growth involve unknown parameters that must be estimated from data for the individual industries. Included among these unknown parameters are biases of productivity growth that indicate the effect of changes in the level of technology on the value shares of each of the four inputs.[11] For example, the bias of productivity growth for capital input gives the change in the share of capital input in the value of output in response to changes in the level of technology, represented by time. Similarly, biases of productivity growth for labor, energy, and materials inputs give changes in the shares of labor, energy, and materials inputs in the value of output that results from changes in the level of technology.

We say that productivity growth is *capital using* if the bias of productivity growth for capital input is positive, that is, if changes in the level of technology result in an increase in the share of capital input in the value of output, holding all input prices constant. Productivity growth involves an increase in the quantity of capital input as technology changes, so that we say that the change in technology is capital using. Similarly, we say that productivity growth is *capital saving* if the bias of productivity growth for capital input is negative. As technology changes, the production process uses less capital input, so that the change in technology is capital saving.

Similarly, we can say that productivity growth is *labor using* or *labor saving* if the bias of productivity growth for labor input is positive or negative. As technology changes, the production process uses more or less labor input, depending on whether the change in technology is labor using or labor saving. We can associate *energy-using* or *energy-saving* productivity growth with positive or negative biases of productivity growth for energy input. Finally, we can associate *materials-using* or *materials-saving* productivity growth with positive or negative biases of productivity growth for materials input. Since the shares of all four inputs—capital, labor, energy, and materials—sum to unity, productivity growth that "uses" or "saves" all four inputs is impossible. In fact, the sum of the biases for all four must be precisely zero, since the changes in all four shares with any change in technology must sum to zero.

We have pointed out that our econometric model for each industrial sector of the U.S. economy includes an equation giving the negative of sectoral productivity growth as a function of the prices of the four inputs and time. The biases of technical change with respect to each of the four inputs appear as the coefficients of time, representing the level of technology, in the four equations for the value shares of all four inputs. The biases also appear as coefficients of the prices in the equation for the negative of sectoral productivity growth. This feature of our econometric model makes it possible to use information about changes in the value shares with time, and changes in the rate of sectoral productivity growth with prices, in determining estimates of the biases of technical change.

The biases of productivity growth express the dependence of value shares of the four inputs on the level of technology and also express the dependence of the negative of productivity growth on the input prices. We can say that capital-using productivity growth, associated with a positive bias of productivity growth for capital input, implies that an increase in the price of capital input decreases the rate of productivity growth (or increases the negative of the rate of productivity growth). Similarly, capital-saving productivity growth, associated with a negative bias for capital input, implies that an increase in the price of capital input increases the rate of productivity growth. Analogous relationships hold between biases of labor, energy, and materials inputs and the direction of the impact of changes in the prices of each of these inputs on the rate of productivity growth.[12]

Jorgenson and Fraumeni [1980] have fitted biases of productivity growth for 35 industrial sectors that make up the whole of the producing sector of the U.S. economy. They have also fitted the other parameters of the econometric model that we have described above. Since our primary concern in this section is to analyze the determinants of productivity growth at the sectoral level, we focus on the patterns of productivity growth revealed in table 2.3. We have listed the industries characterized by each of the possible combinations of biases of productivity growth, consisting of one or more positive biases and one or more negative biases.[13]

The pattern of productivity growth that occurs most frequently in table 2.3 is capital-using, labor-using, energy-using, and materials-

Table 2.3 Classification of Industries by Biases of Productivity Growth

Pattern of Biases	Industries
Capital using Labor using Energy using Materials saving	Agriculture; metal mining; crude petroleum and natural gas; nonmetallic mining; textiles; apparel; lumber; furniture; printing; leather; fabricated metals; electrical machinery; motor vehicles; instruments; miscellaneous manufacturing; transportation; trade; finance; insurance and real estate; services
Capital using Labor using Energy saving Materials saving	Coal mining; tobacco manufactures; communications; government enterprises
Capital using Labor saving Energy using Materials saving	Petroleum refining
Capital using Labor saving Energy saving Materials using	Construction
Capital saving Labor saving Energy using Materials saving	Electric utilities
Capital saving Labor using Energy saving Materials saving	Primary metals
Capital saving Labor using Energy using Materials saving	Paper; chemicals; rubber; stone; clay and glass; machinery except electrical; transportation equipment and ordnance; gas utilities
Capital saving Labor saving Energy using Materials using	Food

saving productivity growth. This pattern occurs for 19 of the 35 industries analyzed by Jorgenson and Fraumeni. For this pattern of productivity growth, the bias of productivity growth for capital input, labor input, and energy input are positive, and the bias of productivity growth for materials input is negative. This pattern implies that increases in the prices of capital input, labor input, and energy input decrease the rate of productivity growth, while increases in the price of materials input increase the rate of productivity growth.

Considering all patterns of productivity growth included in table 2.3, we find that productivity growth is capital using for 25 of the 35 industries included in the study. Productivity growth is capital saving for the remaining 10 industries. Similarly, productivity growth is labor using for 31 of the 35 industries and labor saving for the remaining 4 industries; productivity growth is energy using for 29 of the 35 industries included in table 2.3 and is energy saving for the remaining 6. Finally, productivity growth is materials using for only 2 of the 35 industries and is materials saving for the remaining 33. We conclude that for a very large proportion of industries the rate of productivity growth decreases with increases in the prices of capital, labor, and energy inputs, and increases in the price of materials inputs.

The most striking change in the relative prices of capital, labor, energy, and materials inputs that has taken place since 1973 is the staggering increase in the price of energy. The rise in energy prices began in 1972 before the Arab oil embargo, as the U.S. economy moved toward the double-digit inflation that characterized 1973. In late 1973 and early 1974 the price of petroleum on world markets increased by a factor of four, precipitating a rise in domestic prices of petroleum products, natural gas, coal, and uranium. The impact of higher world petroleum prices was partly deflected by price controls for petroleum and natural gas that resulted in the emergence of shortages of these products during 1974. All industrial sectors of the U.S. economy experienced sharp increases in the price of energy relative to other inputs.

Slower growth in productivity at the sectoral level is associated with higher energy prices for 29 of the 35 industries that make up the producing sector of the U.S. economy. The dramatic increases in energy prices resulted in a slowdown in productivity growth at the sectoral level. In the preceding section we have seen that the fall in sectoral productivity growth after 1973 is the primary explanation for the decline in productivity for the U.S. economy as a whole. Finally, we have shown that the slowdown in productivity growth during the period 1973–1976 is the main source of the fall in the rate of U.S. economic growth since 1973.

We have now provided a solution to the problem posed by the disappointing growth record of the U.S. economy since 1973. By reversing historical trends toward lower prices of energy in the U.S. economy, the aftermath of the Arab oil embargo of 1973 and 1974 has led to an end to rapid economic growth. The remaining task is to draw the implications of our findings for future U.S. economic growth. Projections of future economic growth must take into account the dismal performance of the U.S. economy since 1973 as well as the rapid growth that has characterized the U.S. economy during the postwar period. In particular, such projections must take into account the change in the price of energy input for individual industrial sectors, relative to prices of capital, labor, and materials inputs.

PROGNOSIS

Our objective in this concluding section of the chapter is to provide a prognosis for future U.S. economic growth. For this purpose we cannot rely on the extrapolation of past trends in productivity growth or its components. The year 1973 marks a sharp break in trend associated with a decline in rates of productivity growth at the sectoral level. Comparing the period after 1973 with the rest of the postwar period, we can associate the decline in productivity growth with the dramatic increase in energy prices that followed the Arab oil embargo in late 1973 and early 1974. The remaining task is to analyze the prospects for a return to the high sectoral productivity growth rates of the early 1960s, for moderate growth of sectoral productivity growth such as that of the late 1960s and early 1970s, or for continuation of the disappointing growth since 1973.

During 1979 there was a further sharp increase in world petroleum prices, following the interruption of Iranian petroleum exports that accompanied the revolution that took place in that country in late 1978. Although prices of petroleum sold by different petroleum exporting countries differ widely, the average price of petroleum imported into the United States rose by 130 to 140 percent from December 1978 to mid-1980. In April 1979 President Carter announced that prices of petroleum products would be decontrolled gradually over the period from May 1979 to September 1981. As a consequence, domestic petroleum prices in the United States will move to world levels in a relatively short period of time. Domestic natural gas prices will also be subject to gradual decontrol, moving to world levels as early as 1985 or, at the latest, 1987.

Given the sharp increase in the price of energy relative to the prices of other productive inputs, the prospects for productivity growth at the sectoral level are dismal. In the absence of any reduction in prices of capital and labor inputs during the 1980s, decline in productivity growth for a wide range of U.S. industries, a decline in the growth of productivity for the U.S. economy as a whole, and a further slowdown in the rate of U.S. economic growth can be expected. To avoid a repetition of the unsatisfactory economic performance of the 1970s, it is essential to undertake measures to reduce the price of capital input and labor input. The price of capital input can be reduced by cutting taxes on income from capital.[14] Similarly, payroll taxes can be cut in order to reduce the price of labor input.

The prospects for changes in tax policy that would have a substantial positive impact on productivity growth in the early 1980s are not bright. Any attempt to balance the federal budget during 1981 in the face of a sharp recession during the last half of 1980 and the first half of 1981 will require tax increases rather than tax cuts. Higher inflation rates have resulted in an increase in the effective rate of taxation of capital. Payroll taxes are currently scheduled to rise in 1981. For these reasons it appears that a return to the rapid growth of the early 1960s is out of the question. Even the moderate growth of the late 1960s and early 1970s would be difficult to attain. In the absence of measures to cut taxes on capital and labor inputs, the performance of the U.S. economy during the 1980s could be worse than during the period from 1973 to the present.

For economists the role of productivity in economic growth presents a problem comparable in scientific interest and social importance to the problem of unemployment during the Great Depression of the 1930s. Conventional methods of economic analysis have been tried and have been found to be inadequate. Clearly, a new framework will be required for economic understanding. The findings we have outlined above contain some of the elements that will be required for the new framework for economic analysis as the U.S. economy enters the 1980s.

At first blush, the finding that higher energy prices are an important determinant of the slowdown in U.S. economic growth seems paradoxical. In aggregative studies of sources of economic growth, energy does not appear as an input, since energy is an intermediate good and flows of intermediate goods appear as both outputs and inputs of individual industrial sectors, canceling out for the economy as a whole.[15] It is necessary to disaggregate the sources to economic growth into components that can be identified with output and inputs at the sectoral level in order to define an appropriate role for energy.[16]

Within a framework for analyzing economic growth that is disaggregated to the sectoral level, it is not sufficient to provide a decomposition of the growth of sectoral output among the contributions of sectoral inputs and the growth of sectoral productivity.[17] It is necessary to explain the growth of sectoral productivity by means of an econometric model of productivity growth for each sector. Without such econometric models, the growth of sectoral productivity is simply an unexplained residual between the growth of output and the contributions of capital, labor, energy, and materials inputs.

Finally, the parameters of an econometric model of production must be estimated from empirical data in order to determine the direction and significance of the influence of energy prices on productivity growth at the sectoral level.[18] From a conceptual point of view, a model of production is consistent with positive, negative, or zero impacts of energy prices on sectoral productivity growth. From an empirical point of view, the influence of higher energy prices is negative and highly significant. There is no way to substantiate this empirical finding without estimates of the unknown parameters of the econometric model of productivity growth.

The steps we have outlined—disaggregating the sources of economic growth down to the sectoral level; decomposing the rate of growth of sectoral output into sectoral productivity growth and the contributions of capital, labor, energy, and materials inputs; and modeling the rate of growth of productivity econometrically have been taken only recently. Much additional research will be required to provide an exhaustive explanation of the slowdown of U.S. economic growth within the new framework and to derive the implications of the slowdown for the future growth of the economy.

NOTES

1. The methodology that underlies our decomposition of the growth of output is presented in detail by Jorgenson (1980).
2. The results presented in table 2.1 are those of Fraumeni and Jorgenson (1980), who also provide annual data for output and inputs.
3. This conclusion contrasts sharply with that of Denison (1979). For a comparison of our methodology with that of Denison, see Jorgenson and Griliches (1972).
4. The methodology that underlies our decomposition of productivity growth is presented in detail by Jorgenson (1980).
5. The results presented in table 2.2 are those of Fraumeni and Jorgenson (1980), who also provide annual data for productivity growth.
6. Econometric models for each of the 35 industries are given by Jorgenson and Fraumeni (1980).
7. The price function was introduced by Samuelson (1953). A complete characterization of the sectoral price functions employed in this study is provided by Jorgenson and Fraumeni (1980).
8. Our sectoral price functions are based on the translog price function introduced by Christensen, Jorgenson, and Lau (1971, 1973). The translog price function was first applied at the sectoral level by Berndt and Jorgenson (1973) and Berndt and Wood (1975). References to sectoral production studies incorporating energy and materials inputs are given by Berndt and Wood (1979).
9. Productivity growth is represented by the translog index introduced by Christensen and Jorgenson (1970). The translog index of productivity growth was first derived from the translog price function by Diewert (1980) and by Jorgenson and Lau (1980).
10. This model of sectoral productivity growth is based on that of Jorgenson and Lau (1980).
11. The bias of productivity growth was introduced by Hicks (1932). An alternative definition of the bias of productivity growth was introduced by Binswanger (1974a, 1974b). The definition of the bias of productivity growth employed in our econometric model is due to Jorgenson and Lau 1980.
12. A complete characterization of biases of productivity growth is given by Jorgenson and Fraumeni (1980).
13. The results presented in table 2.3 are those of Jorgenson and Fraumeni (1980). Of the 14 logically possible combinations of biases of productivity growth, only the 8 patterns presented in table 2.3 occur empirically.

14. An analysis of alternative proposals for cutting taxes on income from capital is presented by Auerbach and Jorgenson (1980).
15. See, for example, Denison (1979).
16. Kendrick (1961, 1973) has presented an analysis of productivity growth at the sectoral level. However, his measure of productivity growth is based on value added at the sectoral level, so that no role is provided for energy and materials inputs in productivity growth. For a more detailed discussion, see Jorgenson (1980).
17. Gollop and Jorgenson (1980) have presented an analysis of productivity growth at the sectoral level based on the concept of output that includes both primary factors of production and intermediate inputs.
18. Estimates of the parameters of an econometric model of sectoral productivity growth are presented by Jorgenson and Fraumeni (1980).

REFERENCES

Auerbach, Alan J., and Jorgenson, Dale W. "The First Year Capital Recovery System." *Harvard Business Review*, 1980.

Berndt, Ernst R., and Jorgenson, Dale W. "Production Structure." In *U.S. Energy Resources and Economic Growth*, edited by Dale W. Jorgenson and Henrik S. Houthakker. Washington, D.C.: Energy Policy Project, 1973.

Berndt, Ernst R., and Wood, David O. "Technology, Prices, and the Derived Demand for Energy." *Review of Economics and Statistics* 56 (August 1975): 259–268.

———. "Engineering and Econometric Interpretations of Energy–Capital Complementarity." *American Economic Review* 69 (September 1979): 342–354.

Binswanger, Hans P. "The Measurement of Technical Change Biases with Many Factors of Production." American Economic Review 64 (December 1974a): 964–976.

———. "A Microeconomic Approach to Induced Innovation." *Economic Journal* 84 (December 1974b): 940–958.

Christensen, Laurits R., and Jorgenson, Dale W. "U.S. Real Product and Real Factor Input, 1929–1967." *Review of Income and Wealth* 16 (March 1970): 19–50.

Christensen, Laurits R., Jorgenson, Dale W., and Lau, Lawrence J. "Conjugate Duality and the Transcendental Logarithmic Production Function." *Econometrica* 39 (July 1971): 255–256.

———. "Transcendental Logarithmic Production Frontiers." *Review of Economics and Statistics* 55 (February 1973): 28–45.

Denison, Edward F. *Accounting for Slower Economic Growth*. Washington, D.C.: The Brookings Institution, 1979.

Diewert, W. Erwin. "Aggregation Problems in the Measurement of Capital." In *The Measurement of Capital*, edited by Dan Usher. Chicago: University of Chicago Press, 1980.

Fraumeni, Barbara M., and Jorgenson, Dale W. "The Role of Capital in U.S. Economic Growth, 1948–1976." In *Capital, Efficiency and Growth*, edited by George M. von Furstenberg. Cambridge, Mass.: Ballinger, 1980.

Gollop, Frank M., and Jorgenson, Dale W. "U.S. Productivity Growth by Industry, 1947–1973." In *New Developments in Productivity Measurement*, edited by John W. Kendrick and Beatrice M. Vaccara. Chicago: University of Chicago Press, 1980.

Hicks, John R. *The Theory of Wages*. London: Macmillan, 1932. Second edition, 1963.

Jorgenson, Dale W. "Accounting for Capital." In *Capital, Efficiency and Growth*, edited by George M. von Furstenberg. Cambridge, Mass.: Ballinger, 1980.

Jorgenson, Dale W., and Fraumeni, Barbara M. "Substitution and Technical Change in Production." In *The Economics of Substitution in Production*, edited by Ernst R. Berndt and Barry Field. Cambridge, Mass.: Ballinger, 1980.

Jorgenson, Dale W., and Griliches, Zvi. "Issues in Growth Accounting: A Reply to Edward F. Denison." *Survey of Current Business* 52 (May 1972): 65–94.

Jorgenson, Dale W., and Lau, Lawrence J. *Transcendental Logarithmic Production Functions*. Amsterdam, The Netherlands: North-Holland, forthcoming in 1981.

Kendrick, John W. *Productivity Trends in the United States*. Princeton, N.J.: Princeton University Press, 1961.

———. *Postwar Productivity Trends in the United States, 1948–1969*. New York: National Bureau of Economic Research, 1973.

Samuelson, Paul A. "Prices of Factors and Goods in General Equilibrium." *Review of Economic Studies* 21 (October 1953): 1–20.

3.
Productivity Measurement

Jerome A. Mark
Assistant Commissioner for Productivity and Technology
U.S. Department of Labor

In recent years there has been a great deal of concern about the slowdown in productivity growth. The reasons for this are easy to understand. First, the problem of inflation remains an acute one, and a slowdown in productivity growth, by reducing offsets to increases in costs, does contribute in important ways to this problem.

Second, there is wider understanding that productivity growth has been a major factor in advancing the well-being of the American people, and there is some question about its long-term prospects. Whether we can satisfy all our expectations within the limitations of our resources of labor, capital, energy, and materials is a serious question. If we try to achieve all of our goals fully and quickly, we run the risk of further inflation. If we curtail the demand for goods and services, there is the danger of failing to utilize fully available resources and of risking unemployment. Clearly, greater effectiveness in converting scarce resources into the goods and services we desire—productivity—can help solve this dilemma.

The need for information about productivity movements, therefore, is critical to understanding the magnitude and depth of the potential problems. If adequate policies are to be developed to deal with problems of the economy related to productivity developments, it is essential to have measures that are reasonably accurate, comprehensive, and timely. To provide a basis for understanding where we are with regard to productivity measurement and where we are going, this chapter examines the productivity measures currently available, some of their limitations, how they can be improved, and what attempts are being made to improve them. The examination traces the available measures of the federal government as well as those of the principal private researchers in the field, summarizes the conceptual bases of the indicators, and points out some of the more fundamental differences in approaches employed.

CONCEPTS AND MEASURES OF PRODUCTIVITY

Productivity is loosely interpreted to be the efficiency with which output is produced by the resources utilized. A measure of productivity is generally defined as a ratio relating output (goods and services) to one or more of the inputs (labor, capital, energy, and so on) which were associated with that output. More specifically, it is an expression of the physical or real volume of goods and services, related to the physical or real quantities of inputs.

A variety of plausible productivity measures can be developed, the particular form depending on the purpose to be served. For example, output per labor input, the most familiar measure, is useful in understanding changes in employment or labor costs. A more comprehensive measure of input, using labor and capital combined, is also useful in studying how the economy is utilizing its principal resources. No one measure is the right or best measure.

In general, however, there are two broad classes into which productivity measures can be grouped. One includes those measures which relate output of a producing enterprise, industry, or economy to one type of input, such as labor, capital, and energy; the other includes those which relate output to a combination of inputs, extending to a weighted aggregate of all associated inputs.

Although the former measures relate output to one input, they do not measure only the specific contribution of that factor to production. In addition, they reflect the joint effect of a number of interrelated influences on the use of the factor in the production process—such as changes in technology; substitution of one factor for another; utilization of capacity, layout, and flow of material; the skill levels and efforts of the work force; and managerial and organizational skills.

Whether for an individual establishment, an industry, or the entire economy, the most frequently developed and perhaps most useful productivity measure is an output-per-unit-of-labor-input measure, or what is frequently termed a labor-productivity measure. There are several reasons for this. Perhaps the most important is that labor is almost universally required for carrying through all types of production and distribution. There is a labor element of costs in almost all endeavors generating output. In addition, as a practical matter, labor is the most measurable input. Other factors, such as capital, are much more difficult to quantify.

There are, however, various labor-productivity measures that can be developed, depending on the definition of labor input. A measure may refer to output per person or it may take account of changes in hours of work and be based on total hours. It may cover the hours of the entire employed labor force, including proprietors, unpaid family workers, and employees, or it may be limited to selected groups of workers.

Another set of productivity measures relating output to a single input is output per unit of capital. These measures are particularly useful in understanding movements in unit nonlabor costs by relating the measures to corresponding measures of returns to capital. As in the case of other single-factor productivity measures, capital productivity measures indicate the changes in the use of capital per unit of output and not the contribution of capital alone.

Other single-factor measures, such as output per energy input or output per material input, are relevant for plant and industry study, where these inputs are of considerable importance in the production process or represent relatively scarce resources. For example, in the aluminum industry, where electrical power is an important element in processing bauxite, output per kilowatt-hour (KWH) is useful as an indication of the efficiency with which electricity is being utilized.

As mentioned earlier, all single-factor productivity measures reflect the joint effect of a variety of factors, including the substitution of one factor for another. However, for some purposes, a measure which eliminates the effect of that substitution is useful. This type of measure relates output to a combination of inputs. Thus, a productivity index of output per labor and capital combined eliminates the effects of changes in amounts of capital per worker. These measures have been termed "multifactor," "total factor," or simply "total" productivity measures. For both conceptual and statistical reasons, they have generally been limited to labor and "tangible" capital inputs and have not included as inputs such activities as research and education, which can be viewed as intangible capital.

Output

For all productivity measures, output is measured in physical or real terms. The concept is one of work done, or the amount of product added in the various enterprises, industries, sectors, or economies. It refers not to activity as such, but to the results of activities.

In this sense, at the plant level, production and hence productivity measurement differs from work measurement. Work measurement generally refers to the analysis of the stages of activity under a given technology and the requirements at each of these stages. Productivity refers to the finished product (the result of activities) and its relationship to input—under changing conditions.

In the case of a producing unit making one homogeneous commodity, production in physical terms is merely a count of units produced. For a commodity to be regarded as homogeneous, certain conditions should be fulfilled. The product should be of a specified quality, and it must conform to precise standards of size and volume. Even though the measure of production in this case is a single count, the way of defining the unit of product can have different implications for productivity measurement. For example, carpeting can be measured either in pounds or square yards. A change in the density of the carpeting would affect the weight per yard and, therefore, have a different impact on labor requirements, depending on whether output is measured by the yard or by the pound.

For the more usual case of a plant or an industry producing many heterogeneous products, the different units must be expressed on some common basis. They can be combined in terms of their labor requirements, their capital requirements, their energy requirements, and so on. The diverse products can also be combined in terms of their relative prices, that is, the sum of all factor costs.

When the components are combined with value or price weights, that is, on the basis of their dollar value, then a single-factor productivity measure, such as an output-per-labor-input measure, for the total reflects not only changes in the productivity of the components but shifts in the importance of the components with different value per unit of labor input.

Physical-quantity data are often not readily available, but value data usually are. To develop output measures, these value data have to be separated into their quantity and unit value components. That is, total value of production is adjusted for change in price by use of a price index. This type of index is usually referred to as constant-dollar output, or (since prices generally have been rising) deflated value of output. Such indexes are conceptually equivalent to indexes that use physical quantities combined with price weights.

Labor Input

For all productivity measures where labor is relevant, labor input is also measured in physical terms. The measure can refer either to the total number of individuals engaged in production or to only part of the work force, or it can refer to the hours of workers.

It is usually preferable to include the entire employed work force in the labor-input measure—blue-collar and white-collar workers, corporate officers, and the self-employed. Since the final output of the organization or sector being measured reflects the activities of all individuals involved in the production and distribution processes, complete coverage of labor input is usually appropriate. If it is not complete, an imputation for the uncovered labor input is implied.

To analyze the productive capacity of labor and the effects of changes in working hours, or to project employment requirements, an output-per-labor-input measure is most relevant. The most suitable unit of measure is hours worked. However, there are some ambiguities on what to include or exclude from an hours-worked measure, such as standby time and coffee breaks. In general, "hours worked" refers to "hours at work" or the time spent at the place of employment, and therefore excludes hours paid for but used on leave for vacation, holiday, illness, accident, and other purposes.

In developing a labor-input measure, in many cases, hours of all employees are treated as homogeneous and additive. These measures are particularly relevant to problems of estimating total employee-hour requirements. But merely adding up the number of hours ignores the qualitative aspect of an hour worked by different individuals. Therefore, a productivity measure based on the sum of undifferentiated employee-hours will reflect changes in the composition of the work force with different qualitative characteristics as well as other aspects affecting productivity change.

For some purposes, it may be desirable to develop a productivity measure that takes into account the differences in the "quality" of an hour of labor. That is, an hour of high-quality (high productivity) labor is counted as proportionately more than an hour of low-quality labor. To do this, some methods have to be introduced to differentiate these hours. The differentiation should be reflective of the potential or actual productivity differences among the various groups.

One way that has been utilized is to combine the hours of various employees in terms of pay differentials. The hours of higher-paid workers are given more weight than lower-paid workers. This assumes that differences in earnings reflect differences in productivity of the workers. Workers grouped in terms of education, skill, and experience or by demographic characteristics, such as age and sex, are then combined in terms of their average earnings in some reference period. A related method is to adjust the data to take into account changes in vocational training, length of schooling, or type of education of the work force, assuming there is a close relationship between qualifications and quality. When adjustments are made for changes in the quality of labor input, the resultant productivity measure will not reflect changes in the composition of the work force as a productivity change but rather as a change in labor input.

Capital Input

Capital-stock estimates include the constant-dollar value of structures, plants, and equipment currently available for production. These estimates may also take into account the value of land, inventories, and working capital.

Generally, capital stock measures are derived by adjusting the value of existing plant and equipment for new investment and the retirement of old assets. Since these are physical or real measures, the value of capital stock must be adjusted for price changes.

There are different ways of measuring the real stock of capital; for example, they may be gross measures or net. Net stock estimates are derived by reducing the value of the asset by its depreciation (and there are various methods of assessing depreciation). Gross stock estimates are derived by retaining assets at their full value until they are retired from use. Studies have shown that the output capacity of various types of equipment tends to fall with age, which would imply that a net measure would be preferable to a gross measure. However, depreciation practices for financial purposes may differ from those related to economic efficiency of the assets, and the appropriate measure generally lies between a gross and a net measure.

For productivity analysis, the flow of capital services rather than the stock is in most cases the preferred measure. A capital-stock measure does not account for differences in the intensity of use over time. Equipment, for example, may be used for several shifts during a business expansion or may be idle during a contraction. Then, too, a large part of existing capital capacity may be standby and employed only during periods when the economy is operating at very high rates. A flow measure reflects differences in usage and efficiency and how these affect varying levels of output, which is the basis of productivity estimation. Thus, flow measures should indicate the amount of capital employed to produce current output.

To derive this capital-flow measure, an aggregate of the capital hours used weighted by the rental value of each type of structure and piece of equipment is needed. The data for this measure are generally not available in the detail necessary for a capital-flow measure.

In some instances depreciation has been used as a measure of the flow of capital service. However, this is more a measure of capital consumed, not capital services. Moreover, it is based on accounting principles which often reflect current tax regulations rather than the actual amount of capital involved in current production. Because of the difficulty of estimating a capital-flow measure, however, most analyses of capital and production use capital-stock estimates.

Other Inputs

In addition to labor and capital there has been interest in developing productivity measures with regard to other inputs such as land, materials, and energy. As mentioned earlier, land for most purposes is viewed as a form of capital input and, therefore, the definitions and concepts underlying the development of capital-input measures are applicable to the derivation of land-input measures.

In recent years, because of the concern about energy and material needs, increasing interest has been shown in separate measures of these inputs. As in the case of labor and capital, energy and materials inputs are included in terms of their physical units and are differentiated similarly in terms of their impact on productivity. Consequently, data on energy inputs by type (KWH, HP, BTUs) and materials inputs in physical or constant-dollar terms by type of commodities are called for. Comprehensive data on energy use are limited. Information on materials inputs by industry requires data on separate purchases of commodity inputs by particular industries. Moreover, the price of deflators required should refer to the specific products or product classes purchased by the industries within broader product groupings for which data are generally available. Nevertheless, at higher levels of aggregation these measures can and have been developed.

Multifactor Measures

This group of measures, which relate output to several factors, involve the weighting together of the quantities of the separate inputs into a combined input measure. Just as the separate components of an output index must be combined with appropriate weights, the separate components of the input measure must also be appropriately weighted together. In general, these weights are the proportional share of output that each contributed during a base period. Thus, with a multifactor productivity measure that is limited to labor and capital input, the two elements would be combined in terms of the total cost of capital and labor, each as a proportion of total value of output.

AVAILABLE MEASURES OF PRODUCTIVITY

Because of the different definitions that can be applied to the components or productivity measures and the different analytical uses that involve productivity measures, a wide range of productivity measures can and have been developed. It is not possible in a brief chapter to summarize all measures that are available, so I have limited the description to those which are most prevalent and most commonly used. These are the measures produced by the federal government on a regular basis and some of those produced by private researchers on an occasional basis. Also, since the scope of productivity measures is so broad—extending from the national economy to major economic sectors, and from industries to individual establishments—this discussion concentrates, for purposes of practicality, on the national economy, major-sector, and industry measures.

The Bureau of Labor Statistics (BLS) of the U.S. Department of Labor has the responsibility for developing and publishing the productivity measures of the federal government. Each quarter, the BLS prepares and publishes indexes of output per hour of all persons in the private-business economy and in the nonfarm business, manufacturing, and corporate sectors.[1] For these measures, output per hour refers to the constant-dollar value of goods and services produced in relation to the hours of all persons employed (including proprietors and unpaid family workers).

The output measure for these productivity indexes is real gross national product originating in the private-business economy or in the individual sectors. It comprises the purchase of goods and services by consumers, gross private domestic investment (including the change in business investors), net foreign investment, and government, all deflated separately for changes in prices. Excluded from these measures is the output of general government, households, and institutions.

Final goods and services are differentiated from intermediate products in that they are usually not purchased for further fabrication or resale. In addition to purchases in the market, final goods and services also include some items provided but not actually purchased, such as food furnished to employees and food produced and consumed on farms.

Measures for the nonfarm and manufacturing sectors are derived by subtracting the constant-dollar value of goods and services purchased by the sector from the constant-dollar value of products and services leaving the sector.

In addition to these measures, annual indexes are published for various major economic sectors such as agriculture, mining, transportation, communication, public utilities, and trade. The output measures for these series are also the real gross product originating in the sector.

The labor-input measures for all of these aggregate series are based largely on a monthly survey of establishment payroll records. Since this survey does not cover total employment in the private-business economy and because there are gaps in the hours information, it is necessary to use some supplementary data to derive labor-input estimates for all persons engaged in producing the output of the private-business sector. Various sources are utilized, and data from them are adjusted for consistency with the establishment employee-hours.

The establishment employee-hours are based on an hours-paid rather than an hours-worked concept. That is, the estimates include paid holidays, vacations, sick leave, and other time off paid by the employer in addition to actual hours worked.

In addition to the aggregate indexes for the private-business economy and major sectors, the BLS annually publishes indexes of output per labor input for selected industries. At the present time, measures are prepared for about 90 manufacturing and nonmanufacturing industries, such as steel, motor vehicles, railroad transportation, coal, and so on.[2]

For the most part these indexes are based on output measures derived by combining product information with labor-input weights which in turn are related to corresponding labor-input indexes. The labor-input data for these measures are established employee-hours. As in the aggregate measures, they are derived from payroll records and, for the most part, are based on an hours-paid concept. For manufacturing industries, however, additional hours information is available in terms of hours at the plant. These data, which theoretically exclude vacation, holidays, and other such leave hours, are closer in concept to an hours-worked measure. Unfortunately, the information on plant employee-hours is usually not as current as that of the establishment's hours paid.

The measures indicate the wide dispersion that exists in the productivity growth rates of many industries. In order to ascertain which are lagging and which are leading productivity-growth industries, it is important to have measures on a wide variety of industries.

For analytical purposes, the Bureau of Labor Statistics has developed indexes of output per employee-hour for almost all four-digit standard industrial classification (SIC) industries within manufacturing—about 400 measures. These indexes are useful for examining productivity output, price, and employment relationships. The output measures for these indexes were derived from value data deflated by price indexes. The output indexes, in turn, were related to labor-input measures. These measures are not as reliable as those published by the BLS—primarily because of limitations in the price indexes—but they are useful for general trend measures.

In addition to the current indexes of output per unit of labor input published by BLS, private researchers at various intervals have developed and published indexes of labor and multifactor productivity. For some of these, the output measures and the labor-input measures developed differ from those published by the BLS. The three principal private researchers publishing productivity measures are John W. Kendrick, Edward F. Denison, and Dale Jorgenson and his associates.

Kendrick, of George Washington University, has published a series of output-per-employee-hour indexes as part of a broader set of measures of output per unit of labor and capital combined, or what he has termed total-factor productivity measures.[3] Those series cover the period 1887 to 1969 and recently have been extended to 1976. The output and labor-input measures are virtually the same as those of the BLS, although in an earlier study Kendrick developed a series which made adjustments to the labor-input measures for changes in the composition of employee-hours.[4] Using average hourly earnings for weighting hours at the industry level, he derived an index of output per weighted employee-hour. In his current series, however, the aggregate hours are unweighted.

Kendrick combines his labor-input series with a tangible-capital series to derive the multifactor productivity series. He uses a capital-stock measure that encompasses structures, equipment, land, and inventories. The labor and capital components are combined in terms of their factor shares of output in the base period. Kendrick's measures are annual measures covering the private domestic economy and the major economic sectors.

In a recent publication of the Brookings Institution, Edward F. Denison published measures of output per labor input for the private nonresidential business sector from 1929 through 1978.[5] This series extends earlier work done by Denison and is part of a framework of analyses of the sources of growth in the economy.[6]

As part of that framework he has also published a set of multifactor measures he terms output per unit of input. His output measures refer to national income in constant prices and differ from the gross product measures used by BLS and by Kendrick by excluding the value of capital consumption allowances (depreciation).[7] Denison's labor-input measures are hours at work and provide for adjustments for changes in the composition or quality of labor, but the procedure differs from Kendrick's earlier method. Adjustments are made for changes in age, sex, education, and other changes in the labor force to derive measures of labor input reflecting changes in quality.

Denison's capital-input series is derived by combining a constant-dollar series on structures and equipment with one of inventories. The series on structure and equipment is a weighted average of gross and net stock measures that take into account declining efficiency of capital stock as it ages and increased efficiency of newer capital.

Dale W. Jorgenson and his associate, Frank Gollop, also have published an output-per-unit-of-labor-input series as part of a set of multifactor productivity measures.[8] The series covers the private domestic economy and major economic sectors and industries and extends from 1948 to 1973. The output measure for the economy is a final demand series and is the same as the measures in the BLS and Kendrick series. However, at the sector level, the output measure includes intermediate goods as well as the value added by the sector.

The formulation of the output and input indexes that Jorgenson and Gollop have developed differs from those of the BLS, Denison, and Kendrick, and takes a more complicated form. Also, in contrast to Denison and Kendrick, Jorgenson and Gollop provide adjustments to the data for changes in the composition of capital assets—the quality of capital—as well as for changes in the composition of the work force.

PROBLEMS OF MEASUREMENT

The measurement of productivity trends involves several general problems. First, because of difficulties in obtaining direct-quantity measures of output and input, the coverage of certain sectors must be excluded or, in many cases, substitute measures or approximations must be used. Second, since most data are collected for purposes other than productivity measurement, definitions and procedures already established for reporting information on production and on factor inputs must be used. These may or may not be consistent with concepts appropriate for productivity measurement.

For example, since output is in the GNP framework, some

indicators used in this framework, while adequate as activity indicators, are not appropriate or are weak for productivity measurement.

Three areas where the real product measures as derived from the national accounts are particularly weak for productivity measurement are government, construction, and services (including business and personal services, and finance, insurance, and real estate).

In the absence of market valuation of the services of general government agencies, the practice in national income accounting is to value government output in terms of the wages and salaries of government employees. The deflated, or constant-dollar, measure is derived by multiplying base-year wages and salaries by changes in employment. Such an output measure, when related to a labor-input measure, results in no statistical change in productivity.

This measure of government output in the national accounts may be increasingly difficult to continue in view of the reported increases in output per unit of labor input in certain government operations that are subject to measurement. But because of it, there are no measures of productivity presently published for the entire national economy. Inclusion of these data to develop a measure for the entire national economy would result in a trend of output per hour biased toward no change. As a consequence, the available measures of productivity are limited to the private economy, and we do not at this time have a measure for the total economy.

A similar problem exists in the household and the not-for-profit institution sectors. Employment change in these sectors is the measure of their output change in the accounts. Consequently, these sectors are also excluded from the aggregate productivity measures of the BLS and private researchers, and the highest level of aggregation for which measures are available is the private-business sector.[9]

With the increased importance of government, and with the growth of health services, which are predominantly in the not-for-profit sector, it is important that better measures for these activities be developed in the national accounts to provide more comprehensive productivity measures.

Measuring output in service activities is difficult because of the absence in most cases of a directly quantifiable entity that describes a unit of service. Consequently, various substitute indicators are utilized in the national accounts. These usually involve using some price index for deflating the value of the service activities, or using an employment index to develop trends in producers of services. As in the case of government, the use of employment movements as an indicator of change in real output implies constant labor productivity.

For the bulk of service activities, however, the deflation approach is used, and its validity for the resultant output measure rests on the adequacy of the price indexes. Most of the price indexes used are components of the Consumer Price Index, which in turn have different degrees of reliability.[10] While the price measures for many service activities are reliable indicators, the indexes for some service activities, such as medical services, do not adequately take into account changes in the quality of the services performed.

In construction the real output measure is also obtained by deflation, and while the price indexes for some components are adequate, the price indexes used for many components are predominately cost indexes. As such, they do not take into account savings in the utilization of materials or labor and, as a result, there may be some overstatement of price increases and understatement of real output and, hence, productivity increases for overall construction.

The effects of certain measurement problems are greater at the individual-sector level than at the overall level where there is some tendency for errors and biases to offset each other. In addition, at the overall level, independent measures of final products and services can be developed despite certain weaknesses in the intermediate-sector measures.

Because the output measures of the selected industries are not part of the framework of the national income and product accounts, which require certain definitions and measures not necessarily consistent with the desired productivity measures, greater flexibility is possible in the derivation of these measures. However, three major problems are encountered in developing measures of output from available data for industry-productivity indexes. First, for many industries, the appropriate detailed product data are not available. Second, it is difficult to adequately measure changes in quality which result from the development of new products and the changing specifications of existing products. This problem is more serious for industry measures than for measures covering broader sectors.

Third, appropriate weights often are not available for deriving the desired industry output and, hence, productivity measure.

Some of the presently available industry indexes are based on labor-input (unit employee-hour) weights; others are based on unit value or price. The use of unit value or price weights is not a serious problem among commodities where labor costs or inputs are not a high proportion of total costs. But it is a problem for those industries where labor costs are important or the composition is changing.

With regard to labor-input components, whether for overall measures or for measures of specific industries, there are also some problems with existing measures. First, as mentioned earlier, the current data (based on establishment payroll reports) relate to hours paid, including leave hours that are paid for but not worked. For purposes of relating productivity to hourly compensation trends, the concept of output per hour paid for may be appropriate. But, for purposes of measuring total labor requirements and resource use, a measure based on hours worked would be preferable.

Second, while hours data are available for production workers and for nonsupervisory workers, adequate data are not available for nonproduction and supervisory workers. As a result, estimates have to be made for these workers either by imputing to them the hours of covered workers or by aggregating pieces of information on these types of workers from various unrelated surveys. Because nonproduction workers have become increasingly important over the years, the lack of data is now a greater problem than it used to be.

Third, in the current BLS measures, the total-hours data are an unweighted aggregate which considers the hours of skilled and unskilled workers of equal importance. For purposes of total employment requirements, these are useful measures. However, for some purposes, such as examining the effects of shifts within the work force on output, productivity measures based on labor-input indicators that take account of qualitative differences among workers are needed.

Various approaches have been followed to do this. As mentioned earlier, private researchers have combined the hours of various employee groups in terms of pay differentials. For example, Kendrick's earlier use of industry employee-hours is weighted with industry average hourly earnings. Insofar as earnings of differentials reflect productivity differences among workers, this measure attempts to capture changes in the quality of workers in different industries.

However, this approach has severe limitations. Pay differentials between industries reflect many factors unrelated to productivity differences, such as the degree of unionization or regional and geographical differentials. Moreover, the industry hourly earnings differential does not take into account occupational changes that occur within an industry.

In view of the limited information on occupational detail, another approach to ascertain the impact of shifts and changes in the work force has been to utilize information on changes in age, sex, and education in relation to earnings. Many assumptions have to be made with this approach, partly because of the limited data, and different assumptions can and have resulted in different productivity measures.

With regard to capital input, the measure sought is some count of the numbers and types of physical capital goods combined with appropriate weights. However, since the physical-unit data are available for few types of capital goods, the measures are sometimes derived by deflating book values at acquisition prices that take into account the age of the assets. They are also derived by a perpetual inventory method of cumulating investment adjusted for price change over time, with allowance for retirement of assets.

Changes over time in models, types, and quality of capital goods present serious problems, and the price indexes used to deflate the series must take these changes into account appropriately. There are great difficulties in developing adequate measures of quality change in price indexes, in general, and the approaches necessary for quality adjustments that reflect differences in productive capacity are particularly difficult.

As mentioned earlier in regard to capital-input measurement, there are problems in obtaining estimates of depreciation of the capital assets which are reflective of declines in output-producing capacity. Net measures based on depreciation, following financial accounting procedures, may not be consistent with this requirement. Various assumptions have been made for combining gross and net stock measures but, of necessity, they are somewhat arbitrary.

Finally, there is a serious problem as to the availability of data on capital stock at the sector and industry levels of aggregation.

Moreover, the implications of assumptions which have to be made for an industry measure are much more critical at that level.

Both measurement and data problems are present in the derivation of measures of intermediate inputs, such as energy and materials, which seriously affect the adequacy of productivity measures based on these inputs. The measurement problems are similar to those of other input measures. The need to differentiate among the various types of input with specifications in sufficient detail to take into account differences in productive capacities calls for disaggregate data which generally are not available. Therefore, estimates, or explicit or implicit imputations, are made.

With material and energy input measures, the data problems are somewhat more severe because, for the appropriate industry-input measure a current input/output table with purchases by industries of various inputs is required. These are difficult to develop, in general, and must await the completion of economic censuses. Consequently, the information required at appropriate levels of disaggregation are generally not available. Assumptions, extrapolations, and interpolations have to be made to develop the estimates.

FUTURE DIRECTIONS

For many years the BLS and the various government agencies responsible for collecting basic data related to productivity-measurement needs have been working toward improving the data base. This has taken the form of expanding the coverage of some of the data presently obtained or obtaining more disaggregate information. Progress has been limited because of the complexities described above and because of the costs involved in sharply expanding data collection.

In a recent review of the productivity measures of the federal government, a panel of the National Academy of Sciences' Committee on National Statistics issued a report which made recommendations for the improvement of available measures and suggested some new directions which could be undertaken.[11] Among the recommendations for improvement in the output data, the panel stressed that government agencies, principally the BLS, should improve existing price indexes, particularly by taking quality change into account more adequately. With regard to labor input, the panel recommended that BLS develop data on hours at work and obtain data on nonproduction and supervisory workers. It also proposed that BLS attempt to develop weighted labor-input measures.

On capital-input measures the panel called for the Census Bureau to produce better, more comprehensive and, at the same time, more detailed inventory data as well as fuller coverage on capital outlays, book values of invested capital, and depreciation allowances and retirements.

On intermediate inputs, it also recommended that the Census Bureau obtain data on intermediate purchases of materials, including energy, for detailed industries. These data should be obtained not only for the years of the quinquennial economic censuses, but also annually to the extent possible.

For new directions of government measures the panel recommended that the BLS "experiment with combining labor and other inputs into alternative measures of multifactor productivity." By stressing experimentation, it recognized the complexities and difficulties in developing such a set of measures despite the existence of multifactor measurement efforts by private researchers.

The panel's recommendations are directed to meeting many of the problems described in this chapter, and government agencies have responded to meet these needs. The BLS, for example, has sought funds this year to conduct a special survey of hours at work from a sample of establishments of the current employment survey. Similarly, as part of a general revision of this survey, the possibilities of obtaining hours of nonproduction workers are being explored.

Work on obtaining data for the development of measures of productivity that take into account changes in the composition of the work force, such as changes in age, sex, education, industry attachment, and occupation, has already begun.

The improvement of the capital-input data will not be as rapid since it involves not only expansion of the industry detail for the components of the capital-stock measures, but also resolution of some of the conceptual problems associated with capital-input measurement. This is particularly true with regard to inclusion or exclusion of quality changes in capital input and development of meaningful measures of capital utilization.

The expansion of intermediate input data and particularly the availability of energy input data should accelerate in the near future.

There is a concerted drive in the Department of Energy and in other government agencies involved in data collection to improve the data available in energy input by type. This will contribute greatly to the improvement in the multifactor measures.

Various efforts are being undertaken to improve the data in the sectors that presently are weak for the development of productivity measures—particularly government, construction, and service sectors. For several years, the BLS, in conjunction with the Office of Personnel Management (formerly the Civil Service Commission), has been conducting a program to measure the productivity of agencies in the federal government. At the present time, data have been obtained for 350 agencies, representing 65 percent of federal employees, and the agency measures are grouped into functional areas having common characteristics.

The measures reflect the final output of the government agencies and, since the outputs of one government organization may be consumed wholly or partially by another federal organization, the productivity measures are not final with respect to the entire federal government. Moreover, they do not include state and local government activities, which at present comprise the bulk of government employment. As a result, at present, the measures cannot be used directly to modify the gross national product measures so that a total economy measure, including government, can be developed. Nevertheless, as more data are developed and the possibilities of netting out various activities improve in the future, these measures can perhaps be used in improving the national accounts measures of government output and thus lead to the development of an overall measure.

In construction, the development of an improved price index is expected—toward price measures rather than cost indexes—and an improved productivity measure can be derived. Work has been going on to improve the price indexes in residential construction. Price indexes for multifamily housing not based on costs are being developed to supplement those presently developed for single-family housing.

Similarly, price indexes in service activities are improving, and the extent to which productivity measures in service industries are being developed from physical-output data has been expanding. In recent years BLS has produced reliable measures for hotels, motels, retail food stores, gasoline stations, new car dealers, and so on, to supplement the many other noncommodity activity measures already available, such as public utilities, transportation, and communication industries.

It is expected that over the next decade the coverage and reliability of existing measures will be improved and their scope will be expanded. Comprehensive multifactor measures reflecting the combination of labor, capital, and intermediate inputs should be developed on a quarterly basis, and disaggregate industry multifactor measures should be available on an annual basis.

In view of the deficiencies and limitations in some of the basic data needed for productivity measurement, it is appropriate to ask, "How important are they?" In some cases, output and input data are unquestionably so poor that measures of productivity may never be developed or, if derived, may be quite meaningless. But in other instances, despite the data deficiencies, it may be possible to derive reasonably adequate indicators of productivity change. In many cases, for example, a carefully weighted index shows a trend which differs very little from an unweighted index. This is the case for measures in many manufacturing industries.

The need for precision in a productivity measure depends partly on its purpose. Definitions, weighting, coverage, and adequacy of price deflators may be extremely important for certain types of analysis, such as international comparisons, because of wide variation in structure of industries, changes in product mix, and other factors. For wage and price analysis, perhaps, a higher degree of precision may be required than for other, broader types of analysis.

But for many types of economic analyses, cruder measures of productivity may be acceptable. If one industry is estimated to have a productivity gain of 10 percent and another industry a gain of 100 percent, it may not matter that both measures may be in error by 10 percent. One industry clearly had a much higher gain than the other. If one is interested in determining whether there is a general relationship among industries between productivity change and employment change, a high degree of precision may not be essential. Frequently, the data may be good enough to determine whether a high or low relationship exists. Decision as to the usefulness of a productivity measure should be based not only on the data's statistical limitations but also on their purpose.

Measures of productivity have improved substantially in sophistication and accuracy in recent years. While they are still inadequate to answer all the questions that might be asked of them, they do provide insights into many of the economic problems of the day. The improvements foreseen will serve to provide even more insights.

NOTES

1. Bureau of Labor Statistics press release, "Productivity and Costs," published each quarter, usually the third week in the month following the end of the reference quarter. Also, published in each issue of the *Monthly Labor Review*, table 33.
2. The latest publication in this series is *Productivity for Selected Industries, 1979 Edition*, Bureau of Labor Statistics Bulletin 2054 (Washington, D.C.: U.S. Government Printing Office, 1979).
3. John W. Kendrick, *Postwar Productivity Trends in the United States, 1948–1969* (New York: National Bureau of Economic Research, 1973); and John W. Kendrick, *Productivity Trends and Prospects*, vol. 1 in Joint Economic Committee, *U.S. Economic Growth from 1976 to 1986: Prospects, Problems and Patterns* (Washington, D.C.: U.S. Government Printing Office, 1976).
4. John W. Kendrick, *Productivity Trends in the United States* (Princeton, N.J.: Princeton University Press for the National Bureau of Economic Research, 1961).
5. Edward F. Denison, *Accounting for United States Economic Growth, 1929–1969* (Washington, D.C.: Brookings Institution, 1944); and Edward F. Denison, "Explanations of Declining Productivity Growth," *Survey of Current Business*, part II, August 1979.
6. Edward F. Denison, *Sources of Economic Growth in the United States and the Alternatives before Us* (New York: Committee for Economic Development, 1962).
7. These measures also are at factor cost. This differs from market price used in the BLS output measure by excluding indirect business taxes and including subsidies.
8. Frank M. Gollop and Dale W. Jorgenson, "U.S. Productivity Growth by Industry, 1947–1973," in *New Developments in Productivity Measurement*, edited by John W. Kendrick and Beatrice Vaccara (New York: National Bureau of Economic Research, forthcoming in 1980).
9. Actually, because of the absence of a labor-input component corresponding to the output of returns from foreign investment and owner-occupied housing (in the GNP measure), the rest-of-the-world and resident-owner sectors are also excluded and the measures refer to the private, nonresidential, domestic-business economy.
10. For a description of the extent to which price indexes are used in the service-

sector component of the national accounts, see Martin L. Marimont, "Measuring Real Output for Industries Providing Services: OBE Concepts and Methods," in *Production and Productivity in the Service Industries,* edited by Victor R. Fuchs (New York: National Bureau of Economic Research, 1969).

11. National Research Council, Panel to Review Productivity Statistics, *Measurement and Interpretation of Productivity* (Washington, D.C.: National Academy of Sciences, 1979).

4.
Trade and Productivity: Do They Relate?

Howard D. Samuel
*President, Industrial Union Department, AFL-CIO**

Since international trade has been touted as a miracle cure for all of society's ills, I suppose no one should be surprised if it is dragged into the current discussions about America's declining productivity. After all, international trade has already been awarded curative powers to lower prices and presumably to reduce inflation; to make developed countries out of deserts and jungles; to spread the benefits of a civilized technology far and wide; to raise everyone's living standards.

Under ideal conditions, found usually only in a carefully controlled hothouse, trade could probably go far toward accomplishing all these goals. The fact that it hasn't, and doesn't, and never will, only reflects the cruel realities of our non-hothouse world.

Similarly, international trade probably could—and possibly does—have some beneficial effect on productivity, but trade has been corrupted by so many unsavory influences that the benefits are hard to find and measure, and they come accompanied by some very severe disadvantages.

We start with the given that productivity in the United States, after decades of smooth sailing and regular increases, started turning slightly sour in the late sixties (there were annual increases, but they were lower than before), and headed downward with a vengeance starting in 1974 through 1979—when the productivity level actually

* The author acknowledges the assistance of Brian Turner, director for economic policy of the Industrial Unions Department, AFL-CIO, in preparing this chapter.

produced a negative result for the year. The figures are stated in table 4.1.

What were the reasons? A number of experts have examined the situation, even more nonexperts have issued judgments, but no consensus has emerged. One of the most relevant analyses was done by Edward F. Denison in a book published by The Brookings Institution (*Accounting for Slower Growth: The United States in the 1970s*) and summarized in several articles in the *Survey of Current Business*. In an article in the August 1979 issue, Denison examines 17 possible causes of the decline in U.S. productivity and arrives at the following conclusions:

> I rejected a few suggestions, expressed skepticism about some, had no opinion about others, and characterized the rest as probably correct but individually able to explain only a small part of the

Table 4.1. GNP in 1973 in Constant (1972) Prices and Growth Rates of GNP per Hour Worked, 1948–73, and 1973–78, by Industry[1]

Industry[2]	GNP, 1973 (billions of 1972 dollars)	Growth rates (percent) GNP per hour worked		
		1948–73	1973–76	1973–78
Agriculture, forestry, and fisheries	35.9	4.5	1.1	2.0
Mining	19.2	3.6	−6.6	−4.8
Contract construction[3]	58.3	1.6	.9	−1.1
Manufacturing: nondurable goods	124.1	3.3	2.0	2.3
Manufacturing: durable goods	189.0	2.6	1.1	1.1
Transportation	50.6	3.0	.1	.8
Communication	32.0	5.2	8.4	7.1
Electric, gas, and sanitary services	30.0	5.4	1.4	.7
Wholesale trade[3]	88.9	3.3	−1.3	− .6
Retail trade[3]	123.1	2.4	1.1	1.1
Services[4]	137.9	1.0	− .2	.1

1. Denominator of GNP per hour worked excludes hours worked by unpaid family workers.
2. Excludes finance, insurance, and real estate; private households; and government enterprises.
3. Classification for 1948–73 growth rate differs slightly from classification used for 1973–76 and 1973–78 rates.
4. Excludes private households; includes nonprofit institutions.

Source: Edward F. Denison, "Explanations of Declining Productivity Growth," *Survey of Current Business*, pt. II, August 1979, p. 20. Calculated from national income and product account tables 6.2, 6.11, and (to eliminate hours in private households) 6.10.

slowdown. No single hypothesis seems to provide a probable explanation of the sharp change after 1973.[1]

Denison also makes it clear that the drop in the productivity rate is not unique to the United States. The same drop also occurred in six other major industrialized countries, and only in Germany was it smaller. It was about the same in Canada, France, and the United Kingdom. It was much larger in Japan and Italy.

Not surprisingly, Denison did not include foreign competition among the 17 issues he analyzed. Foreign trade as a percentage of gross national product (GNP) has been steadily advancing, partly fueled by the tremendous growth in the prices paid for petroleum

Table 4.2. Selected Growth Rates in Industrial Countries Selected Periods

Country	Growth Rates (percent)				
	1950–73	1960–73	1973–76	1973–77	1973–78
Real gross domestic product per employed civilian:					
United States	2.1	2.1	−0.1	0.3	n.a.
Canada	2.6	2.4	.4	.5	n.a.
Japan	7.8	8.8	2.3	2.7	n.a.
France	4.6	4.6	2.7	2.9	n.a.
West Germany	5.0	4.4	3.3	3.3	n.a.
Italy	5.3	5.8	.8	− .2	n.a.
United Kingdom	2.5	2.6	.4	.4	n.a.
Output per hour in manufacturing:					
United States	2.7	3.2	1.2	1.5	1.7
Canada	4.2	4.6	1.3	2.1	2.5
Japan	9.7	10.0	1.4	2.4	3.5
Belgium	n.a.	7.0	6.7	6.6	n.a.
Denmark	5.2	7.0	6.2	5.2	4.7
France	5.3	5.7	4.7	4.8	4.8
West Germany	5.8	5.5	6.0	5.5	5.1
Italy	6.6	7.2	3.0	2.4	2.6
Netherlands	6.2	7.4	5.4	4.9	n.a.
Sweden	5.3	6.7	.9	.5	1.5
United Kingdom	3.1	3.9	.6	− .2	.2

n.a. Not available.

Source: Edward F. Denison, "Explanations of Declining Productivity Growth," *Survey of Current Business*, pt. II, August 1979, p. 20.

products, partly by the increases in levels of manufactured products imported. In other words, international trade has been increasing, so if it has had an effect on U.S. productivity, one would have to assume either that the effect has been unfavorable, or that, on the contrary, it has stopped productivity levels from deteriorating even further.

There doesn't seem to be any yardstick one can devise to measure the effect of foreign competition on productivity. Presumably it could go either way, and probably does. It could force economies and efficiencies in trade-impacted domestic industries, thereby improving productivity. It could also discourage trade-impacted industries from investing to modernize, or actually make it impossible for them to obtain needed capital. By forcing a reduction of domestic production, it could also lead to diseconomies of scale, further reducing productivity, and leading to a circular path, all downward to bankruptcy. In addition, the special factor of increased oil prices has had some downward effect, it is widely agreed, on productivity generally, although the specific extent or even direction is in dispute.

If it is unclear how foreign competition affects productivity, it is clear that there are some special kinds of foreign competition which by and large are distinctly unhelpful to the United States. I would classify these disadvantageous kinds of imports under three headings: fair trade which is unduly disruptive—and as a result may act to retard domestic productivity; unfair trade because of labor exploitation; unfair trade because of violations of international agreements.

FAIR BUT DISRUPTIVE IMPORTS

Some quotes from a chapter in a book, *The New International Economic Order,* one of the Policy Studies series of the United Nations Association of the United States, could well set the stage, particularly since the chapter in question, "Current International Trade Policy," has been written by three economists not known as protectionists.

> Two questions thus go unanswered: "Is free trade better than restricted trade?" and "Is free trade better than the status quo?" Neither question can be answered glibly, although both free traders and protectionists sometimes try to do so in the heat of

controversy. . . . There is no universal, timeless answer to either practical trade policy question.

The list of circumstances under which restricted trade can conceivably make an economy stronger (and freer trade can make it weaker) is quite long. It includes exploiting national monopolistic power in export sales, or monopolistic power in import purchases. It includes using trade policy to combat foreign monopoly, felt perhaps through predatory dumping, when superior antimonopoly policy is unavailable or administratively more costly. It includes protecting economic sectors that possess positive production external ties (e.g., national defense, or high-technology industries with significant spillovers into the rest of the economy), when more direct, first-best production subsidies are infeasible or sufficiently costly to implement. And most important in current world conditions, it includes defending the status quo when trade liberalization would lead to a sufficiently large and enduring rise in national unemployment and excess capacity—one that could not be alleviated quickly (or at all) by conventional government policies.[2]

The authors continue:

Except in ideal worlds, there are always gainers and losers from trade liberalization. To design and carry out practical mechanisms whereby *every* loser was duly compensated (and more) would require a frightening diversion of resources from wealth-producing to wealth-transferring activity. Yet in the absence of such mechanisms, there may be instances in which trade liberalization should be rejected because it undermines a society's sense of equity.[3]

It would be useful to distinguish two different kinds of situations where trade liberalization undermines society's sense of equity. One is the classic case of the so-called sunset industry, which traditionally refers, in a developed country, to the more labor-intensive, less technologically advanced industry such as apparel, footwear, and so on. In recent years we have found to our horror that a sunset industry may include steel, electronics, and other pillars of what we thought was an advanced economy.

A sample of the kinds of industries which might be regarded as sunset was drawn up by the U.S. Department of Labor in connection with an examination of the effects of tariff reductions in the Multilateral Trade Negotiations. The industries listed in table 4.3 include the stereotypical labor-intensive industries, such as artificial flowers, apparel, jewelry, and musical instruments. But, it also includes motorcycles and bicycles, optical instruments, plywood, elevators and moving stairs, and radio and TV sets, products which we had thought were ornaments of advanced societies.[4]

In these industries it is doubtful that intensive, uncontrolled foreign competition would lead to much in the way of increased productivity. It would result, instead, in a decline in the ability of the industry to take needed steps to modernize itself, to generate the needed capital either from its own profits or from outside sources to make itself competitive.

I am not suggesting that we should try to repeal the law of comparative advantage and give all these industries a free ride into the future. Competition has been accepted as a key ingredient in the economy's growth. But the ability of foreign countries to create a kind of competitive pressure which is stifling, rather than invigorating, is not particularly useful to the economy. It leads, instead, to precipitous disruption and truly undermines society's sense of equity.

The other kind of inequity produced by trade liberalization affects not an industry but only discrete parts of it, often located in a certain geographical area, and usually the older segments. These older segments of an industry may be doomed in the long run anyway, but again the pace of change could mean the difference between disruption for an entire community and a slow adjustment to optional products or services.

What I suggest in both these cases is that the undisturbed operation of competition from abroad, according to the laws of comparative advantage, might well be interrupted to permit the adjustment process—and adjustment programs—to cushion the effect on workers, on companies, on communities. What is needed in these cases is a combination of import restraint, aimed at the particular problem but effective enough to do the job, with a flexible program of adjustment assistance. Too often in the recent past, import restraints have been designed more to meet a perceived political problem rather than to provide a legitimate breathing spell for economic recovery. The restraints imposed on imported shoes

Table 4.3. Selected 4-Digit Manufacturing Industries Experiencing Net Losses of Employment Opportunities as a Result of the Multilateral Trade Negotiations Tariff Reductions

I/O Code§	Industries with Losses of Employment Opportunities of At Least 0.5 Percent of Their Respective Labor Forces	Net Loss of Employment Opportunities			
		Number of Jobs	Percent of Industry Labor Force	Annual Rate of Decline of Employment Opportunities	Annual Rate of Growth Employment (%)
3609	Pottery Products, not elsewhere classified	1269	11.97	1.50	1.09
6406	Artificial Flowers	319	6.02	0.75	−2.85
1703	Lace Goods	130	5.65	0.71	−5.71
*6401	Jewelry	3639	4.55	0.57	0.83
3607	Food Utensils, Pottery†	551	4.11	0.51	−1.65
*6207	Watches, Clocks and Parts	1304	3.86	0.48	1.56
1426	Vegetable Oil Mills	50	2.94	0.37	−2.23
1708	Scouring, Combing Plants	302	2.75	0.34	0.00
*6105	Motorcycles, Bicycles	570	2.62	0.33	2.07
*4201	Cutlery	349	1.96	0.25	1.10
*6412	Miscellaneous Manufactures	1095	1.74	0.22	2.23
6403	Games and Toys	1164	1.69	0.21	0.00
6301	Optical Instruments	343	1.56	0.20	0.00
*6404	Sport, Athletic Goods	879	1.40	0.18	2.89
6407	Buttons, Pins, Fasteners	342	1.31	0.16	0.00
1710	Textile Goods, nec	90	1.27	0.16	0.00
5601	Radio and TV Sets	1377	1.19	0.15	0.00
3603	Ceramic Wall, Floor Tile	112	1.12	0.14	−3.10
3403	Other Leather Products	734	1.11	0.14	0.00
*2006	Veneer, Plywood	816	1.09	0.14	1.06
1709	Cordage and Twine	90	0.85	0.11	0.00
1707	Tire Cord, Fabric	94	0.84	0.11	0.00
*3608	Porcelain Electric Supplies	114	0.75	0.09	2.16
1705	Processed Textile Waste	27	0.69	0.09	−1.88
*6402	Musical Instruments	189	0.69	0.09	2.18

continued

Table 4.3. Selected 4-Digit Manufacturing Industries (*continued*)

I/O Code§	Industries with Losses of Employment Opportunities of At Least 0.5 Percent of Their Respective Labor Forces	Net Loss of Employment Opportunities			Annual Rate of Growth Employment (%)
		Number of Jobs	Percent of Industry Labor Force	Annual Rate of Decline of Employment Opportunities	
3300	Industrial Leather, Tanning	149	0.63	0.08	−2.85
1702	Felt Goods	21	0.60	0.08	0.00
1601	Broadwoven Fabric Mills	2327 (1114)‡	0.59 (0.28)	0.07 (0.04)	−1.50
1604	Thread Mills	54	0.59	0.07	0.00
1804	Apparel, Purchased Material	6800 (2945)‡	0.58 (0.25)	0.07 (0.03)	0.00
*6302	Ophthalmic Goods	237	0.57	0.07	2.47
*1803	Knit Fabric Mills	366	0.53	0.07	6.60
4601	Elevators, Moving Stairs	87	0.52	0.07	0.00

Note: * Indicates industries where annual rates of growth in employment are capable of absorbing all Multilateral Trade Negotiations–related employment declines.

The net losses in industry employment opportunities resulting from the Multilateral Trade Negotiations will not occur at once but rather will typically occur over the next 8 years as the tariff reductions are phased in. See the text for a discussion of the staging of the tariff cuts in industries 16, 17, 18, and 36.

† Negotiators and industry specialists in the Office of the Special Trade Representative (STR) feel strongly that buyers of certain Tariff Schedules of the U.S. (TSUS) items in I-O 3607, food utensils and pottery, are relatively insensitive to price changes. In order to minimize the employment impact of the tariff cuts, STR's negotiators tended to concentrate the tariff cuts on those TSUS items for which demand is inelastic and STR made smaller cuts (or granted exceptions) on those TSUS items for which demand is more elastic. We attempted to incorporate this into our trade and employment estimates for I-O 3607 by using a range of import elasticities. The estimate reported in the table is based on an elasticity estimated by the ITC (1.06). Using an elasticity calculated by R. Baldwin (4.6), the employment impact is estimated to be 2292 jobs or 17.9% of the industry labor force. In a separate calculation, STR estimates a net gain of 694 jobs in I-O 3607.

‡ The estimated losses in apparel and textiles due to tariff cuts tend to be overstated because tariff effects are constrained by existing quotas. It was not possible to fully quantify the restraining effects that the recently tightened textile quotas will have on U.S. imports. Because Taiwan, Korea, and Hong Kong have already reached their overall import-quota limits, it was estimated that the tariff cuts would not lead to additional imports from these countries. The same assumption was not made for the remaining countries with which the United States has bilateral textile agreements. Yet the full impact of the tariff cuts will not be felt for all of the textile and apparel products imported from these other countries. Quota limits have already been reached for certain products, and therefore no additional imports will occur for these products. For some of the remaining products, the quotas will prevent the full impact of the tariff cuts from taking place. This is particularly true in light of a new agreement which will limit the carryover of unfilled quotas frm one year to the next. Thus, if the quotas also prevent increases in imports from the remaining Multifiber Arrangement (MFA) suppliers as tariffs are reduced, the estimated loss of job opportunities in the textile and apparel sectors (input-output codes 16 and 18) would be cut by over 50 percent to the levels shown in brackets. In addition, larger gains (or smaller losses) would occur in industries which supply inputs to the textile and apparel sectors. Accordingly, the job impact reported here must be appropriately discounted.

§ Based on Bureau of Economic Analysis 1967 Input-Output Codes.

Source: "Trade and Employment Effects of Tariff Reductions Agreed to in the Multilateral Trade Negotiations," U.S. Department of Labor, Bureau of International Affairs, June 15, 1979.

and color TVs are two examples. In both cases, the restraints were so severely limited that other sources, unaffected by restraints, quickly stepped in to fill the vacuum. It took months to extend the restraints to these new sources of imports. By the end of the original three-year breathing spell, the affected industries found that total import levels had hardly been affected.

Coupled with an honest restraint system should be an honest adjustment-assistance program. It should cover all workers affected, including those providing components and services to the company directly affected. It should recognize the special problems of skilled workers, who are likely to have to settle for replacement jobs at lower levels than those they lost, thus affecting family living standards; of less skilled workers, often disadvantaged and from minority groups, who may have special problems in finding new jobs at all; and of older workers, who may have to be carried at government expense for a period until they retire. It should provide job-creation machinery to communities that have lost major segments of their industrial base. And we might as well recognize that adjustment assistance has little meaning in anything but a full-employment economy. Sending workers unemployed because of imports to look for jobs that are already in short supply is what has led trade-union leaders to label adjustment assistance "burial insurance."

Traditional economists would shudder at these recommendations, suggesting that they represent a return to protectionism. The doctrinaire free traders—if there are any around anymore—tell us that unalloyed free trade leads to a useful rationalization of industry and to price advantages to the consumer, among other benefits. About a year ago the U.S. Department of Labor, Bureau of International Labor Affairs, took a close look at four industries which had been preserved from instant destruction, in violation of the dicta of pure free trade, to see what had happened. I suppose we should have expected the dreary fulfillment of the classicists' prediction: higher prices for the community, accompanied by declining productivity in the industries. But this is not what happened. In the words of the report:

> The imposition of import relief need not have the expected inflationary consequences if the affected domestic industry is able to use the relief period to improve its technology, productivity,

> and price competitiveness. Import relief gives a domestic industry seriously injured by imports a breathing spell during which it can take steps to increase efficiency and improve its competitive position. Conventional analysis of import relief typically ignores this possibility of increased efficiency on the part of the industry which will have a moderating effect upon prices.
>
> Conventional analysis predicts that, other things being equal, import restraints will cause price increases. Other things do not remain constant, however, when the industry granted relief responds by upgrading technology, expanding investment, and increasing capacity utilization. Increased competitive efforts, such as these, can result in improvements in productivity and greater domestic supply.[5]

The Labor Department specifically examined the "price and efficiency performance" of four industries under import relief in 1979: textiles and apparel, specialty steel, nonrubber footwear, and color TVs. The study found, first, that the four industries indeed did have smaller price increases during the period of import relief than in earlier years, and smaller price increases than in comparable industries in the U.S. economy. Capacity utilization rates rose in these four industries, and all four industries had increased investment rates and "brought in new technology with the effect of increasing efficiency."[6]

The example of the specialty steel industry is especially instructive—and damaging to classical trade theory. The industry won a measure of import relief in July 1976. Price increases in 1977 were below those for 1974 or 1975, and, in 1978, price increases in this industry were less than half the rise in the wholesale price index (WPI) for durable manufactured goods.

More significantly, the imposition of import restraints was followed by a sharp rise in capital investment, initially in 1976, followed by a second round in 1978. Output per employee-hour in 1976 and 1977 was significantly higher than it had been in earlier years, and in 1978 it rose to an all-time industry high. These levels were also higher than the increases for the economy as a whole and higher than the increases in the steel industry as a whole.

Import restraints in the textile and apparel industry for the first decade (1962–71) covered only products made of cotton. The effectiveness of the restraints eroded as foreign sources switched to products made of manmade fabrics and wool. It was not until 1971 that a series of bilateral agreements were negotiated to cover all textiles and apparel made of the three principal fibers. In 1974, a multinational agreement succeeded the bilaterals. In the period 1971–78, textile prices increased less than wholesale price index (WPI) consumer nondurable prices in six out of eight years. Particularly in the manmade fibers industry, the imposition of import controls was followed by a marked increase in productivity. In 1972, output per employee-hour increased by 15 percent; it went up 8 percent in 1975, 6 percent in 1976, and 14 percent in 1977. In each year since 1974, productivity in this branch of the industry increased more rapidly than overall industrial productivity.

At the time of the Labor Department study, footwear and color TVs had been under relief for only about 18 months. But, there were some indications then that import restraints were followed, not by unrestrained price increases, but by a falling off of increases. For the entire year following the imposition of import relief, the consumer price index (CPI) for footwear rose by 3.9 percent compared with the overall CPI increase of 6.7 percent. At that time, the federal government also instituted a program of technical assistance and loan guarantees for the industry designed to "promote the vitality and competitiveness of the industry during the 'breathing spell' " afforded by the controls on imports. During that first year, the first efforts led to some success. "Although domestic production of shoes had fallen in 12 of the last 13 years, it increased by 1.9 percent in the year since relief was instituted in July 1977. Meanwhile, the Office of Science and Technology of the Department of Commerce had identified new technologies in shoe production which are just beginning to be adopted by the industry."[7]

In color TVs, wholesale prices fell in the first year following signing of an agreement limiting imports of sets from Japan—despite an increase in domestic demand and a decline in import penetration. The final word on productivity is not yet in, but the Department of Labor (DOL) report states that "news accounts of the intense competition in the color TV industry have stressed substantial new investment and improved technology employed by domestic industry and the new marketing strategies of domestic suppliers."[8]

The conclusions of the Labor Department study are surrounded with the appropriate caveats. In some cases, the evidence covers too short a span to be entirely reliable. In all cases, many factors could have influenced the results besides international trade. But the same caveats should now, as a result of the Department of Labor study, be applied to classical economists who made unsupported forecasts pointing to the inflationary, antiproductivity effects of import controls. An example of this occurred during the Carter Administration's consideration of the International Trade Commission (ITC) recommendation in respect to nonrubber footwear in early 1977. The administration was confronted by a number of estimates of the cost to consumers, ranging from the ITC estimate of $194 million to the $3,200 million submitted by the Council on Wage and Price Stability. The Department of Labor report comments with laudable restraint: "Clearly, the methodology for making such estimates needs to be reexamined. One method of examination is to see what the actual price performance and adjustment efforts have been in industries granted import relief in the past."[9]

It seems clear that, despite the caveats, certain conclusions are inescapable. Imports may lead to price advantages for consumers, but, on the other hand, import restraints do not necessarily lead to domestic manufacturers' extracting "monopoly rents" and raising prices promiscuously. In addition, the increased foreign competition does not always necessarily improve productivity. In the example of four industries under study, just the opposite occurred: restraints on imports appear to have led to greater productivity.

UNFAIR TRADE BECAUSE OF LABOR EXPLOITATION

It is apparent that foreign competition—far from necessarily improving productivity—may instead undermine our "sense of equity" or may hinder productivity growth by blocking investment in impacted industries. Another category of trade which may have an equally damaging result consists of products which are made under exploitive labor conditions. Again, let me make it clear that I am not advocating repeal of the law of comparative advantage. There will obviously be differences in wages and conditions between developing and developed countries, even in comparable industries making the same products with the same capital. But comparative advantage should not serve as camouflage to hide aggravated exploitation, such as child labor in factories, forced labor, or the uncontrolled use in the workplace of toxic substances or dangerous conditions. The standards of humanity accepted by all of civilization do not bestow a license on anyone to damage young children or kill adult workers, even those working in the least developed nations. Products which are designed for sale to other nations should be required to have been made under minimally reasonable standards.

Some commentators, whose principal concern is the improvement of the international trading system, reject such international standards on the basis that they would be used only to disguise a new kind of protectionism. But, the standards would have to be accepted by a multilateral organ, such as the General Agreement on Tariffs and Trade (GATT), and implementation would presumably be in full view of all. It might be possible to twist labor standards into a protectionist pretzel, but the process would be neither silent nor invisible and could be met with the same steps that the community of nations takes against unwarranted restrictions of trade wherever they occur.

In the meantime, it would appear to be difficult logically to protest against the imposition of minimum labor standards for international trade. After all, a principal rationale for increasing international trade is that it is supposed to enhance the living and working conditions of all parties, for both those who sell and those who buy. But when a building-supply manufacturer in a developed country moves an asbestos plant to a less-developed country (LDC) in order to avoid health regulations, neither the workers in the old plant—who have lost their jobs—nor the workers in the new plant—who are doomed to lung cancer—can boast of any particular benefit from the resulting flow of trade.

The question is raised, why inflict on international trade the obligation to assure minimum labor standards? Why not leave it to the International Labour Organisation? The answer is simple: Because the ILO cannot do the job. Like other elements in the United Nations system, the ILO depends on voluntary cooperation for implementation of its conventions. The ILO is proud of its record over the years, but it is a record which has depended on exhortation, example, and education. There is no means of effective enforcement. Abused workers suffering exploitation in uncounted shops and factories throughout the world deserve a better, more muscular system of implementation that will remove the profit from intolerable conditions by making it impossible for exploiters to peddle their fruits on the world market.

UNFAIR TRADE PRACTICES

The third category of trade that I would suggest is counterproductive are imports which worm their way into our market on the basis of irregular pricing or special privilege bestowed by their home governments. Such trade succeeds not on the basis of comparative advantage, but in violation of comparative advantage. In effect, the sources of these imports have given up on comparative advantage and instead are resorting to cheating the system. The international trading community recognizes the dangers posed by such practices and has erected barriers in the form of international codes against dumping and subsidies. But, the implementation of these codes remains very much in question; it has been a constant struggle for those who believe in comparative advantage to hold the fort against those who would prefer to cheat.

There is good reason to fear that such unfair trade practices—the new GATT codes notwithstanding—will be very much on the rise during the 1980s. Tariffs are no longer the major barrier to trade they once were, at least for most industries in developed countries; successive tariff reductions since the Smoot–Hawley rates of 1930 were established have largely accomplished their intended goal. Nontariff practices—less visible and more difficult to circumvent—have become the weapon of choice for governments and firms seeking to beggar their neighbors by bending comparative advantage to their benefit.

The expanding use of dumping and subsidies can take place because of higher levels of government in industry in almost every industrialized nation—other than the United States. While a Chrysler loan guarantee is very much the exception on the American scene, even more profound government involvement in industry is the rule in Japan, Germany, and our other key trading partners—especially the developing countries. The frequency of dumping violations is rising. Although carried out by private firms, the chronic dumping apparent in industries like steel is indicative of government support, that is, direct or indirect subsidies. Such government support is needed to allow foreign producers to sell persistently below their costs of production in the large U.S. market.

The economic impact of dumped or subsidized imports on the U.S. economy and U.S. productivity growth are unfortunately clear. Highly productive American producers can be undermined by dumped imports whose price advantage results only from illegal pricing practices. (Discovering and proving illegal dumping, of course, is no easy task.) While some consumers may draw a temporary gain from dumping, disruption of profitability, output, employment, and investment in competing domestic firms will not help improve the national productivity track record.

A new species of unfair trade practices has recently emerged with enormous potential for damaging U.S. investment and productivity growth. "Performance requirements" imposed on international investors have an almost unlimited potential to pull investment and jobs—and new productivity growth—from the United States because of the absence of any international rules limiting such government intervention. These trade-distorting performance requirements are becoming a major factor in international commerce generally, particularly from countries like Brazil, Australia, New Zealand, Canada, and Mexico.

Investment-performance requirements are measures that governments impose either as a condition of entry for incoming direct investment or as a condition of continued operation for already established investors. Performance requirements can be explicitly stated legal requirements, such as those set forth in the Mexican automotive decree, or they can depend on administrative procedures and be negotiated on a case-by-case basis, as happens with the Canadian Foreign Investment Review Agency.

Trade-related performance requirements include:

1. Requirements regarding export (or import substitution) performance.
2. Requirements related to local content or value added.

Minimum export requirements are very similar to export subsidies since both aim to directly improve the trade balance. Local content requirements specify that a given percentage of the value of the final output (either output as a whole or specified by product category) must be locally sourced. The effect is to reduce imports and increase domestic production at the expense of other countries. The Mexican Decree for Developing of the Automotive Industry included both of these trade-distorting performance requirements in its provisions. This decree, promulgated in 1977 and scheduled to take full effect by 1982, has already affected investment and trade flows between the United States and Mexico. Its economic repercussions will increase significantly as the automotive decree takes full effect, leading to the import of an estimated $2 billion of additional auto parts from Mexico and the loss of some 86,000 jobs in the automobile and supplying industries.

Performance requirements that distort trade are a matter of great concern because of their negative economic effects. They result in a direct transfer of jobs and production to the country which imposes them. The international changes in employment, production, and trade which they cause are not a response to market forces. These changes are the result of government fiat. The purpose is to increase the imposing country's economic welfare directly at the expense of other countries. Such government-directed economic decisions not only injure other countries, they also result in the misallocation of resources internationally with consequent results on efficiency and inflation.

Performance requirements that artificially expand exports threaten to grow into the most important distortions of global trade, investment, and production because they are not proscribed in present international agreements. The recently completed Multilateral Trade Negotiations addressed the issues of subsidies, counterfeiting, dumping, and other unfair trade practices. Investment-performance requirements which unfairly expand exports were not addressed. This gap means that governments which seek to expand their exports will increase their use of these measures because other means are effectively closed off. Because the United States is the source for approximately 50 percent of international direct investment, a large share of the trade effects of these measures will be experienced in the U.S. economy. Mexico and Brazil, two developing countries which use these measures most extensively, are also the major host countries for U.S. direct investment in the developing world, as is Canada among developed countries. This distortion of economic resource allocation will appropriate U.S. jobs and production and push down productivity growth.

THE MIRROR IMAGE: IMPACT OF U.S. PRODUCTIVITY ON TRADE

Reversing the optics of the impact of international competition on productivity reveals the ill-understood impact of productivity growth on international competitiveness—the ability of the United States to compete effectively against the goods of other countries.

Lower productivity growth affects U.S. international competitiveness directly by raising our costs relative to production costs in competing countries.

U.S. productivity growth, however, is only half the story of relative costs. The other half is the growth of wage costs, and very low American wage gains have more than offset this country's poor productivity record to yield a very strong U.S. position in relative costs.

The economic facts and figures show that America's slow productivity growth is wrongly blamed for the nation's declining competitive position in international trade and for the falling value of the dollar. It is important to understand why this increasingly common belief is untrue, because its proponents often blame labor for both our productivity and trade problems. Our productivity track records have been much lower than in the other advanced western economies (see figure 4.1). In manufacturing, the area that is most important for trade and in which productivity can be most accurately measured, U.S. annual productivity gains averaged only 2.2 percent during the 1970s. Japan's productivity growth averaged 5.8 percent annually and Germany's averaged 5.9 percent annually during the same decade. Even the beleaguered United Kingdom had a productivity track record that exceeded that of the United States.

During the 1970s as during the 1960s, the extreme modesty of U.S. wage gains (figure 4.2) more than offset the relatively poor productivity performance of the United States. The result: a dramatic strengthening of U.S. industry in relative costs of production (figure 4.3). While U.S. hourly compensation went up 130 percent from 1967 to 1978, German hourly compensation was rising 216 percent (in marks); British, 353 percent (in pounds); and Japanese, 400 percent (in yen).

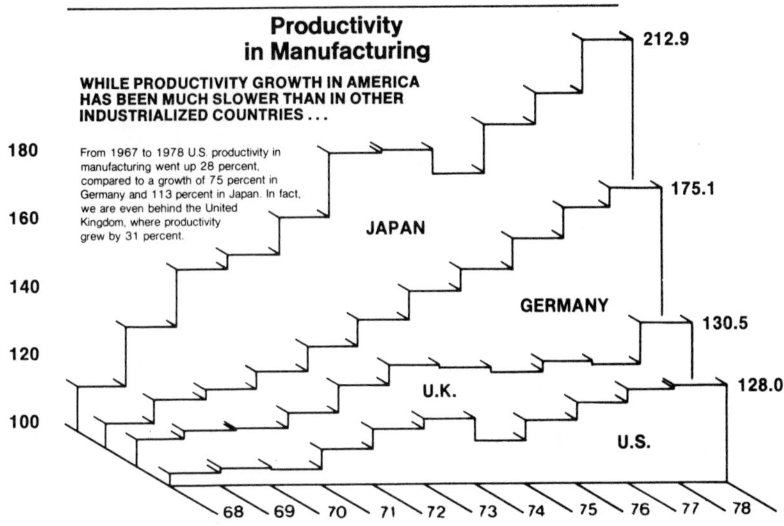

Figure 4.1

Source: Bureau of Labor Statistics.

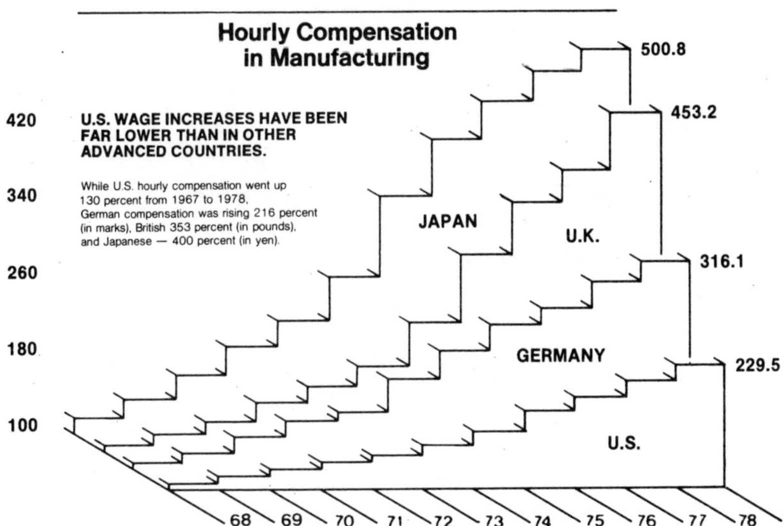

Figure 4.2

Source: Bureau of Labor Statistics.

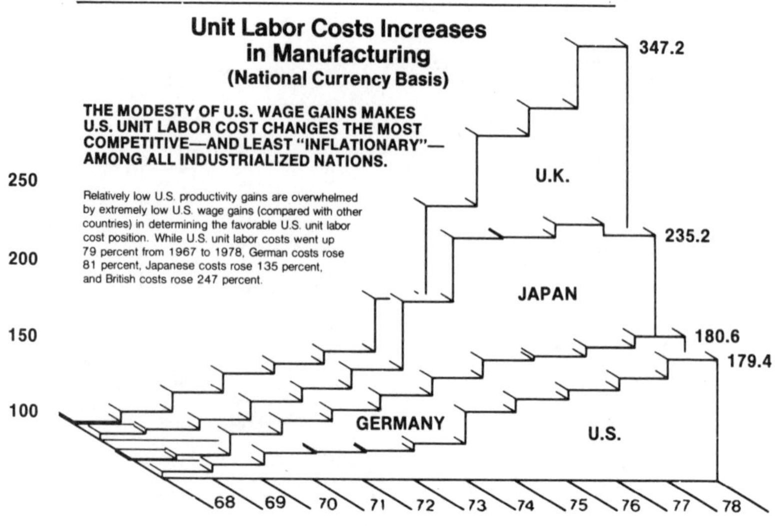

Figure 4.3

Source: Bureau of Labor Statistics.

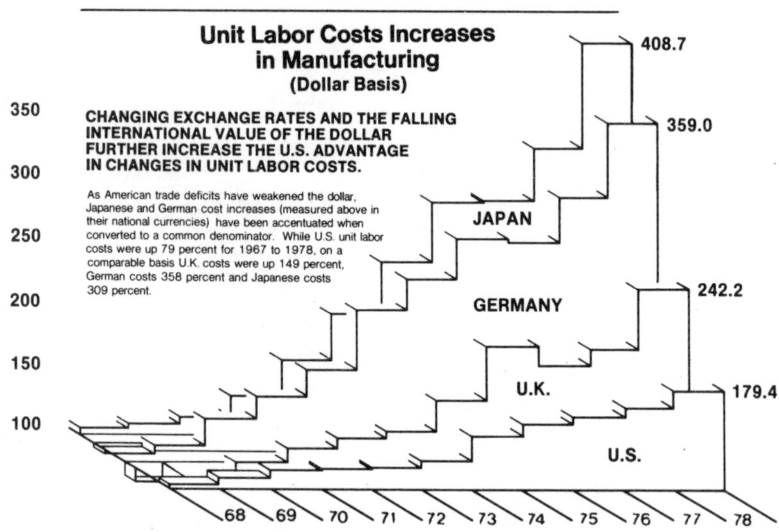

Figure 4.4

Source: Bureau of Labor Statistics.

The declining value of the dollar against most other currencies further strengthens the American advantage in relative costs (figure 4.4).

As a result, unit costs (measured in dollars) have increased only half as much in the United States as in other industrialized countries since 1967. While U.S. unit labor costs were up 79 percent from 1967 to 1978, UK costs were up 149 percent, German costs were up 358 percent, and Japanese costs were up 309 percent.

These international comparisons suggest we have to rethink many common misapprehensions about the impact of slow U.S. productivity growth on U.S. trade. Far from undermining U.S. competitiveness, U.S. labor has contributed tremendously to American trade competitiveness through relative restraint in wage gains.

The decline in U.S. trade and the value of the dollar since the mid-1960s, then, has to be laid to causes other than slow productivity growth. One fundamental cause for our declining trade competitiveness may lie in the falling rates of innovation in American industry—a decline in our ability to invent new products and bring them to the marketplace. This lag can be seen in consumer electronics (video tape recorders), machine tools (where U.S. imports are now soaring), automobiles (efficient cars with modern technology), and other sectors.

Is there a specific answer to the question of how foreign competition affects productivity? Probably not. There must even be a question as to whether foreign competition has any discernible or important effect on productivity at all. As indicated in the preceding pages, foreign competition can encourage efficiency or discourage it and may do both simultaneously. At the same time, there may be certain varieties of foreign competition that are so distinctly unhealthy for the welfare of most people that their effect on productivity is irrelevant. This kind of competition is unwanted in the United States.

So far as foreign competition is concerned, it's back to old-fashioned comparative advantage—provided that it is honest comparative advantage, untarnished by chiseling or exploitation, and provided that we realize that every doctrine should be modified occasionally for the greatest good of the greatest number.

NOTES

1. Edward F. Denison, "Explanations of Declining Productivity Growth," *Survey of Current Business*, pt. II, August 1979, p. 20.
2. Robert E. Baldwin, John H. Mutti, and J. David Richardson, "Crucial Issues for Current International Trade Policy," in *The New International Economic Order: A U.S. Response*, edited by David B.H. Denoon (New York: United Nations Association of the U.S.A., 1979), pp. 40–41.
3. Ibid., p. 42.
4. U.S. Department of Labor, Bureau of International Affairs, *Trade and Employment Effects of Tariff Reductions Agreed to in the Multilateral Trade Negotiations* (Washington, D.C.: U.S. Government Printing Office, 1979).
5. U.S. Department of Labor, Bureau of International Affairs, *Price Behavior of Products under Import Relief* (Washington, D.C.: U.S. Government Printing Office, 1979), p. 1.
6. Ibid., p. 2.
7. Ibid., p. 6.
8. Ibid., p. 7.
9. Ibid., p. 2.

5.
Unions and Productivity

Rudy Oswald
Director of Research, AFL-CIO

There is a need to understand why productivity increases, because that understanding can help shape policies which lead to better living standards. But too often, the call for "increased productivity" is a catch phrase used to justify attacks on unions, laws protecting worker safety and health, and laws protecting the environment, or to undermine the tax structure and essential public investment and services.

Productivity increases when better ways are found to produce and distribute goods and services, raising the output of each worker for each hour worked. Productivity increases when new machinery is installed, the flow of work is improved, or when workers are better trained and educated.

Productivity does not mean working harder. If productivity were measured by the total of human energy expended during the workday, then the construction of the ancient Egyptian pyramids would represent the peak period of productivity. Unfortunately, when some people say they want to increase productivity they just mean they want to increase someone's work load.

Human capital is the most important element in productivity growth. Educated, experienced, and skilled workers are highly productive workers.

American workers are better educated than they were a generation ago as the United States has continued to emphasize education. In 1900, very few adults had a high school education. By 1950, only 34 percent of Americans, aged 25 and older, had finished high school.

In 1975, 63 percent of the adult population had finished high school, and more than half now receive some schooling beyond high school.[1]

The importance of education to Americans is illustrated by the comparison of spending by Americans on education with that spent by other nations. Americans spend about 35 percent more per person on education than Japan and 40 percent more than West Germany.[2]

Better education and the spread of knowledge—through schools, training programs, books, magazines, newspapers, television, and so on—account for 40 percent of U.S. economic growth in recent decades, according to a study by Edward Denison.[3] Education provides the basis for inventions, new materials, and the improved flow of work from one operation to another. And education provides the work force with the basic skills for applying such advances in technology and know-how.

The more than one million patents issued in the United States since World War II testify to the scientific progress and abilities of the American people and have consistently provided new ways of producing more and better goods and services.

TRADE UNIONS AND PRODUCTIVITY

Trade unions make an important contribution to the efficient utilization of human capital. Recent studies show that union workers are much more productive than nonunion workers.

Charles Brown and James Medoff compared union and nonunion establishments in 20 two-digit standard industrial classification (SIC) manufacturing industries. Holding other factors constant to measure productivity differences, they found that:

> These regressions imply that even when the characteristics of workers most frequently associated with productivity differentials are held constant, unionized establishments are about 22 percent more productive than those that are not. If we attribute the effect entirely to labor. . .we find a union productivity effect of about 30 percent.[4]

Kim Clark did a study of the productivity of union and nonunion establishments in the cement industry. Clark concludes:

> The results suggest that unionized establishments are 6 to 8 percent more productive than their nonunion counterparts. . . . Since the statistical analysis controls for capital, labor substitution, scale effects and technological change, the evidence suggests that unionization leads to productive changes in the operation of the enterprise.[5]

Clark also looked at firms which changed their status from nonunion to union. He says:

> The evidence supports the conclusion, however, that unionization leads to gains in productivity within an establishment, with the size of the effect ranging from eight to ten percent.[6]

Steven Allen compared productivity of union and nonunion construction workers using 1972 Census of Construction covering all sectors of the industry nationwide. Allen found:

> Output per employee is at least 29 percent greater in unionized establishments in construction. If this extra productivity is entirely attributed to labor, then union members are at least 38 percent more productive than other workers in construction.[7]

Allen goes on to say:

> Differences in capital, capital recentness, firm size, measurable labor quality (age, schooling, and occupation), geographical price differences, sector within construction, and region have been held constant in the study. Such controls are necessary so that one cannot then claim that union members are more productive merely because unions tend to organize, for example, the largest firms or the capital-intensive sectors.[8]

Allen points out two reasons why union members are most productive:

> First, union members are likely to receive more training, and this results in part from their tendency to be tied to a craft rather than a firm. Rees and Dunlop both note the pride craft-union members

take in the skills which provide them with a group identity. Superior training also results from the active role union members take in developing apprenticeship programs. Second, union hiring halls reduce recruiting and screening costs to contractors.[9]

Discussing the commonly held attitude that unions hurt productivity, Allen says:

If these are the sources of the union productivity effect in construction, we have further reason to move away from the view that unions are monopoly institutions whose sole purpose is the creation and protection of economic rents for their members. The evidence presented here seems more consistent with models of unionization which emphasize the efficient provision of public goods at the workplace.[10]

Brown and Medoff give several reasons why unionized establishments are more productive, citing several sources on this topic.

High turnover can reduce the productivity of a work force through both a reduction of investment in and a loss of firm specific training, interference with the functioning of a work group and the costs (e.g., personnel) securing the requisite amount of labor. Unionized workers have lower turnover rates than do otherwise comparable workers in the nonunion portion of the industry.[11]

Brown and Medoff also say that the seniority system put in place by the union can raise productivity.

One way unions can affect workers' perception of their co-workers is by pressuring firms to let seniority govern the relative ranking of individuals relative to each other. . . . Seniority can greatly weaken the feeling of rivalry among workers. This can increase the amount of informal training and assistance that workers are willing to provide others.[12]

The union effect of raising morale is also mentioned by Brown and Medoff as a possible source of increased productivity.

Unionization can raise morale and motivation of a work force by improving the nature of jobs or by changing workers' perceptions of their jobs. Unions can effect these changes by securing greater material rewards (both wages and fringe benefits), reducing the potentially arbitrary nature of decisions as promotions and layoffs (through seniority), and by attempting to insure that workers' grievances are heard and fairly adjusted. It is plausible that the increase in morale can be transformed into an increase in worker productivity.[13]

The utilization of human capital can also be improved by eliminating discrimination based on race, age, and sex. Discrimination prevents people from making their best contribution to output and productivity.

Other basic causes of increased productivity include scientific research and development; business investment in high-technology plants and equipment; and investment by federal, state, and local governments.

High wages in the United States and the large size of the American market also are factors in productivity. Higher wages are both a cause and a result of highly productive mass production, which features large-scale plants and assembly lines utilizing the latest technology.

PROBLEMS OF MEASURING PRODUCTIVITY

Evaluating the productivity trend is complicated by problems of measuring productivity. There are a number of problems that are encountered in efforts to measure output and, therefore, productivity on an economy-wide scale. These problems are made more difficult by inflation, when output has to be adjusted by price indexes that may not be appropriate for the series being deflated. The widely bemoaned slowdown in productivity is due in large part to the understatement of output due to measurement difficulties for most nonmanufacturing output.

When details of the Bureau of Labor Statistics (BLS) data are looked at in the unpublished tables, major questions and discrepancies arise. The poorest measures of output are for construction, finance, insurance, and real estate and services. It is difficult to determine real output in these sectors of the economy.

The faulty nature of construction industry productivity data is due primarily to the use of inaccurate corrections for inflation. These inflation-adjusted data understate output and, therefore, productivity. Unpublished BLS figures based on overall gross national product (GNP) data show an average 2.5 percent yearly decline in construction productivity from 1969–78. This result contradicts all detailed BLS construction productivity studies, including those for single-family homes, office buildings, sewer and water systems, and apartment houses.[14] Each of these studies indicates a substantial positive productivity increase. A study done by the Institute for Defense Analysis for the U.S. Labor Department on construction productivity criticizes the GNP-based construction productivity measure and recommends using a productivity figure of 2.0 percent per year increase based on the detailed BLS construction studies.[15] This is a difference of 4.5 percent per year.

It is also difficult to measure the "output" of finance, insurance, real estate, and other services, such as health, legal, and repair services. Output is not appropriately measured by gross income or the number of persons employed. But these indirect measures are the procedures now being used to measure output. They do not accurately measure changes in output and, therefore, productivity. No reliable basis exists for adjusting "gross income" figures for inflation.

Construction and services account for about 23 percent of the hours used for measuring productivity in the overall productivity measure. The growth of these inadequately measured sectors and the decline of manufacturing add a downward bias to the measurement of productivity of the total private economy.

The productivity measure for manufacturing is more accurate because in many cases there is physical output which can be counted, and more and better information is available on output and prices.

Although overall productivity measures show a sharp slowdown in the 1970s, productivity in the basic manufacturing sector has slipped less substantially and, when adjusted for the decreases in two recessions of the 1970s, the change is minor.

For all of the 1970s, manufacturing productivity increased an average of 2.2 percent per year—less than the 3.0 percent average of the 1960s, but almost the same as the 2.4 percent average yearly growth of the 1950s.

The respectable rate of manufacturing productivity growth during the 1970s occurred despite two back-to-back recessions and an underutilization of plant and equipment during most of the 1970s. The 1973–75 recession was so severe that it caused a 5.2 percent drop in manufacturing productivity, the largest drop for any year since World War II. The recession of 1970 also caused a drop in manufacturing productivity.

The decade of the 1950s also had two recessions, but neither was as severe as the 1973–75 recession. The decade of the 1960s was a long period of continuous expansion of output with only a slight slowing of growth in 1967 and late in 1969.

Plant, equipment, and manpower were seriously underutilized during the 1970s and this lessened the need for expansion, thereby slowing productivity growth. Plant and equipment utilization in manufacturing averaged only 82 percent in the 1970s compared to 85 percent in the 1960s and 84 percent in the 1950s, according to Federal Reserve Board figures.

So the recessions and low utilization rates of the 1970s make it remarkable that productivity growth in manufacturing did as well then as compared to the 1950s. And considering the marked difference in the economic climate, it is even more remarkable that the 1970s growth rate came so close to that of the 1960s.

Productivity in manufacturing is increasing much more rapidly than in nonmanufacturing, but manufactured goods are a declining share of total output, and manufacturing now accounts for only 29 percent of total hours of work in the private business economy.

The slowdown in measured productivity for the total private business economy results primarily from nonmanufacturing data, which do not have the reliability of manufacturing data.

The inadequacies of measurement of productivity in these sectors and the probability that productivity is vastly understated in these sectors means that the downturn in productivity in the 1970s may be a problem of measurement and not reality.

Concentration on doubtful statistics concerning productivity growth and unit-labor costs for the total private economy may seriously distort an understanding of inflationary pressures in the economy. Productivity has been increasing in manufacturing and continues to contribute substantial real gains to the economy.

COMMON EXPLANATIONS FOR THE PRODUCTIVITY SLOWDOWN

Many explanations have been given for a slowdown in the overall measure of productivity. The fact that there is so much trouble with the explanations is still further evidence that the method of measuring, and not productivity itself, should be getting the scrutiny. Among the explanations commonly cited are these:

- Regulations that require business to reduce safety hazards in the workplace, or the related environmental regulations to protect the quality of air and water.
- Reduced emphasis on research and development funding.
- A shortage of capital investment and lack of modern machinery and equipment.
- The increased number of women and teen-agers in the labor force.
- A general U.S. decline in the work ethic.

Environmental and Safety and Health Regulations

Regulations in the 1970s have required business to provide safer workplaces, to be more responsive to customer complaints, and to reduce pollution of the air and water and to dispose of wastes in a safe manner. These regulations have come in response to public demands for solutions to serious health and safety problems. But 58 percent of the funds spent for plant and equipment for pollution control are spent in manufacturing—the sector which has shown the least ill effects in the 1970s.[16]

The increased expenditures for worker health and safety due to OSHA regulation amount to about one-tenth of one percent of the nation's income, too small to have a significant impact on productivity.[17]

The expenditure to comply with pollution-control regulations has been larger, and some have assumed this came at the expense of other investment. This assumption is open to question, but even if true, the BLS estimates that investment spending on pollution-control equipment would reduce productivity growth by about one-tenth of one percent per year from 1975 to 1985.[18] A study by Data Resources, Inc. (DRI), agrees with the BLS result that the impact of these regulations on productivity is small and also concludes that spending for pollution control actually stimulated the economy because business spent funds that otherwise would not have been invested. The DRI study concludes that the additional business-investment spending for pollution control has created about 200,000 new jobs.[19]

These estimates of the effect of pollution control regulations on productivity consider only the negative impacts, and unfortunately do not attempt to include the positive effect on future productivity from improved worker and community living standards.

Increase of Women and Teen-agers in the Labor Force

Another reason given for declining productivity is the increase in women in the labor force. Women now hold about 42 percent of all U.S. jobs, up from only 29 percent in 1950. But this growth has not occurred suddenly in the 1970s but rather has occurred gradually since World War II. Women are concentrated in clerical occupations, and 85 percent hold white-collar or service jobs. Fifteen percent hold blue-collar jobs, as craft workers, machine operators, drivers, and laborers. The rapid increase in white-collar jobs has enabled women to enter the labor force more rapidly. There is no evidence that women are less productive in the jobs they hold than men. The studies asserting that women are less productive assume that the lower pay of women indicates their lower productivity. But the lower pay is often a reflection of the generally lower pay levels of service jobs or may actually reflect wage discrimination against women rather than lower productivity.

Teen-agers do require training when they enter the work force, and too little attention has been paid to the need to provide training, skills, and employment opportunities to young people. But the impact of teen-agers on the work force is not large enough to have much effect on pulling down productivity growth in the 1970s compared to other periods. The rate of increase of teen-agers entering the labor force in the 1970s is not very different than it was in the 1960s when productivity was high and no one was citing their "detrimental" impact.

Decline in the Work Ethic

The contention that the work ethic has declined is a generalization refuted by the healthy productivity gains in many industries. In five industries, productivity rose more than 5 percent per year from 1973 through 1978. These include telephone communications, synthetic fibers, air transportation, copper mining, and corn milling. Motor vehicle and several other industries had productivity growth rates of about 3 percent. For manufacturing as a whole, productivity grew 1.8 percent in the year 1979. The workers in high-productivity industries are no different from those in low-productivity industries—so there is simply no support for the notion of a fundamental decline in the "work ethic."

Accusations abound that the work ethic has declined, but workers rarely get to tell their side of the story. A recent article in the *New York Times* by auto worker John Jones expresses some of the complaints that trade-union leaders often hear from their constituents.[20]

Jones complains that management fails to keep the equipment that workers use in good repair, to provide the correct tools for the job, and that managers ignore faulty products produced by poorly functioning equipment.

On one occasion Jones told his supervisor that his air wrench was not getting bolts tight enough. His complaint was ignored, causing a whole day's production to go out with bolts that looked tight but were not. On another occasion Jones was told to allow faulty products produced by an imprecise welding machine at breakneck speed to pass inspection when they should have been scrapped.

Jones believes that the problems consumers have with their products are generally due to poor engineering and design or poor materials rather than poor workmanship.

These kinds of events are frustrating to workers and have an obvious impact on morale, but despite his frustration, John Jones says he does his best because, "There is more self-respect in doing even this type of work well than in doing it poorly."

Shortage of Capital Investment

There is a similar lack of evidence of an economy-wide shortfall of savings, or "capital shortage," that deters investment and therefore lowers productivity growth. Returns to corporate investors and savings are more than ample to supply funds for business investment. Corporate cash flow—the key measure of funds available to replace old equipment and invest in new equipment—totaled $276 billion in 1979, almost double the $140.9 billion cash flow in 1973. Cash flow in 1979 was a higher share of the nation's income than in 24 of the past 25 years.[21]

People who say that there is a shortage of savings often misinterpret the savings rate published by the Department of Commerce as financial savings. Actually, the Commerce Department savings include only those savings borrowed by businesses for investment in plant and equipment. Money put aside for saving does not count if businesses or individuals borrow the money for speculation, if the money is borrowed by government, or if the money is borrowed for the purchase of existing homes or for the purchase of automobiles, appliances, or other "consumption" spending.

Financial savings have been greatly supplemented by the rapid growth in pension funds and life insurance reserves.

In 1979, borrowers raised $481.7 billion in U.S. credit markets, or about 20.3 percent of GNP, a much greater share than the 13.5 percent raised ten years ago.

Savings have been high in recent years, but speculative loans for corporate acquisitions and for speculation in commodities and real estate have diverted funds from productive investment.

The adverse effect on the economy of the use of funds for corporate acquisitions was pointed out by Harold Williams, chairman of the Securities and Exchange Commission, in testimony before the Senate Anti-Trust Subcommittee. As quoted in a *New York Times* article, Williams estimates that $100 billion in acquisitions and mergers took place from 1975–79. Williams points out that:

> The $100 billion could have been devoted to new production and employment opportunities. This money, he emphasized, does not

flow back as new capacity, improvements in productivity, innovations, new products, or new jobs.[22]

A thorough analysis of speculative loans is needed to assess their impact on the economy and to determine how those investments can be curbed.

The growth and size of the pool of financial savings indicates that savings are adequate to provide funds for housing loans, business investment in productive capacity, and consumer purchases of automobiles, home appliances, and other goods, but they may not be large enough to satisfy the demands for speculative loans as well.

Some people have argued that tax cuts to business are needed to provide funds for investment. Investment, however, expanded at a rapid pace in 1979, with no additional tax cuts. Plant and equipment have become increasingly more modern since World War II. The average age of plant and equipment in U.S. manufacturing, according to the Commerce Department, has fallen from 7.4 years in 1950 to 6.3 years in 1979, the lowest figure in the postwar period.[23] The average age of equipment—excluding plant—has varied between 4.4 and 5.3 years since 1950 and now stands at 4.5 years. The average age of equipment does fall during times of expansion and rise during recessions. So it was at its lowest in the expansion of the 1940s and 1960s and fell again in the past four years during the recovery from the 1974–75 recession. A survey done by McGraw-Hill also found U.S. plant and equipment to be quite modern.[24] Durable-goods manufacturers reported that 49 percent of their plant and equipment was less than five years old, and nondurable manufacturers reported 39 percent of theirs to be that new.

Reduced Emphasis on R&D Funding

The National Science Foundation estimates that, in dollars adjusted for inflation, overall spending for research and development (R&D) was higher in 1979 than for any previous year but has declined as a share of GNP because of a decline in federal spending on R&D.[25] Spending by private industry for R&D in 1979 was also higher than in any previous year. Private industry in 1979 spent about the same share of GNP for R&D as 15 years ago, and a significantly higher share than 25 years ago. But R&D spending by the federal government, as a share of GNP, has fallen as a result of cutbacks in the space programs and a decrease in research and development for national defense.

Research and development spending has declined as a percent of the nation's GNP because of reduced commitment by the federal government. And there are reasons why private R&D spending has been below what it could be. Such expenditures, for example, are very much affected by recessions—being one of the first items to be cut when the economy falters. During the economic recovery of 1975 to 1979, real R&D spending by private industry increased 24 percent, and a strong economy would continue that trend.

Furthermore, research and development in U.S. manufacturing industries has been harshly affected by imports. Foreign firms that capture large parts of the U.S. market replace U.S. research and development. For example, the Japanese now do the most R&D in consumer electronics goods because they produce a large share of those products sold in the United States. To the extent that U.S. firms are protected from unfair foreign competition, they will be encouraged to further R&D expenditures.

The sale of technology to foreign countries, or the use of technology developed in the United States to produce in overseas plants owned by U.S. firms, has hurt the ability of the United States to compete abroad. It has also affected adversely the growth of jobs and production in the United States. Often the technology—and, therefore, the productivity—transferred out of the United States was paid for by the U.S. taxpayer.

The rapid growth of imports over the last decade has not allowed U.S. productivity to reach its full potential. Imports have added to the problem of excess capacity and reduced the incentive for investment in new plant and equipment in many industries.

Imports have created apprehension about the impact of productivity growth on jobs and employment opportunities in many industries. In steel, heavy subsidies to producers by foreign governments and dumping of steel by foreign producers in U.S. markets has dramatically reduced the growth prospects of the American steel industry. American steel producers are now investing a large portion of their funds in other industries.

The rate of growth of productivity in the United States has been slower than the growth of productivity in other industrialized nations, but the American worker is still the most productive in the world. The American worker produces 24 percent more than the German worker and 32 percent more than the Japanese worker, according to a study by Dresdner Bank.[26]

Other industrialized nations have generally done better in keeping unemployment low and productive capacity more fully utilized. Also, these nations rely to a great extent on building production facilities that are like those already in use in the United States. The transfer of technology from the United States has played a major role in the growth of productivity in other industrialized nations.

The problems of the trade balance have not been caused by the difference in productivity growth rates. In fact, U.S. unit labor costs have risen more slowly in the United States than in competing industrialized nations. Unit labor costs rose 74 percent in the United States from 1968 to 1978, a much slower rise than the 297 percent increase in Japan and the 264 percent increase in German unit labor costs.[27]

The productivity growth of the American economy is not at its full potential, and policies can be constructed to raise productivity growth.

The greatest hindrances to productivity growth have been the policies for slow economic growth and recessions. The 1970 recession and the 1974 recession each caused a drop in productivity. Productivity in manufacturing declined 5.2 percent in 1974, the largest drop since World War II.

A decline or slowdown in consumer demand leaves workers, plant, and equipment idle. High overhead costs discourage the investment that can increase productivity. The slower operation of business retards the introduction of new plant and equipment that embodies the latest technology.

The best productivity growth is achieved when unemployment is falling and consumer demand is strong. Businesses expand more rapidly in a healthy economy, and the latest technology and machinery are brought into the workplace more quickly. In that climate, on-the-job training programs are also stepped up, and schools and universities expand programs to train workers in the newest skills for expanded job opportunities.

The recession and slow-growth policies stem from misguided attempts to cure inflation with unemployment. The Federal Reserve

Board over the last year has raised interest rates as a way to combat inflation as they did in 1970 and again in 1974.

The inflation of the 1970s has resulted primarily from rising prices of energy, food, housing, and medical care. The only way to reduce inflation is to apply corrective policies to these sectors. Raising interest rates will not solve the problems in these sectors and will make inflation worse by raising the cost of credit, an important cost in any investment decision.

Consumer demand is below the level necessary for the economy to realize its potential growth in productivity. With unemployment above six million and rising and production in manufacturing at only 83 percent of capacity, business managers have little incentive to invest in new equipment.

The trend of productivity cannot be fully assessed because of the doubtful accuracy of productivity statistics. Using the manufacturing data as a more accurate guide, productivity has slowed only slightly in the 1970s. And this slowdown is largely attributable to the recessions in the 1970s. A return to a more healthy economy should substantially raise productivity.

The prospects for productivity growth depend fundamentally on the performance of the economy. If inflation is fought with recession and slow growth, the prospects for productivity are poor. If policies are put into place to attack the specific causes of inflation—energy, food, housing, and medical care—and to achieve full employment of the nation's resources, the prospects for productivity growth will be bright.

NOTES

1. U.S. Bureau of the Census, *Educational Attainment in the U.S.-1977 and 1976*, Current Population Report, Series P-20, No. 314 (Washington, D.C.: U.S. Government Printing Office, 1977).
2. Irving B. Kraus, Alan Heston, and Robert Summers, *International Comparisons of Real Product and Purchasing Power* (Baltimore: Johns Hopkins University Press, 1978).
3. Edward F. Denison, *The Sources of Economic Growth in the United States and the Alternatives before Us* (New York: Committee for Economic Development, 1962).
4. Charles Brown, and James Medoff, "Trade Unions in the Production Process," *Journal of Political Economy* 86 (1978): 368.

5. Kim B. Clark, "Unionization and Productivity: Microeconomic Evidence," National Bureau of Economic Research (NBER) Working Paper Series No. 333 (Washington, D.C.: National Bureau of Economic Research, 1979).
6. Ibid, p. ii.
7. Steven G. Allen, *Unionized Construction Workers Are More Productive* (Washington, D.C.: Center to Protect Worker Rights, 1979), p. ii.
8. Ibid, p. ii.
9. Ibid, p. 5.
10. Ibid, p. 16.
11. Brown and Medoff, p. 357.
12. Ibid, p. 358.
13. Ibid, p. 358.
14. U.S. Department of Labor, Bureau of Labor Statistics, *Labor and Material Requirements for Construction of Single-Family Houses,* BLS Bulletin 1755 (Washington, D.C.: U.S. Government Printing Office, 1972).

    U.S. Department of Labor, Bureau of Labor Statistics, *Labor and Material Requirements for Private Multi-Family Housing Construction,* BLS Bulletin 1892 (Washington, D.C.: U.S. Government Printing Office, 1976).

    U.S. Department of Labor, Bureau of Labor Statistics, *Labor and Material Requirements for Sewer Works Construction*, BLS Bulletin 2003 (Washington, D.C.: U.S. Government Printing Office, 1979).

    John G. Olsen, "Decline Noted in Hours Required to Erect Federal Office Buildings," *Monthly Labor Review,* October 1976, pp. 18–22.
15. Douglas C. Dacy, *An Evaluation of the Treatment of Labor Productivity in the Construction Labor Demand System* (Arlington, Va.: Institute for Defense Analysis, 1978).
16. Gary L. Rutledge, and Betsy D. O'Connor, "Capital Expenditures by Business for Pollution Abatement, 1977, 1978, and Planned 1979," *Survey of Current Business* 59 (June 1979): 20–22.
17. Economic Department, McGraw Hill Publications Company, *Sixth Annual McGraw-Hill Survey of Investment in Employee Safety and Health* (New York: McGraw-Hill, 1977).
18. R.E. Kutscher, J.A. Mark, and J.R. Norsworthy, "The Productivity Slowdown and the Outlook to 1985," *Monthly Labor Review*, May 1977, pp. 3–8.
19. Data Resources, Inc. *The Macroeconomic Impact of Federal Pollution Control Programs: 1978 Assessment* (Cambridge, Mass.: Data Resources, Inc., 1978).
20. John Jones, "Company Line," *The New York Times,* April 9, 1980.
21. U.S. Department of Commerce, *Survey of Current Business,* February 1980.
22. Morton Mintz, "Playing the Takeover Game," *Washington Post,* April 18, 1980.
23. U.S. Department of Commerce, Bureau of Economic Analysis, *Fixed Nonresidential Business and Residential Capital in the United States 1925–1975* (Washington, D.C.: U.S. Government Printing Office, 1976), pp. 52–53.

24. Economics Department, McGraw Hill Publications Company, *How Modern is American Industry: A Progress Report* (New York: McGraw Hill, 1978).
25. National Science Foundation, *National Patterns of R&D Resources, Funds, and Personnel in the United States: 1953, 1978, 1979,* National Science Foundation No. 78–313 (Washington, D.C.: U.S. Government Printing Office, 1978).
26. *International Comparison of Labor Productivity,* Economic Quarterly No. 58, Dresdner Bank Aktiengesellschaft, New York, August 1978.
27. U.S. Department of Labor, Bureau of Labor Statistics, *Comparative Growth of Manufacturing Productivity and Labor Costs in Selected Industrialized Countries,* Bulletin 1958 (Washington, D.C.: U.S. Government Printing Office, 1977).

U.S. Department of Labor, *Productivity and Labor Costs: Preliminary Measures for 1978,* USDL 79–489 (Washington, D.C.: U.S. Government Printing Office, 1979).

II.
CORPORATE DECISIONS

6.
The Role of the Chief Executive in Productivity

John Fenlon Donnelly
Chairman, Donnelly Mirrors, Inc.

THE NATURE OF THE PROBLEM OF PRODUCTIVITY

Ordinarily, problems with lack of productivity would be handled expeditiously by the appropriate functions of a company and would not call for the special attention of the chief executive. Today we see the problem in a new light. Executives see that many causes of the problem lie outside of the company, as in government regulation. Furthermore, the problcm is so acute and so widespread as to threaten national and international economies, jeopardizing the free enterprise system and, with that, political freedom. It is only natural, then, that the chief executive officer should feel the responsibility for taking appropriate action. But what action? When we look at the influences which are suggested as causes of lower productivity, it appears that the avenues for CEO activity would be limited. These influences appear to cluster into five groups: (1) government regulation, (2) taxes, inflation, and other disincentives to investment, (3) high energy costs, (4) lack of innovation, and (5) employee indifference. I would tend to put employee indifference first. Indeed, I believe that if we use our full capabilities in reducing this problem, we will be better able to deal with the others. High energy costs, however, may really be something that we must adjust to, rather than cure, in that previous energy costs were artificially low. (Today's are artificial too, but probably not much above what a free market would support.)

This chapter will endeavor to show that the CEO holds the key to changing employees from being indifferent to being responsible and creative. To do this it will look for a definition of productivity suitable for the needs of the CEO, then identify the forces working against productivity, look for their origin, discuss models for offsetting these forces and why they seem to work and, finally, describe how the CEO can implement such a course of action. This fundamental treatment seems necessary because the problems are so deeply ingrained in our systems of management and in society at large that an understanding of the causal factors is necessary before we can understand what to do about them.

One definition of productivity is, "Output per worker-hour, quality considered." Such a definition is, in my opinion, much too narrow for the purposes of a chief executive. This is really not productivity, but only one measure of productivity. Under this definition, we could make increases in output per worker-hour through the work of added engineers and other specialists, but the output per hour of total effort would decrease, while showing that the output per direct hour improved. To correct this, we could specify that "worker-hour" covers all work in the company, whether managerial or specialist, whether indirect or direct production effort. This would help, but still would not sufficiently define what should engage the attention of the chief executive. The definition ignores other factors of production, such as capital. It does not consider depletion of the resources used. For instance, are productivity gains made at the expense of prematurely incapacitating the producing people, or by not maintaining equipment? These later phenomena are common means of "improving" productivity.

What should challenge the chief executive is how to make the organization more effective in using all of its resources, human, physical, and financial. At the level of the chief executive, attention is focused, as it should be, much more on the company as a system operating within larger systems, such as an industry or national and international economies, as well as various societies, from the very local to the national on several continents. CEOs have to consider the many inputs and outputs to and from the systems which they head. Shareholders, customers, suppliers, employees, unions, and governments make inputs to the system and expect something in return. The CEO's responsibility is to work out a plan for utilizing these varying inputs in such a way that more value goes out than comes in, and then distributing this output so that the various groups willingly continue making their inputs. This is a rather abstract way of describing the role of the CEO, but a little reflection will reveal that this is necessary if a company is to continue to prosper.

Productivity is a rather narrow concept when viewed from the CEO's chair. A better term would be organizational effectiveness. This has been defined as "the extent to which an organization, as a social system, maximizes its output without incapacitating its means and resources, and without placing undue strain on its members."[1] While we will continue to use the term productivity in this chapter, we are looking at this broader definition since this is the assignment of the CEO. While the CEO's efforts must result in product going out the door, he or she must also work toward profits, job satisfactions, innovation, and a host of other benefits.

It might put the problem into perspective to list some of the major forces at work pushing toward or against more productivity.

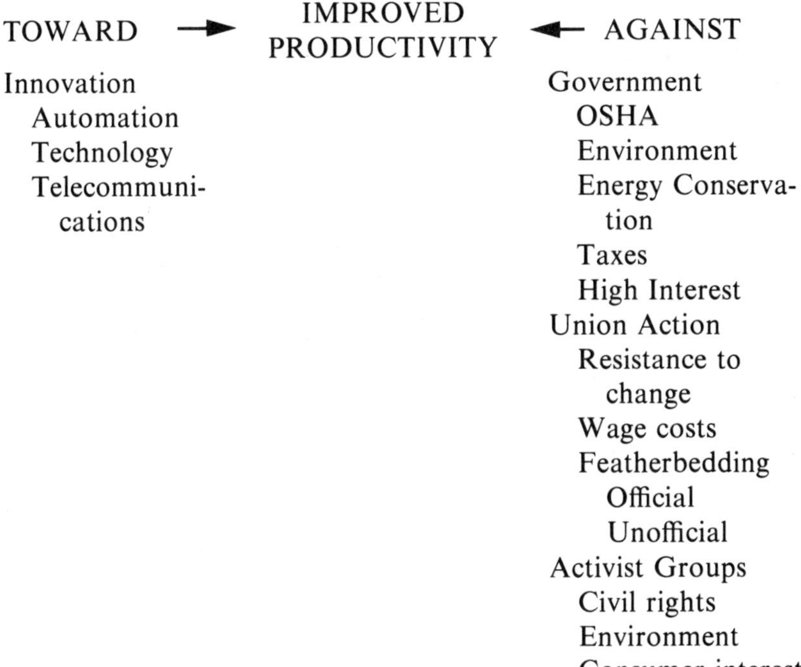

Employee
  Indifference
  Irresponsibility
  Hostility
Energy
  Cost
  Scarcity
Inflation

This is a lopsided list, although I did not deliberately make it so. At least, a reading of business literature would cause one to think that this is the way business leaders see the situation. We see more problems than helps at hand. Moreover, the "against" list contains many forces that an individual company cannot do much about. We cannot stop government regulation or inflation. Even if we were to give in to the demands of activist groups, the mood is such that we would likely be faced with a whole new set of demands.

The one area in which companies might have some effect is in dealing with their employees and any unions they may have. This, too, seems to be an intractable problem that appears to be getting worse instead of better. I do not believe it is intractable. I believe we have models for dealing with it. I believe that there are examples of definite change in the attitudes and work habits of employees in some companies, and there are examples of good union-management collaboration in improving productivity, even where a bad relationship has existed. I also recognize how hopeless this situation seems to managers who feel they are in a state of siege. The world seems to be going socialist, even in the West. We seem to be fighting a rearguard action, merely delaying the day of disaster. In spite of this prevailing gloomy view, there are several types of activities that show that a change is possible. The type which has the longest history and the greatest amount of research is the Scanlon Plan. It has been in use since the mid-thirties and periodically attracts public attention.

As long ago as 1952, *Life Magazine,* then in its heyday, pointed to the need for management and labor to put their mutual interests to work and suggested that the Scanlon Plan could be a useful tool to that end. *Life* referred to this voluntary cooperation as "freedom's secret weapon."[2] Freedom's secret weapon is a way of galvanizing an organization into action to make work more meaningful and productive. Such a promise should at least provide a ray of sunshine in the gloom, for if enough companies find this mutuality, not only the working climate in the companies, but the larger environment in which these companies operate will be changed.

If we are to be effective in making these changes, I believe we should have a clearer perspective on why many solid American citizens behave irresponsibly in their daily work and why government, which could not live in the style to which it has become accustomed without business, appears so hostile to it. As business managers, we are in the midst of a struggle, and such a climate is not conducive to clear thinking regarding the intentions of our opponents. It is vital for us to take some time to understand how this struggle came to be.

The great rise of government regulation of—and hostility toward—business began with the New Deal in 1933. This period completely upset traditional thinking patterns. During the twenties, business and the Republican Party were very much in the saddle. Republican philosophy called for a strong central government, but during the twenties the government merely did the bidding of business. The Democrats were traditionally for states' rights, which meant a weak federal government, but weak government is not what Franklin Roosevelt instituted when he took office in 1933.

Roosevelt came into power promising to balance the budget, but because the banking system was in great disarray and closed in much of the country, Roosevelt took the drastic step of closing all banks, making a crash audit of the major ones and reopening in a few days those with a chance for survival. This was a bold first step toward government assistance to business but also a step toward control of business; and having taken that step, Roosevelt decided not to turn back. The National Recovery Administration (NRA) was established to revive manufacturing and merchandising. The Home Owners Loan Corporation (HOLC) and other acronymic agencies sprang up to rescue sector after sector of American economic life.

Now how could a Democratic president get away with such a shift in philosophy? This was indeed a strong central government, and there were cries of alarm from unconverted states' righters. A case can be made that the president was forced to do so because of the desperate plight of this country. Therefore, most people listened to FDR's fireside chats sympathetically as he explained, step by step, how government was going to get things moving, first of all, and then control the malfeasance of big business, which had caused the Crash of 1929 and the Great Depression by its excessive speculation.

By 1936, Roosevelt's electoral support was so overwhelming that Postmaster General Jim Farley could quip, "As Maine goes, so goes Vermont." Not everyone liked the shift in emphasis from reviving business to controlling it. There was still resistance and it grew. Roosevelt protected his position by cementing a relationship between the Democratic Party and the unions, which is still largely intact. The Wagner Labor Relations Act was the cement. Labor became the ally of big government and gained a strong voice in how to regulate big business. Since business was largely unrepentant for the sins of the twenties, it opposed the new laws and fought regulatory commissions all the way to the Supreme Court, earning the personal enmity of the government and the unions. Because of its attitude, government and the unions became more harsh in their treatment of business. Business, naturally, fought back harder. If there ever had been a possibility for business to say, "We were wrong in the twenties and we are going to start policing ourselves," that chance was gone. In this hostile climate, business was preoccupied and thus overlooked new problems where their leadership could have helped, as for example, in race relations, pollution, and product safety. As the problems worsened, business became part of the problem instead of the solution, and today it has a new load of unacknowledged guilt, more punitive laws, and more public animosity.

This account of the origin of our present situation is one-sided, in that it seems to place all the blame on business. The only justification for holding business responsible is that it was the major leadership force in society up to 1929 or thereabouts, and others reacted to it. I believe that this narration, while neither complete nor balanced, generally describes how business became the scapegoat of society. This analysis doesn't make its position any happier, but it does make it somewhat understandable, and it may offer some clues as to how to change the situation. It should help us understand that feelings are so deep-seated that business cannot expect much public acceptance; even when it does something genuinely good, not many people will stand up and cheer.

Most employees will have grown up hearing about the struggle between business and government and business and labor—and they will be suspicious of business. In addition, they will have some problems concerning how business manages people.

In this respect, it is worth putting ourselves in the place of a production worker to see how the job is presented. Suppose the worker is a young man who has been self-employed in a gas station, but decides he can make more money in a factory. He is somewhat self-reliant and wants to get ahead. He is instructed in what to do and learns very quickly because of his experience with machinery and tools. After a couple of days on the job, he has a bright idea for an improvement on the fixture that holds his work. At home that night, he puts the idea into metal and next morning arrives at work a little early so the new fixture will be ready for the start of the shift. Lo and behold, it works! Parts come popping out about 15 percent faster than usual. He runs out of parts and calls for more. The lugger's only comment is, "What are you doing? Eating those parts?" By midafternoon, a scheduler notices the extra production. His comment, "You're going to get me all screwed up producing more than the others." Then a safety engineer says, "What the hell have you got on your machine?" The young man proudly tells him. But the response is, "That's a safety violation and I'll get a millwright to take it off." The employee replies that he can take it off himself but that this fixture is really safer than the old one. At this point, the foreman comes along and decides that the incident may result in a safety citation and a union grievance, so he orders the offending fixture removed and reprimands the employee in front of the crowd now looking on. When, do you suppose, that company will have another suggestion from that ambitious young man?

This example calls attention to the fact that the climate within industry may not be conducive to the exercise of responsibility and initiative. Granted, the behavior of the young man was disruptive. There is a need for appropriate procedures, and people can't just make changes indiscriminately. However, the treatment which we imagined him receiving was not necessary. He could have been congratulated at every step of the way and then advised about appropriate ways of carrying out his ideas. We get a glimpse in this story of what needs to be done within a company if we want to encourage responsible action. Each of the people in the story has an important function that is supposed to serve the production function.

The actual manner of operating, however, tends to stifle creativity and responsibility. The young man was effectively isolated from any real relationship to his work and became an adjunct to the machine. He perceived, of course, that people seem to be concerned with following procedures and not with the end result of the production effort.

The situation that the young employee found himself in may be extreme, but it reflects the climate that has developed under traditional management. At one time, most people would have felt the young man got what he had coming. Today, we know that that is not the way to manage people. Still, that is what happens all too often. This climate developed gradually in the factory system. As factories became larger and processes more complex, there was more need for standardization. As more controls were added, people felt less responsible for their work which, in turn, brought on more control. People then tried to beat the system, and this brought on punishment, which was resisted by unions. A frightful amount of time is now spent in trying to settle how much work will be done for what wages and who can do the work. Each side uses tricks and loopholes for every little advantage it can get. Little time or energy is left for improving productivity.

The factory floor is where the problem first became noticeable, but it has spread. Sociologists refer to the attitude of the worker as a symptom of alienation, a word that describes the feelings of people who are estranged from the organization in which they work. As work becomes more specialized, people have a hard time seeing that their work achieves anything. A clerk can say, "All I did today was type 100 invoices." These invoices may be the source of thousands of dollars of income for the company and this money will support many jobs, but if this isn't perceived, the invoices are meaningless pieces of paper to the typist. The pervasiveness of this problem is testified to by a New York psychiatrist, who claims his practice largely consists of treating executives for the same sort of alienation as a result of the meaningless work they do.

MODELS FOR DEALING WITH PRODUCTIVITY PROBLEMS

A Scanlon Plan can do something about these problems, but are there other models too—and what is a "Scanlon Plan?" The experience of Japan comes quickly to mind. The Japanese have developed very large, but apparently very effective, organizations. They have had victory after victory in the marketplace. Stories from Japan indicate a very different mode of operation than is the custom in the United States. The whole organization development movement was beginning to be heard in the postwar years and the Japanese listened, I think, a bit better than we did. Books suggesting ways of making organizations more productive, like the *Managerial Grid,* were quickly translated into Japanese. I don't know how much these books influenced the results in Japan, but they had the information.

There are innovative companies in America which do not follow traditional patterns. William Ouchi has called these companies Type Z and points out the similarity to highly productive Japanese companies. The quality-of-work-life programs here in America are also achieving improved relations between companies and their employees, together with unions. The organization development people have worked out methods of dealing with this problem. For example, a few years ago, executives from a Far Eastern refinery, belonging to one of the "seven sisters" oil companies, visited our company to exchange experiences on organization development. They told of an extremely stressful bargaining session they had had and indicated that they were determined to establish a better relationship with their union. Organization development people from their headquarters came and worked out a joint program to enable each side to understand, first, the motivations of the other, and then, their expectations. Gradually, trust developed. The next wage negotiations were embarrassingly smooth. After ratification, the union astounded management by asking if company organization development people could help the union with an internal problem. So even severe friction can be lubricated.

My own experience has been in using the Scanlon Plan in our company since 1952. The structure of the Scanlon Plan is so simple that one has difficulty in seeing how it can achieve much. It is the *process* of installing a plan that can, if done properly, transform a company from being a virtual cockpit to being a purposeful, cooperative enterprise. While the suggestions made in this chapter will reflect this experience, the principles used will also apply to other plans, such as Type Z, quality of working life, the managerial grid, organization development, and quality control circles. The

Scanlon Plan has been used in many types of companies for a long time. Many of the leaders in organization development recognize, in their writings, how the plan is congruent with the best thinking in the field. These efforts are designed to change people's attitudes and work habits so that they will expend their energies in support of company objectives—because they see that that is the way to achieve their own objectives. In general, these plans are forms of participative management.

In a Scanlon Plan each department has a committee, usually called the production committee, which is charged with communicating information on department goals and problems to others in the department and asking for suggestions on how to meet or solve them. Depending on the size of the company, one or more upper layers of committees are chosen to coordinate the work of lower committees. The top committee has been called the screening committee.

Then there is a bonus. Scanlon bonuses have been based on a wide variety of production measures, all the way from tons of material produced to profits. They apply uniformly to everyone in a company or division as a percentage of pay. The formula agreed upon is usually for improvement, in the measure chosen, from a period of, for example, five years prior to the start of the plan. The formula should be such that it can be stable over a long period. It is paid monthly.

These committees and the bonus are not sufficient in themselves to account for the changes brought about by a Scanlon Plan. The process of establishing the plan must effect a change in attitudes and behavior that will allow the committees and the bonus to function. This would hold true, whether the Scanlon Plan or some other form of participation were chosen.

THEORETICAL BASIS OF MODELS

To gain a thorough understanding of the change required in both the actions of the CEO and the response from the organization, one should take a quick look at three important pieces of theoretical work. These writings attempt to explain the attitudes of managers toward worker behavior, what motivates people to act and, finally, how this information can be brought to bear on the problem of initiating an action program which would improve productivity through the innate abilities and needs of the people producing.

The first of these is the work of Douglas McGregor. By observing effective and less effective managers at work in several large companies, he found the effective managers had different assumptions regarding the attitude toward work of their subordinates than those of the less effective managers. The assumptions of the less effective managers, he called Theory X. It is easily recognized in the treatment of the inventive young man described earlier in this chapter. If you were to ask a group of people how the manager should act to improve that situation, the answer would be something like Theory Y. Theories X and Y are part of the folklore of management. Theory X is still alive and busy, in spite of the fact that managers generally like to think that they are using Theory Y.

An abbreviated list of assumptions for Theory X and Theory Y follows:[3]

THEORY X	THEORY Y
1. The average person has an inherent dislike of work.	1. Work is as natural to people as play or rest.
2. People must be coerced, controlled, directed, and threatened to perform adequately.	2. People will exercise self-direction and self-control in the service of objectives to which they are committed.
3. People prefer to be directed and to avoid responsibility.	3. Commitment to goals is a function of the rewards associated with their achievement.
	4. Under favorable conditions, people learn to seek responsibility.
	5. Imagination, creativity, and ingenuity are widely distributed in the work force.
	6. In business, generally, the intellectual potential of people is only partially used.

There appears to be general agreement that Theory X leads to alienation and its attendant problems, and Theory Y yields better results. Incidentally, McGregor uses the Scanlon Plan as a prime way of implementing Theory Y in a company.

The second piece of work deals with motivation. It also is well known, and is the work of Abraham Maslow. He suggests that when people act purposefully, including work, they do so to meet needs that are currently felt. This does not sound earth shattering, but it is followed by the proposition that people tend to have a schedule of needs which must be met in a specified order. The first are the basic physical needs of food, shelter, and clothing. When these are satisfied, people seek security against the hazards of unemployment, sickness, old age, and so on. Then they desire to be part of a worthwhile group, church, company, union, club, or other organization. When this is reasonably met, recognition for achievement is sought. The highest goal that Maslow identified was self-actualization, that is, becoming the fullest person one is capable of being.

The theory sounds, at first, a bit ethereal, but Maslow was down to earth. He insisted that the higher needs are largely unfelt until the earlier one is reasonably met. If, for some reason, people are blocked from meeting a newly felt need in one way, they try alternate ways, or seek an excess of an already met need. For example, blue-collar workers who feel no sense of belonging to their company may satisfy this need by joining a union. They may also demand an excess fulfillment of physical and security needs by demanding more pay.

So far as the issue of productivity is concerned, this failure to recognize needs as a motivating factor has resulted in businesses losing the affiliation of their employees and paying extra wages without asking anything in return. The appropriate procedure, assuming Maslow makes sense, would be to survey peoples' needs and strike a bargain with them. "We will help you meet 'A,' but we need 'B' in return." The nonrecognition of this fact of life has led to businesses paying more and more and asking for nothing in return—a prime prescription for low productivity. That business too often overlooks motivation, participation, and appropriate managerial behavior as keys to better productivity is witnessed by a brochure recently published by a giant corporation, entitled *U.S. Productivity—What Can Be Done to Improve It*? The brochure points out how taxes and regulations hurt productivity and states that, "Technology, work flow, product standardization, and human resources are the four areas for improving productivity." But what do they have to say about human resources? They will train people. There is no thought given to motivation or creating a climate in which people can work effectively, or to the fact that the present situation is the result of how we have managed our businesses.

The third theoretical effort is that of Dr. Carl Frost, formerly of Michigan State University and a one-time associate of Joseph Scanlon at Massachusetts Institute of Technology. He has spent over thirty years studying, teaching, and consulting on Scanlon Plans and has developed a framework for understanding the essentials of the Scanlon Plan. Dr. Frost theorizes that if we want to modify the system to minimize alienation and increase both productivity and job satisfaction through the Scanlon Plan, three factors are necessary: identity, participation, and equity. Indeed, any plan to deal with productivity by improving the climate for work would entail these factors in some way. The three considerations are related, with each dependent on the other two for its full realization. *Identity* is a clear statement of the way in which the company hopes to organize itself to serve its customers. To accomplish this goal, the company needs the full use of its human resources as well as its financial, technical, and marketing resources. This marshaling of human resources is achieved through *participation*. People can be led, rather easily, to more responsible and creative action toward company goals when there are threats to the organization. Under normal circumstances, more skill would be needed to gain cooperation. Even then, cooperation would not last long if all the benefits of the extra performance were to be shared by customers and shareholders only. To avoid this, the company needs to develop a comprehensive system of *equity*. By comprehensive, I mean that three main groups—shareholders, customers, and employees—must be considered in establishing what is equitable. The three groups must be treated in such a way that they will willingly continue to make the inputs of capital, markets, and work so that more can be gained for all three groups. Identity and participation can provide added benefits. There must be a plan for sharing these additional gains if the process of producing them is to continue. This is what we mean by a comprehensive system of equity.

INSTALLATION OF A PRODUCTIVITY PLAN

We can now look at the three considerations in more detail and, at the same time, see how the proper installation of a program of participation, or specifically the Scanlon Plan, improves the work climate, and thus productivity. Identity—what is the company there for? Everyone knows its purpose is to make a profit, but this is an oversimplification because it puts results before causes. We are interested in what the company intends to do to earn the profit. Overemphasis on profits is something like overemphasis on winning. When winning is stressed in sports, all sorts of mischief replace the original intent. The degree to which winning approaches "everything" is a measure of how many referees are needed to prevent mayhem and trickery, and what begins as fun, as a game, or as healthful exercise, ends up as a deadly serious business. Winning is important, just as profit is, but when disproportionate emphasis is placed on either, we tend to skimp on the basic objectives. In football, the game often becomes, "We have to incapacitate the opposing quarterback." In business, it can be, "We cannot afford to dispose of these poisons in a safe manner." In addition, if people realize that their welfare is subordinate to profits, they naturally have to consider themselves as not part of the enterprise. This attitude is not confined to blue-collar people.

On the other hand, if the head of a company can state clearly what the company is about, several good things happen. The chief executive will probably better understand what he (or she) is trying to do, and people all through a company can exercise intelligent discretion more easily when an occasion arises. Assuming that the identity is respectable, people see a goal toward which they can work. The work of Likert points out that this is one of the chief responsibilities of leadership. People respond well to high goals set by their leaders. This overall identity statement has to be interpreted and amplified as it is carried through the organization, because each department and level must see how its work contributes to the goals of the identity statement.

Establishing a corporate identity would seem like eminent good sense in any business, and I am sure it is often done. The big question is, what does the leader do with the statement of identity or purpose? If the leader expects people to be indifferent and irresponsible, the information can be confined to the corporation's key people. If the leadership expects people to be capable of using ingenuity and imagination in working toward high goals, it will want to propagate the identity statement widely, encouraging department heads to take the lead from it and to interpret and expand it for their people. This is a way of giving direction to the whole organization, of galvanizing it for action. If people do show an interest, and if the leadership really is interested in these stated purposes, it will want to encourage the full use of all its resources—financial, technical, and human—in meeting these objectives. The full use of finances and technology is pretty standard operating procedure, but the marshaling of human resources is seldom encouraged. The failure to go this next step is a prime cause of the alienation that is referred to so often in this chapter. To make identity operational, we will want to be serious about encouraging participation, which is our second consideration.

Merely decreeing that participation is wanted will not automatically do away with the lethargy that is bothering our companies, our economy, and life in general. Old habits are hard to overcome. There are too many verbal and nonverbal signals in the organization that have to be eliminated.

The very first step is to make a decision. We must decide, "Is there a need to change?" This is perhaps the hardest single step to take correctly, because it is easy to do without conviction. It is always others who need changing, not we. However, it is not enough for top leaders just to decide; the decision process must also lead to an understanding of, and answers to, such questions as:

- Does participation destroy authority?
- How will decisions be made?
- What will be the role of authority?
- In what areas should participation be encouraged?

This is an imposing group of questions. They don't answer themselves. The honesty and thoroughness with which they are addressed will measure the probability of success. This process will go a long way in preparing the organization for change.

At this point the reader will realize that guiding this process is not everybody's job. It requires understanding, tact, persistence, and the ability to see through pretense. A competent consultant from outside the organization is the preferred choice to provide guidance. However, the work must be done by the organization, including top management.

This process should have led to a consensus in the organization that there is a need to change, and to an understanding of what things must change if company goals are to be pursued with full vigor. A steering committee is the typical vehicle to move toward the next stage, which would be a formal planning of the structures needed to make participation feasible. The production and screening committees might need restructuring for the needs peculiar to each company.

While this is going on, we need to prepare managers for their new roles. They need to know, "How do you encourage suggestions and responsible behavior? How do you turn a complaint into a suggestion? How do you encourage trust, or, in words that are more to the point, how do you yourself become trustworthy?" These questions must be answered at every level of management, because each level has its own set of biases and problems. Sensitivity training or the managerial grid are examples of the kind of training that can help. Formal training in listening also helps. In our organization, all managers attend managerial grid rather early in our efforts.

We usually think of participation being needed on the shop floor, but there is adequate evidence that people in middle management can be just as alienated as the blue-collar worker. As the ratio of white-collar employees in the company passes the 50 percent mark, the need for white-collar involvement and effectiveness becomes even more necessary. Upper management needs the training, as well as do other levels. In fact, training consultants generally insist that training for middle- and first-line managers is wasted if top managers do not take the training first.

Even though the final plan for participation may not yet be formulated by the steering committee, a great deal of participation is exercised in the organization through the process of deciding and getting started. This process is the first chance to see participation at work. It usually provides exciting and gratifying results—and a clear signal that a change is happening, that all shots are no longer called from on high.

This discussion has had little to say about how to deal with a situation in which one or more unions are present and the relationship is adversarial or even hostile. The example of the oil refinery shows that improvement is possible, but great insight into the problem and skill are equally required. It is essential that the union be involved before the organization as a whole is involved, and it must be demonstrated very early that there is no intention to displace the union or to divide its members from it. There are models for dealing with this problem which a good industrial relations department should know. The key to change is the identity statement, which should clarify the powerful marketplace demands which the company can only meet if it can draw fully upon the abilities of its people, not only to perform their allotted tasks, but also to think, to innovate, to cooperate, and to be responsible. The competition is not just from companies making the same products locally, but from companies throughout the world. Furthermore, competition can arise from other products, since one type of product can displace other types, as today's electronic equipment is displacing countless mechanical devices. The grounds for the company and union making common cause are real. It remains for the CEO to make the needs explicit and to clear away past differences, enabling the company and union to get on with the joint task at hand. One thing that can pave the way for more openness with the union is a clear acknowledgement that unions have become a part of industrial life because past managers have not sufficiently regarded the needs of their people. They continue to exist because of more recent failures of managers.

With managers more or less trained, with a plan developed by the steering committee, and with the assistance of any unions that have agreed to cooperate, we can begin to involve the whole organization in a series of meetings which will explain the program that is being proposed. These meetings should culminate in a secret vote, yes or no. It is not sufficient to get a simple majority or even a two-thirds majority. For a change of this magnitude, we need the wholehearted support of people. Ninety percent or even 95 percent of the votes are usually required to carry us through the inevitable misunderstandings and backsliding that occur as we proceed.

I am sure that I appear to be demanding a lot of work from the organization. I can only counter with the reminder that this problem has been a long time coming. When we look back over the century and a half or two centuries during which this problem has been building, we can be a bit more patient if the cure takes some doing. Furthermore, the magnitude of the present problem and the benefits available through the development of a cooperative work force are great enough to justify the managerial effort required.

What distinguishes this effort from more conventional approaches is that we are looking for an organizational change more than a patching up, a clarification of company goals, and the marshaling of everyone's efforts and talents toward reaching those goals. This involves a fundamental shift in emphasis from a focus on rewards and punishments to a focus on the job to be done. While I am labeling this a fundamental shift, I have some difficulty making the shift apparent. It often appears to be a chicken-and-egg argument. When we say that the work is more important than the pay, the answer comes quickly that people really work for the pay. This relationship between work and pay must be clarified if we want to understand the process.

For example, what is the purpose of the medical profession? A ready answer might be to cure illnesses, or at least to help the patient be as comfortable as possible if the cure cannot be effected at once. Surely the focus is on the well-being of the patient. If we ask, "Why does a person undertake this work?" we would hope the answer is because he or she wants to help people be healthy. This must be a factor in the choice of many people when they enter the profession. There is, however, a strong suspicion abroad in the land that it is not the only factor. The profession is also generally well paid, and this fact appears to be something of a magnet to the profession. Indeed, there are repeated studies which point to the phenomenon of surgeons being so anxious to help people that they perform 10 percent to 30 percent more operations than people need. This could be brushed off as being purely a difference in diagnosis, which still has a bit of art to it. But there is a haunting question, "If the surgeons were on salary and not on fee, would the diagnosis be the same?" Committees of doctors are themselves raising this same kind of question when they examine statistically the purposes and results of operations. The only case I want to make here is that pay seems to affect the judgment of some doctors in some cases, but not all doctors and not in all cases.

If this can occur in so vital a profession as medicine, what would happen in the case of more prosaic work, such as making parts for automobiles? Do people enter this or similar occupations out of dedication to serving the public, or out of a desire to make money? The answer, a desire to make money, would probably come through much more clearly in industry than in medicine. Indeed, people all the way up to top managers feel quite ready to leave industry "A" and move to industry "Z" if they can make more money. The work is not that important.

This indifference to the end product of work and focus on the money to be earned should not surprise us. The leaders of industry and, indeed, their leading theoreticians, the economists, insist that profit is the purpose of business. It would seem quite reasonable, then, for employees to look upon money as the prime purpose for their work. This emphasis on money is, as we have seen earlier, the cause of a great deal of mischief that exists in the world of work today. I would like to restress this point.

If our main focus is on the pay that our work brings in, why should we not focus on ways to get more pay for less work? The ultimate is very high pay for no work at all, and many people have achieved this. Healthy people who live on unemployment benefits or who feign illness and get workmen's compensation are one type of example. At the other end of the scale are people who are paid handsomely for not competing, or ineffective executives who are given jobs with high pay and few duties to get them out of the way.

As a business manager I am taught to make judgments, not on the basis of the welfare of the employees, whose loyalty I expect, nor the needs of the customers, whom I say I serve, nor out of respect for natural resources or the society, which make my business possible, but on the basis of what will give my company the largest profit—provided, of course, that I share in that profit. From this, it would seem that there is an imbalance in business regarding what is said about money.

This does not imply that profits or money should not be important, but that they should be a result of work well done. We hope the surgeon will decide to operate only on the basis that the patient needs the surgery, not because the fee will buy the surgeon a set of golf clubs or the success will enhance his reputation. So also, if work in industry is to be interesting, challenging, or satisfying, the output of the industry as a whole should be something that can attract our interest, challenge our abilities, or satisfy our need to feel worthwhile. My job should appear to me as a significant contribution to these company purposes. If we can switch our main emphasis to the work to be done, then we can galvanize the organization into action. It will seem reasonable to ask people to dedicate more of their attention and skills to the work. But to ask for more care and dedication only so that the company can make more money is not a compelling argument. To say that we need this or that extra effort from you so we can get this new customer, or increase our business from that old customer, has a little more rationale. To let people know that we are changing this operation so product "A" can be safer for the customer or last longer can elicit a positive response. John Ruskin came close to summing up this notion in saying, "The highest reward for man's work is not what he gets for it, but what he becomes by it." Unfortunately, when we hire people or when we look for work ourselves, that is, too often, not foremost in our minds.

There is another saying whose source I do not know, which also sums up my thinking and introduces my final statement. The saying goes, "Unless the work means more than the pay, it will never pay more." This opens up the idea that good work will or should pay more, and it starts to balance the emphasis on good work with a reward or payoff of some sort. We do, after all, work to live. Today, most of our needs, such as food, shelter, medicine, and education, do not come directly from the work itself, but through the medium of money earned. It is easier for us to focus on the money rather than the work, especially when we are told that the prime or sole purpose of the enterprise is money.

If a person who has dedicated himself or herself to doing the work better, to taking more responsibility, and to being creative, and then sees only the company prosper as a result of these efforts, that person might reasonably sit back and wonder if the whole pitch had been a con game. This is where equity comes in. I believe that people can be led to dedicate themselves to company goals for a long time without special reward, when survival is the only benefit. But, in those happy times when these dedicated efforts result in prosperity for the company, it is not unreasonable for people to ask for some share in that prosperity. Indeed, one of Joseph Scanlon's best moves was to develop ways of determining, ahead of time, how that sharing was to take place.

Several beneficial results occur. First of all, it is usually easier to establish a formula for sharing before there is something to divide. It is usually safer for people to inquire about price before they say they will buy. Similarly, people like to know what they will be paid before they do a job. If the decision about sharing the results of improvements is delayed until the improvements have been made and the results are in, each person will have been busy totaling up what his or her contribution is worth. The sum of these evaluations tends to exceed the actual improvements made. Scanlon recognized that, regardless of what each individual did, the improvements had to be a group effort, and the group included everyone in the company. His formulas shared the savings between the company and the employees. The employees' bonus was shared on the basis of their base pay, so everyone received the same percent bonus. The important consideration is whether or not people accept the formula as fair before they are asked to go about their work in a more responsible fashion. If this agreement is hammered out early in the process of moving the company into a participative mode of operation, the question of equity becomes less traumatic and less divisive. People can get on with the work without wondering whether they will be fairly treated in the end.

In other words, this prior agreement has been a major move in developing a feeling of trust in the organization. Trust makes a world of difference, since both the managers and the managed have been operating in a mode without trust, or even with positive distrust. Requests from either side have been scrutinized for hidden objectives. Before we can substitute wholehearted cooperation, this climate must be changed. In fact, there can be no agreement to begin the process of participation unless some measure of trust is first established. The bonus formula is a major contribution to this building of trust.

The elimination of arguments and the establishment of trust are two benefits of settling the bonus formula ahead of time. There is, however, one problem with this, namely, the tendency for everyone to look forever after on the bonus as the motivator of all further activities. If this is allowed to happen, all the early work of encouraging a focus on the work itself as the important consideration is undone. In our company, we go to considerable efforts to keep this priority straight. Bonuses and pay are not incidental considerations when we go about work, but we must try to keep our focus on the work first. Unless the work means more than the pay, it should never pay more.

Equity means more than a fair share of monetary rewards, since there is more to life than money. According to Maslow's hierarchy of needs, the typical job is seen to provide satisfactions for physical needs through pay, and for safety needs through insurance and pensions. The need to belong, the need for recognition, and the need for self-fulfillment are seldom considered when jobs are designed and rewards are provided. A little thought will reveal many possibilities for bettering this situation when a company decides to go through the steps of identity, participation, and equity in establishing a Scanlon Plan or any other plan of participation. The very act of communicating to the company what leadership believes the company's purpose to be will signal people that leadership regards them in a new light. They are not hands or hirelings, but people, important for the company's success. They can begin to feel that they have some membership in the company, and the company itself has taken on more value to them because its purpose is better understood.

As ideas for improving operations are solicited in the participation process, there will be opportunities for recognizing good work. The changed attitudes of people toward their work will help them make better use of their skills and motivate higher performance, creating more opportunities for advancement.

Finally, the entire experience, from serving the genuine needs of people through participation to meeting company goals and serving one another by this cooperative effort, brings with it a new sense of worth and self-fulfillment. These opportunities for belonging, for recognition, and for self-fulfillment are an added output of the company and are powerful motivators. They are sometimes called the psychic profit or psychic increment of the company. People in the company then have an enlarged equity by receiving a share of this psychic increment.

This is still not the whole story, because if the process of participation means a genuine change in attitude toward people, the people will be seen to be less expendable. There will be a desire to find ways of improving job security for people. Human resource accounting, for instance, would have greater meaning for a company which really believes its people are important. In our company, for example, we have adopted a policy protecting people whose jobs are eliminated by technology. This policy, far from slowing up change, tends to foster it, because people do not fear the results of new technology.

Our company has been in the process of adopting the Scanlon Plan for 27 years. We are not finished, because each year's experience and current research in the social sciences give us new insight into what the process means. Have we eliminated alienation and all the attendant problems? Not entirely. We have certainly reduced the problems to manageable levels. There is less alienation and more responsible involvement. Work does have some meaning for most people. There is less politics and more cooperation.

In this sketch of the executive's role in improving the climate for work and productivity, we have suggested that the symptoms of alienation and indifferent work result, at least partially, from the continued use of Theory X assumptions. If we want to change this situation, we should attempt to operate our business systems with the assumptions of Theory Y. The Scanlon Plan was suggested by McGregor as an effective way of doing this, but there are other good plans. This entails a clear statement by leaders as to the purpose of the company, or how it intends to earn its profit by serving its customers and how it relates to its employees and shareholders. This set of goals can best be achieved if all human resources can be drawn upon, making use of their intelligence, cooperation, and responsibility in the furtherance of the company's goals. To this end, a structure for participation must be established. To make the whole process rational, a system of equity is established to let people see that their added efforts will be fairly rewarded. The goals of company identity are achieved through participation and through encouraging people to assume the added responsibility and creativity called for. Equity makes it rational to assume these added tasks and has the added dimension of identity and participation, because they provide a psychic as well as monetary profit.

Early in this chapter, I elected to put the people problem at the head of the list and suggested that its solution might help on all the others. As *Life* suggested, the solution of our problems in industrial relations would remove a great deal of friction from society. Business would be seen in a more wholesome light. Business leaders would be more relaxed and could approach the political arena with more confidence. Because of their regained public respect, business leaders could hope for a more sympathetic hearing on changes in regulations. In addition, one of the strongest disincentives to investment is the fear that people in the company will not allow the investment to produce well. With participation effectively working, this fear should be lessened. At the same time, participation encourages widespread small innovations and makes the arrival of the major innovations more welcome. Participative management won't bring heaven to earth, but it can make the business world much less like the hell we hear so much about. Top executives can bring this about if they are willing to lead rather than command.

NOTES

1. Robert A. Sutermeister, *People and Productivity* (New York: McGraw-Hill, 1963), p. 2.
2. "Good News from LaPointe," *Life Magazine* (editorial), December 22, 1952, p. 14.
3. Douglas McGregor, *The Human Side of Enterprise* (New York: McGraw-Hill, 1960), pp. 33–35, 47, 48.

REFERENCES

The Effect of Managerial Style on Productivity

Blake, Robert Rogers; Avis, Warren E.; and Mouton, Jane S. *Corporate Darwinism: An Evolutionary Perspective on Organizing Work in the Dynamic Corporation.* Houston, Texas: Gulf, 1966.

Follett, Mary Parker; Metcalf, Henry C.; and Urwick, L. *Dynamic Administration: The Collected Papers of Mary Parker Follett*, edited by Henry C. Metcalf and L. Urwick. New York: Harper, n.d.

Greenleaf, Robert K. *Servant Leadership: A Journey into the Nature of Legitimate Power and Greatness.* New York: Paulist Press, 1977.

Likert, Rensis. *New Patterns of Management.* New York: McGraw-Hill, 1961.

———. *The Human Organization: Its Management and Value.* New York: McGraw-Hill, 1967.

McGregor, Douglas. *The Human Side of Enterprise.* New York: McGraw-Hill, 1960.

Application of the Scanlon Plan

Frost, Carl F.; Wakely, John H.; and Ruh, Robert A. *The Scanlon Plan for Organization Development: Identity, Participation, and Equity*. East Lansing, Michigan: Michigan State University Press, 1974.

Application of Other Plans of Participation

Blake, Robert Rogers, and Mouton, Jane S. *The Managerial Grid: Key Orientation for Achieving Production Through People*. Houston, Texas: Gulf, 1964.

Cole, Robert E. *Work, Mobility and Participation*. Berkeley: University of California Press, 1979.

Davis, Louis E.; Cherns, Albert B.; and Associates. *The Quality of Working Life*. 2 vols. New York: The Free Press, 1975.

Ouchi, W. G., and Jaeger, A. M. *Type Z Organization: A Better Match for a Mobile Society*. Research Paper 314. Palo Alto, Calif.: Stanford University Press, 1977.

Cooperation with the Unions

Bisanz, F. F. *Towards Understanding Organization Change in Situations Involving Unionized Employees—An Open Systems Approach*. An unpublished doctoral dissertation. Cleveland, Ohio: Case Western Reserve University, 1977. Also available through International University Microfilms.

7.
Capital Investment and Tax Policy

Alfred C. Neal
Former President, Committee for Economic Development

It is a commonplace truth that investment in capital goods, in technological research, and in education and training share the same precondition in a period of high employment. That precondition is the deferral of current consumption (or production for current consumption) and the use of the economic resources so diverted to provide goods or services that are usable only in the future. In considering the question of improving productivity, therefore, the contribution of capital investment can take tangible or intangible form. Capital can be embodied in physical form (plants, equipment, and inventories) or in human form (improvement of knowledge, education, and training). While comparable data are not available on the productivity of all forms of investment, some of the most important information is available.

It is useful to consider briefly the role that capital investment has played in the decline in productivity in recent years. As other chapters have treated the problems of measurement, all that is appropriate here is a summary statement.

Using Denison's[1] most recent summary of sources of productivity growth (national income per person employed), the contribution of capital by sources selected to match the definition above in the period 1948–73 accounted for 2.73 percent annual growth in productivity, or more than the net annual average growth rate from all sources per person employed of 2.43 percent (see table 7.1).

There was an unprecedented decline in the growth rate of pro-

Table 7.1. Growth Rates and Selected Sources of Growth, 1948–73 and 1973–76 in National Income per Person Employed

	1948–73	1973–76
Growth rate (annual average, all sources)	2.43	−0.54
Selected contributions to growth rates, percentage points		
Education	.52	.88
Inventories	.10	.02
Nonresidential structures and equipment	.29	.25
Economies of scale	.41	.24
Advances in knowledge and miscellaneous determinants	1.41	−0.75
Total contribution of selected sources	2.73	0.64

Source: Derived from Edward F. Denison, "Explanations of Declining Productivity Growth," *Survey of Current Business*, pt. II, August 1979, table 1.

ductivity per person in the period 1973–76 from the 1948–73 average, a change of +2.43 to −0.54, a drop of nearly three percentage points.

An important factor in the total decline was in the category "advances in knowledge and miscellaneous determinants," which dropped from +1.41 to −.75. This category is not self-explanatory. Denison notes that "capital input is so defined and measured that changes in output that result from advances in the design of capital goods are classified as contributions of advances in knowledge, not of capital." Advances in knowledge "measure gains in measured output that result from the incorporation into production of new knowledge of any type—managerial and organizational as well as technological." But this classification is a residual which also includes "miscellaneous determinants." So far, the factors that account for the large drop in the growth rate of "advances in knowledge and miscellaneous determinants" beginning in 1973 have not been identified.

It should be clear from the foregoing paragraphs that the role of "capital," as I have broadly defined it, will be of critical importance in reversing the slowdown in productivity. Of the nearly 3 percent drop in productivity growth from 1948–73 to 1973–76, more than two thirds was in the capital and "miscellaneous determinants" categories shown in table 7.1.

The maintenance of gains in structures and equipment should also not be misunderstood. Changes from *economies of scale*, from *improvements in plant and equipment*, and from *new products* are all included in other categories, and not in the "structures and equipment" sector as defined.

A striking feature of the slowing in U.S. productivity growth in the period beginning in 1973 was that it was accompanied by slowdowns in other industrial countries, although these were usually less drastic than the U.S. slowdown. Students of the problem have suggested that this is a clue to a common cause, or set of causes. The year 1973 witnessed some major shocks to the U.S. and world economies.

The first and outstanding shock to the world economy in 1973 was the run-up of oil prices by OPEC. This and a run-up of grain prices triggered a new and large ratchet of inflation in the United States to double-digit level and similar movements elsewhere. A third wave of shocks followed two devaluations of the dollar and the subsequent shift to a moderated floating exchange-rate system. A fourth ripple of shocks emanated from the drastic use of restrictive monetary policies as a response to these inflationary developments, with a rise in interest rates around the world in consequence.

The theoretical consequences of these shocks can easily be sketched. The inflation of oil prices had far-reaching consequences on productivity. These included acceleration of energy conservation, requiring unexpected investment outlays that did not add to productivity, and a step-up in gasoline conservation resulting in everything from reduced highway speed limits to a sudden increase in investment in equipment for making more energy-efficient automobiles, air conditioners, buildings, and so on.

The change in expectations toward inflation and interest rates stirred people to "buy now" with borrowed money those things that were expected to rise most in price. Housing became a primary inflation hedge that soaked up personal savings (and credit usage) that might have gone into other things. Expansion of consumer credit for buying consumer goods also lowered the savings rate. To these changes there was added an unknown amount of speculation in gold and silver holdings, antiques, and art which added nothing to productivity.

High interest rates and the expectation of their continuance had important consequences for business investment. Expected returns on business investment had to be higher to offset higher interest rates, the risk of tying up funds in long pay-out projects was increased, and the desirability of short pay-out investments was enhanced. Equipment investment was favored over structures, and low investment-to-sales uses of capital were favored over high. Mergers shifted investment funds toward acquiring finance and insurance companies, retail merchandising, fast-food chains, and other enterprises that were more labor intensive. Many heavy investment-per-worker lines with long pay-out times, such as utilities, steel, paper, and chemicals, were deferred or scaled back.

In this process of adjustment, capital was substituted for fuel and energy—but without improvement in productivity—and labor was substituted for both capital and energy because wages did not increase nearly as fast as the costs of energy and capital. Substitution took such forms as investing in insulation to save energy, and using overtime or adding shifts in manufacturing and processing instead of expanding plants.

Foreign competitors, often U.S. owned, equipped with newer and technologically more advanced plants as a consequence of their long-continued higher savings and investment rates, stepped up their sales to the United States despite their appreciated currencies. Export drives abroad were assisted by the rebating of value-added taxes on exports and government-assisted financing. Import competition reduced investment prospects in the United States for such industries as steel and producers' equipment.

The large additions to the labor force of young people and women had productivity-reducing effects, a factor noted by all investigators. Almost unnoted was the increased rate of retirement at earlier ages by older persons whose embodiment of human capital was high. The proportion of male workers between ages 55 and 64 in the labor force dropped from 83 percent to 74 percent between 1970 and 1977 and is expected to fall to 68 percent by 1985.[2]

It will take a long time to sort out and to quantify the effects of the changes described above on U.S. productivity, but it is in such monolithic shifts as those described that I believe the mystery of the disproportionate lowering of U.S. productivity since 1973 will be found. That the role of business capital investment in productivity growth is important has been demonstrated beyond question.

INVESTMENT INADEQUATE FOR GROWTH

On the surface, it would appear that the volume of investment was not a factor in explaining declining productivity. The rate of capital investment in the U.S. business sector has not declined; gross business plant and equipment investment in relation to gross business product has since 1945 remained close to an average of 10 percent. This ratio holds even after deduction of investments for environmental protection. But the relatively well-maintained ratio of gross investment to GNP is misleading. A large part of such investment must be devoted to replacing worn-out plant and equipment and used-up inventory. When these replacements, valued at current cost, are subtracted from gross investment, it was found that a diminishing portion had been devoted to making additions in the form of new physical capital. In the five years ending in 1969, the ratio of net new investment, after subtracting the current cost of replacements from gross investment, was nearly 64 percent of the total. In the five years ending in 1978, this ratio of net additions to capital stock had fallen to 49 percent. Thus, net additions of new physical capital fell drastically in the 1970s.

Moreover, during the period 1960–73, for which comparable data are readily available for the United States and some of its leading competitors, ratios of investment to output in manufacturing by other industrial countries far exceeded those for the United States and so did their growth rate of productivity (see table 7.2). This relationship is not clearly one of cause and effect because of the intercorrelation involved, nevertheless it is significant.

A later study based on Organization for Economic Cooperation and Development (OECD) data comparing productivity growth with gross savings in the United States and nine other industrial countries reinforces the findings for the manufacturing sector.[3] Since investment depends on savings, there should be a relationship between gross savings and investment, and indeed there is. There should also be a relationship between savings (as the proxy for investment) and productivity growth. For the period 1960–77, a comparison of gross domestic product per civilian employee and gross savings as a percent of gross domestic product yields the expected results. Japan ranks first in productivity growth and ratio of savings to gross product. The United States ranks last in both,

Table 7.2. Ratio of Manufacturing Investment to Output versus Growth in Manufacturing Productivity

Seven Industrial Countries*—1960–1973

	Investment Ratio	Productivity Growth—%	Country Ranking: Investment Ratio	Country Ranking: Productivity Growth
Japan	24.4	10.5	1	1
Netherlands	19.0	7.5	2	2
Sweden	17.1	7.0	3	3
Belgium	17.1	6.6	4	4
Canada	14.6	4.3	5	5
United Kingdom	13.6	4.0	6	6
United States	11.2	3.3	7	7

* Comparable data for fixed investment to output limit the number of comparisons. However, recent OECD estimates for the United States, Japan, West Germany, France, United Kingdom, Canada, and Italy, comparing nonresidential fixed-investment ratios with productivity growth rates, show a similar pattern.

Sources: Organization for Economic Cooperation and Development and U.S. Bureau of Labor Statistics.

Adapted from *Capital Goods Review*, Machinery and Allied Products Institute, February 1976.

with the United Kingdom and Canada only a little higher. The other six industrial countries fall in between on both counts. The lesson is clear: countries that saved and invested more had more growth in productivity.

In addition to a lower rate of investment to output than that of our industrial competitors, there are some other disturbing trends in the pattern of U.S. investment. World War II gave enormous impetus to research and technological advance in the United States as well as to many types of industrial investment. One needs only to name nuclear fission, computers, radar, space exploration and communication satellites, microwave and laser-beam transmission, and jet engine aircraft (some, of course, adapted from work in other countries). With its industrial base undamaged by war and peacetime markets eager to be served, the United States was prepared for and enjoyed at the end of the war two decades of technological and industrial supremacy. In this period Western European countries and Japan caught up technologically in fields where they had lagged and began to make advances of their own, while the United States reduced its rate of growth in government research and development

(R&D) expenditures. While the ratio of industrial investment to gross output in the United States was maintained, as has been noted, its effect upon economic growth after the mid-1960s was due almost entirely to labor and capital inputs, and not to extra efficiencies resulting from advances in management and application of innovations derived from government-financed research.[4] To restore the productivity growth rate calls not only for more investment, but for a better allocation to uses embodying new technology and higher efficiency. In particular, the subsidies that induce an overallocation of capital to housing have not yet been offset by tax changes for business permitting recovery of the replacement cost of plant and equipment investment.[5] The governments of most other industrial countries have long permitted business to recover replacement costs in one way or another, including heavy reliance on indirect taxation rather than on corporate-profits taxes.

UNDERCOSTING AND EROSION OF CAPITAL

The disadvantage of antique cost-recovery allowances under U.S. tax laws (and of undercosting pursued voluntarily by business) is larger than is generally realized. Undercosting of inventory and depreciation overstates profits and gives the wrong signals for both the direction and volume of investment. Overstated profits have led to payment of excessive income taxes, to dividends paid that were in many cases in excess of real profits, and to starvation of internal sources of funds for investment.

Table 7.3 summarizes major differences between reported and inflation-adjusted results for nonfinancial corporations in the years 1968 through 1978.

In a period of high inflation, depreciation for tax purposes based on original cost and specified useful lives falls increasingly short of recovering enough through depreciation to replace plant and equipment. Inventory costing based on first-in, first-out (FIFO) does the same with respect to inventory sold, but in this case the fault lies with business because it is permitted to use last-in, first-out (LIFO) costing for inventory, and most companies do. When reported profits, taxes, and retained earnings (after payment of dividends) are corrected for these shortcomings, it is apparent that nonfinancial corporations in the last decade have:

Table 7.3. Nonfinancial Corporations' Profits before and after Taxes and Retained Earnings, Adjusted for Inflation, 1968–1978 (in billions of dollars)

	(1) Profits before Taxes		(2) Profits after Taxes		(3) Retained Earnings	
	Reported	Adjusted	Reported	Adjusted	Reported	Adjusted
1968	71.9	72.1	38.3	38.5	17.6	17.8
1969	68.4	66.4	35.1	33.1	14.4	12.4
1970	55.1	51.5	27.8	24.2	7.9	4.3
1971	63.3	58.8	33.4	28.9	13.4	8.9
1972	75.9	72.0	42.4	38.5	20.7	16.8
			Total 1968–72		74.0	60.2
1973	92.7	75.9	53.1	36.3	29.2	12.4
1974	102.9	59.5	60.2	16.8	34.2	(−9.2)
1975	101.3	77.0	60.7	36.4	32.2	7.9
1976	130.2	101.4	77.2	48.4	43.7	14.9
1977	143.5	114.0	84.5	55.0	45.4	15.9
1978	167.1	125.0	98.6	56.5	53.6	11.5
			Total 1974–78		209.1	41.0
			Total 1973–78		238.3	53.4

Source: Derived from George Terborgh, "Inflation and Profits," a paper published by the Machinery and Allied Products Institute, Washington, D.C., April 1979. This series, extending back to 1965 is probably the most useful set of data published on the magnitude and effect of inflation on corporate results in the United States.

- Paid taxes at much higher rates than reported.
- Paid a much higher proportion of after-tax profits as dividends than reported. In 1974 nonfinancial business as a whole paid dividends in excess of after-tax, adjusted-for-inflation profits.
- Realized retained earnings in the period 1968–78 almost $200 billion less than they would have if they had not undercosted inventory, had been allowed to depreciate plant and equipment at current cost, and had not in consequence overpaid income taxes.

Moreover, the capital dissipation from the causes identified increased greatly in 1973 and in the years following, the same years that evidenced the slowdown in productivity. Retained earnings were about $14 billion below the full-costing optimum in the five years preceding 1973, but $168 billion below in the five years after 1973. The $168 billion of unrealized earnings retention amounted to about a year and one-third of plant and equipment investment at the rate prevailing in the five-year period. It amounted to an annual average about 2.5 times the amount of so-called "tax expenditures" provided in the tax laws in favor of corporations.

The full effect of the $168 billion deficiency of retained earnings unavailable for investment was much greater than the amount implies. This sum was in *equity funds*, which management can use more readily than borrowed funds for risk investment in new and less proved ways.

The market value of net corporate assets reflected the malaise just described. Whereas in most of the 20 years before 1974 the corporate market value (equity plus interest-bearing debt) had exceeded current replacement costs of net assets, beginning in 1974 the ratio dropped to .725 and has dropped further in 1978 and 1979.[6] Corporate assets as a whole can be bought at a discount of one-third from their replacement cost.

These findings stand in contrast to results obtained by using aggregate savings and investment trends for the economy as a whole. Personal savings as a proportion of disposable personal income held up well until 1976 and, after a drop in 1976–77, even recovered somewhat in 1978–79. Gross private domestic investment as a proportion of GNP has followed a similar pattern. The gross savings and investment totals provide poor clues for identifying an investment deficiency. In contrast, the decline in adjusted retained earnings of nonfinancial corporations began in the early 1970s and increased during the decade, reflecting the increase in inflation-adjusted depreciation and inventory valuations. It must be emphasized again that internally generated funds finance a major part of plant and equipment investment in the nonfinancial business sector. The earlier impact of inflation and taxes on internal sources of financing suggests that tax policies designed to regenerate internal sources of business investment would be more prompt and effective than tax changes aimed at increasing aggregate savings and investment.

There are worse secondary effects of undercosting than paying taxes on profits not really there and dividends not justified by real earnings. One is encouragement of wage increases beyond productivity gains. The effect of overstated profits on labor negotiations is obvious. Companies that are presumably reporting large profits can afford large wage increases. To the upward pressure on prices from externally imposed oil price increases must be added the pressure of wage increases not even partially offset by productivity gains. Just to stay in business under such pressures, companies must raise prices. There is no choice.

But previously overstated profits have already triggered adverse public, labor, and political reactions to price increases. The whole process has planted an unexploded bomb. Rising costs that reflect the replacement of productivity gains by productivity losses, accompanied by wage increases to catch up with inflation, drain off the real earnings, which in the major industries can be only partially restored by price increases. This alarming state of affairs will finally be exposed in large companies (with assets of $1 billion or more) in annual reports for 1979 under terms of a new rule of the Financial Accounting Standards Board that requires publication in company reports of depreciation and inventory valuation adjustments for inflation.

The deterioration of our economic strength in recent years compounds a long-term decline in our competitiveness in the world. Other countries have had a more rapid rate of growth in world trade compared with our own. In 1960 the United States accounted for 14.9 percent of world exports. By 1978 this figure had dropped to 10.9 percent. By contrast, in imports from the rest of the world, the U.S. accounted for 11.5 percent in 1960 and 13.5 percent in 1978. Obviously the United States has become a better country in which to sell and a poorer country from which to buy. The record of Japan offers an interesting contrast. In 1960 Japan accounted for 4.2 percent of world exports, but by 1978 its share was 7.5 percent and still going up. Its share of world imports paralleled at a lower level the increase in its share of world exports.

The diagnosis of the debilitating productivity disease to this point is that it results from an anemia of physical and human capital compounded by large doses of high-priced oil and a strangulating monetary policy. Enhancement of the already large contribution of human capital is the subject of part III of this book as well as of another study by the Work in America Institute, *The Future of Older*

Workers in America (Scarsdale, N.Y.: Work in America Institute, 1980). The contribution of research and development to knowledge which will be incorporated in new plant, equipment, processes, and products is also treated in another chapter of this book. While there may be tax changes that will accelerate desirable changes in these areas, it is more likely that the assistance needed will come from more government support and less regulation rather than from tax changes. Therefore, the paragraphs that follow will concentrate on those tax reforms that offer the most promise of relief from the anemia of capital investment.

Compared with the past, business has experienced a serious deterioration in its ability to retain internally generated funds, which have accounted for the bulk of its financing of plant and equipment. In the four years 1969–72 that preceded the most recent surge of inflation, depreciation and retained earnings generated *three-fourths* of the cash that nonfinancial companies invested in plant, equipment, inventory, and mineral rights. In subsequent years, undercosting inventories and depreciation, as has been shown, seriously diminished the capacity to finance investment from internal sources. Not surprisingly, the growth rate of real fixed capital of business per employee fell by more than 1 percent a year in 1975–78 after averaging an increase of more than 2 percent per year in the preceding decade.

TAX CHANGES TO STIMULATE INVESTMENT

The volume and direction of investment are influenced by many forces, both in the economy as a whole and among the multitude of possible lines of investment opportunity. Since the preceding diagnostic discussion has identified plant and equipment investment as being of critical importance to the maintenance and growth of productivity, the following discussion will concentrate upon tax incentives and obstacles in that area, not on aggregate flows of savings and investment that are distributed among business fixed investment and investments in homes, consumer durable goods, and other uses that have little to do with productivity. Moreover, considering that the federal and state governments throughout our history have provided grants and subsidies for stimulating banks, roads, canals, railroads, land settlement, conservation, housing, and many other purposes deemed worthy, the discussion will be confined to the recent past and will not attempt to resolve philosophical issues regarding the government's role in stimulating investment, but will only concern itself with the role of tax policy in doing so.

Investment Tax Credit

The most recent major experiment in tax policy to stimulate investment, now made permanent, is the investment tax credit. A tax credit (first of 7 percent and later of 10 percent) for new investment in equipment (not plant) was inaugurated in 1962 as a countercyclical measure. It was subject to reduction or withdrawal to help stabilize the economy. In its original form, its effect was hard to measure and was weakened by uncertainty as to when and to what extent it would be available. The credit was made permanent in 1978, and the amount that might be taken was expanded in stages from 50 percent of the company's total tax liability to a top rate of 90 percent, to become effective in 1982. It was also expanded to include rehabilitation of nonresidential structures.

The 10 percent tax credit was used to the extent of $8.26 billion in 1977, covering about 6.5 percent of that year's expenditures for new equipment. Its value to business in that year was equal to about one-quarter of that year's amount of undercosting of depreciation and inventory. At current rates of use, it would be worth less than one year's inflation in the cost of the investments to which it applied. The credit does lower the initial cost of an eligible investment and provides funds for it, thus raising the rate of return, but it is not known how much investment would have been made anyway without benefit of the credit. It did make funds available that would otherwise have been paid in taxes, but it is clearly not addressed to ending the erosion of capital by undercosting in a period of inflation. Still, it is a useful stimulant and deserves to be continued.

Double Taxation of Corporate Profits

It is often argued that if stockholders own the company, they also own the profits that it earns and should pay the taxes on them. According to that reasoning, the corporate profits tax should be eliminated. It is argued that to tax corporate profits and then to tax dividends derived from them is double taxation. (By contrast, partnerships are taxed but once on the profits realized by the partners.)

If stockholders were taxed on *all* corporate reported profits, whether or not paid out, the pressure to include all costs, including current cost depreciation, would become almost irresistible. There is very little support for the full integration into one tax of both corporate and personal income taxes on profits. Such an integrated tax on profits would put great pressure on companies to pay out profits and decrease retained earnings. Retention of earnings by companies adds to company net worth and should eventually lead to higher values for shareholders' stock and make them subject only to a capital-gains tax on the increased value of the stock. By the same argument, dissipation of capital by undercosting inventories and depreciation deprives shareholders of possible capital gains, as indicated, and results in overpayment of dividends and taxes.

The root of the trouble with the argument about double taxation of dividends is a misguided concept of the nature of corporate profits and of who pays the tax on them. In a purely competitive economic system, one in which many sellers of each product compete with one another and therefore sell at the lowest prices that they can afford and still stay in business, some sellers will be covering only their costs (including a market rate of return on capital) and would make no returns beyond that except as management income, equivalent to salary. Only those fortunate sellers with total costs lower than prices would realize a profit, something over and above that necessary to keep them in business. Such profit is a "surplus," a return (by definition) above what is really needed to keep the marginal seller's supply coming to market. A tax on such profit is a tax on a surplus and is a tax which cannot be passed on to others. If most such profits are taxed away, there will be no change in supply, but sellers having to pay the profits tax will probably have to borrow or otherwise pay the cost of additions to capital in the marketplace.

Business executives have a view of profits that is quite different from seeing them as a true surplus (or rent). The name of the game that companies play is the bottom line. After the company has paid all its costs and its taxes, what is left is profits. What keeps the company going is the rate of return those profits provide on invested capital. For a growing economy, the rate of return on invested capital has to be high enough not only to retain capital in the company, but to attract additional capital for financing additional investment in plant, equipment, and working capital. In a growing economy, the "after-tax return" on the company's investment must be at least equal to what it could get by investing elsewhere—in other companies, in other countries, or by liquidating and putting the proceeds into loans, real estate, securities, or other investments (as some companies have done). Executives continually argue that products are necessarily priced to bring a satisfactory return after taxes. This means that the corporate profits tax is passed on, usually in prices. Both because it raises or holds up prices and because it requires higher returns on new investment, the corporate profits tax may be bad for the economy and probably should be reduced, even if the revenue loss has to be made up by substituting a broad-based excise tax to maintain government revenues. Executives see the corporate tax and excise taxes as having the same incidence on prices; both are passed on. And *a tax that is passed on is not a "double tax."*

If, as I think it is, the foregoing argument is correct, then corporate profits taxes are for the most part not taxes on profits but a part of the cost of doing business. Profits after taxes are a return on the equity that on the average should be high enough to yield the going rate of return on capital, that return being also a cost of doing business similar to the interest on borrowed money. If it does not earn that much, the market value of equity plus debt will fall below the replacement cost of net assets, the condition that has existed since 1973, as was noted above. That condition is itself a basis for corporate tax relief in one form or another.[7]

Current Cost Depreciation

The erosion of physical capital by failing to make financial provision for its renewal can be reduced, and in most cases eliminated, by appropriate tax policies. It cannot be stopped altogether, nor should it be, because companies that do not earn enough will not have a cash counterpart to their depreciation cost and, if that condition continues, will go out of business, as they should.

One part of the tax reform is already in place: the option to use

LIFO costing for inventory. While this method results in accelerating the timing of price increases, it does preserve capital invested in inventory. The fact that many companies still do not use LIFO is incomprehensible. Ignorance and unwillingness to take the loss involved in shifting may be partially responsible. Also, some companies may be unable to construct an index for price adjustment acceptable to the Internal Revenue Service.[8]

The principle involved in extending current costing to depreciation could be similar to that used for inventory. An inflation index could be applied to book costs of structures and equipment annually to put them on an inflation-adjusted basis.[9] From the inflation-adjusted book cost, depreciation already taken in prior years would be deducted. The remainder would be the new base which could be depreciated (using the same depreciation formula) to obtain the current year's depreciation. The same procedure could be repeated in succeeding years if inflation continued.

The foregoing is but one of many possibilities. It is often opposed because of opposition in principle to indexing, despite already widespread use of indexing for wages, Social Security, government pensions, inventories (LIFO), commercial-space leases, and many other payments and transactions.

If it is firmly expected that inflation will be brought under control, a one-time revaluation of depreciable assets could be carried out, with subsequent depreciation being based on the new values. One-time revaluations were commonly used in European countries after major wartime and postwar inflations. This method may result in failure to make up underdepreciation for the years preceding revaluation.

Adoption of current cost depreciation all at once could result in a large increase in the cash flow of business and a loss of tax revenue to the Treasury. On a national income accounts basis, the increased cash flow to business could be $15–20 billion in the first year and the tax loss to the government about 40 percent of that amount. Amounts of this size should not upset the economy. If the addition to the federal deficit were deemed excessive, the additional amount claimed for the inflation adjustment of depreciation could be held in escrow by the Treasury until used by business for capital expenditures, the procedure now followed for the 10 percent investment tax credit.

Capital Cost Recovery and 10/5/3

Until recently, organizations that represent business have been reluctant to face up to the capital erosion problem by supporting current cost depreciation and wider use of LIFO. As the problem became more acute, however, a coalition was formed around a compromise directed at shortening the tax lives of physical assets, regardless of their so-called useful lives. This proposal, named 10/5/3 for short, is the proposed Capital Cost Recovery Act. It provides 10-year depreciation for structures, including commercial real estate, that draw support from the construction industry and real estate investors, supermarkets, stores, and service outlets, all of whom have investment concentrated in structures. Five-year write-offs would be available for equipment and would provide relief for manufacturing and mining as well as for machinery and equipment industries. A three-year write-off, up to $100,000, would be provided for automobiles and trucks and would attract the support of small business. These periods of depreciation are all shorter than is now permitted, especially for structures, and the 10-year rule may cause a ballooning of an already large tax shelter.

It should be noted especially that the shortened depreciation periods proposed apply only to property acquired after January 1, 1980. They would provide no relief for underdepreciation of capital goods already on hand.

There is no doubt that the financial returns expected from investment decisions would be improved by shorter periods for recovering capital. A shorter income stream has a higher present value than a longer one of equal size, and a longer deferral of taxes costs a company less than a short deferral or none at all.

Shorter lives for depreciable assets will also reduce the bite of future inflation but will not eliminate it. And just as the investment tax credit favored investments in equipment over those in structures, an unbalanced shortening of depreciation periods will favor some lines of investment over others that might make a much greater contribution to improving productivity.

The lowest published estimates of the annual cost of tax revenues to be lost by the Treasury by adopting 10/5/3 are more than double the tax revenue that might be lost from granting current-cost tax treatment to depreciation. As 10/5/3 does nothing to correct the erosion of existing capital by underdepreciation and seems to be costly in terms of tax revenues lost, it would appear to be a second- or third-best alternative to allowing current cost depreciation. Coupled with the latter, it would be highly desirable although highly expensive in terms of tax revenues lost.

The Choice of Alternatives

There are many other ways that the tax system could be modified to improve the supply of capital to American business. For example, further cuts could be made in the corporate tax rate; capital-gains taxes could be reduced further; incentives to save, such as a tax credit for interest on savings, could be introduced (and is incorporated in the windfall-tax measure adopted early in 1980). A more fundamental reform, such as the substitution of a value-added tax (VAT) for all or part of the corporate income tax, also deserves serious consideration.

All of these proposals suffer from a common defect. They do not directly remedy what is in effect a tax on physical capital imposed by tax laws and regulations limiting capital recovery to original cost, a tax that becomes increasingly onerous as inflation continues. Most proposals, except that for a shift from a corporate income tax to a value-added tax, give relief in general, leaving uncorrected the imposition of corporate income taxes on the illusory profits resulting from undercosting depreciation and inventory. Tax relief should be targeted to that objective if it is to contribute the most per dollar of reduced tax revenues toward improving productivity.

A complete substitution of a value-added tax for the corporate income tax would eliminate the tax on capital. Substitution for the corporate income tax of the most common form of the VAT using a consumption base would impose a value-added tax as a percentage of sales. Taxpayers would remit the tax that they add to sales reduced by the amount they have paid on purchases. Deduction of VAT paid prevents duplication of the tax as goods pass forward in the production and distribution system and in the process offsets any tax paid on capital equipment. Elimination of the tax on capital that is inherent in the corporate income tax would in itself improve corporate cash flow and the supply of investment funds. Promising as this proposal might seem, its far-reaching effects on the whole tax system, one of which is that the change might make the tax system more regressive, give a low probability to its adoption anytime soon.

Investment Incentives and the Fight against Inflation

Depreciation reform, however, should not be undertaken in such a way as to weaken the role of fiscal policy in the fight against inflation. It is inflation, after all, that makes depreciation reform so necessary. Reducing inflation will reduce the loss of tax revenues from depreciation reform. The Congress early in 1980 earmarked about $136 billion from new windfall profits taxes on oil for tax relief in the 1980s. Part of windfall profits tax revenues might well be dedicated to depreciation reform. In any event, a fiscal policy that produces a federal budget surplus is an essential complement to depreciation reform. Unfortunately, the administration's fiscal program for 1981, announced in March of 1980, called only for a balanced budget, not a surplus.

Budget surpluses, by making possible retirement of government debt, would contribute toward three anti-inflation objectives. First, a budget surplus would reduce the banking system's holdings of government securities (by paying them off) and thereby reduce credit creation, which adds to inflationary pressures. Second, funds made available to the private sector from retiring government debt, together with accompanying lower interest rates, would provide additional means to finance new investment. Third, increased investment would lower costs and prices (or reduce their rate of increase) and therefore, over a period of time, would put downward pressure on the price level. Whatever tax reforms are adopted to stimulate investment should be within the context of a fiscal policy aimed at achieving an overall budget surplus under conditions of high employment.

Notes

1. Edward F. Denison, "Explanations of Declining Productivity Growth," *Survey of Current Business*, part II, August 1979. Denison uses output per employed person as his measure of productivity, not output per employee-hour, nor other concepts which are used in some other studies. Therefore, absolute numbers of derived productivity growth rates will differ among sources, depending on the concepts and measures used.

2. A cogent analysis of these changes is included in a report by the Work in America Institute, Inc., *The Future of Older Workers in America* (Scarsdale, N.Y.: Work in America Institute, 1980).
3. Summarized in "Savings Levels and Productivity Growth," *Capital Goods Review*, April 1980. The Machinery and Allied Products Institute, Washington, D.C., publishes this periodical.
4. This thesis depends heavily on a paper summarizing a research study for the National Council on Life Insurance presented by its director, George M. von Furstenberg, before the International Business Economics Association, New York City, October 10, 1979.
5. Some of these subsidies are mortgage-interest deduction from personal income, mortgage guarantees, exclusion of capital gains on house sales if reinvested in homes, and one-time exclusion of up to $100,000 on gains from sales of personal residences, as well as government-subsidized secondary markets for mortgages.
6. *Economic Report of the President* (Washington, D.C.: U. S. Government Printing Office, 1979), p. 128; *Economic Report of the President* (Washington, D.C.: U. S. Government Printing Office, 1980), p. 141.
7. There is one basis for a tax credit or exemption for dividends received that is thoroughly consistent with the "passed-on" view of the corporate profits tax. When a company can be shown to have paid dividends out of capital (i.e., through failure to use LIFO or current cost depreciation), the stockholder should be exempt from tax on such dividends as, in effect, they are a return of capital. As noted in table 7.3, this would have called for a tax credit to stockholders totaling possibly $9.2 billion in 1974, the amount paid out in dividends in excess of real profits after taxes.
8. The amount of undercosting reflected in the Commerce Department's inventory valuation adjustment for business as a whole was $25 billion in 1978 and was running at a $40 billion annual rate in the first three quarters of 1979.
9. It is not necessary to employ cost indexes related to particular classes of capital equipment, structures, and so on, because what is needed is only to restore the purchasing power of the dollars frozen into such investments. This subject is admirably treated by George Terborgh, "The Indexation Issue in Inflation Accounting," a paper published by the Machinery and Allied Products Institute, Washington, D.C., in January 1980.

8.
How Do We Revitalize Our Technological Infrastructure?

Reginald H. Jones
Chairman and Chief Executive Officer,
General Electric Company

The United States in the past century has been the technological society par excellence. More than any other people, Americans have exuberantly sought, bought, and used the products of technology. We've made folk heroes of scientists and inventors like Albert Einstein and Thomas Edison.

This friendly atmosphere has helped us build a broad and deep technological infrastructure. The United States has bred or attracted the best scientists in the world, to judge by the Nobel Prize record, and great industrial-research laboratories and first-class schools of science and engineering have flourished here. Our long experience with machines has produced not only superb engineers, but also a nation of do-it-yourself mechanics.

High technology is still our special strength in world trade, and high productivity is still the basis of our $2 trillion economy. As a symbolic proof of our people's deep love affair with technology, we were the first nation to send human beings to the moon and back, an engineering feat eagerly monitored on TV by almost every American.

LOSING GROUND

But the country that accomplished all this is slipping—badly. In the past few years, our feet have become firmly planted in last place in productivity growth among all major industrial nations.

Our factories are aging: the average U.S. factory is 20 years old, while Japan's is only 10 and West Germany's is 12. France and West Germany have been investing about two times, and Japan about three times, as much of their gross national product (GNP) in new plant and equipment as has the United States. With half as many people, Japan invested, in 1978, almost as much in new plant and equipment as did the United States.

The cliché for research and development (R&D) used to be an American in a white lab coat, but here, too, we've been faltering. While many other industrial nations have been increasing their share of GNP spent on R&D—a critical factor in technical innovation—this country actually decreased R&D expenditures from 3 percent of GNP to 2 percent in the last decade.

And finally, we have seen policies of our own government inhibit the development of our technological infrastructure and our ability to compete worldwide in the high-technology arena.

The question is, can we turn the tide? Can we avoid losing our preeminent position in technology? Can we regain the momentum in productivity growth which, until recently, made the United States the pacesetter for the industrial world?

Productivity and technology are closely linked, with some experts claiming that technology accounts for 60 percent to 70 percent of all productivity improvement. If that is so, then the means are now at hand for dramatic productivity growth.

REVOLUTION IN THE FACTORY

There is a revolution going on in both the design and manufacture of products. It is a revolution fired by the computer, applied to design through the advent of interactive graphics, and to manufacturing with the development of automated systems, flexible robotics, and computerized controls. The paperless factory, talked about for three decades, will soon be a reality.

Consider these projections compiled by the Society of Manufacturing Engineers in their 1978 Delphi forecasts. By 1990:

- Computer-aided design techniques will be used for 50 percent of new assemblies.[1]
- Development of sensory techniques will enable robots to approximate human capability in assembly.[2]

- Half the workers on the manufacturing floor will be highly trained engineers and technicians keeping robots and computers working.[3]

If these projections sound revolutionary, consider that the Japanese plan to have an unmanned, fully automated factory in operation not by 1990, but by 1984. And it will not be for high-volume, low-variety production. The government-sponsored project will produce machinery components ranging from hydraulic pumps to heavy-duty transmissions, at maximum runs of only 300 units.

FORCES BEHIND A TECHNOLOGICAL RENAISSANCE

We have the technology—heralded since the fifties—to transform the way goods are designed and made. The United States has created much of this technology, but until now we have been slow to utilize it—slow to do things better. We have also been slow in doing more of the right things, the things we do best—slow to aggressively market our preeminent high-technology products on a global scale.

The question remains, can we turn the tide? I believe we can and will. Three major driving forces in the world are pushing us to reassess our current priorities and direction. These forces could move us into a new technological renaissance.

1. *Increasing competition from foreign multinationals.* With newer, more highly automated plants; cooperation from their own governments; aggressive global strategies; and sometimes a greater commitment to the product quality desired by the American consumer, these foreign multinationals should be driving U.S. companies into greater technological efficiencies, innovation, and quality in order to remain competitive.
2. *Energy and materials shortages.* Higher costs for energy and materials will also force new, more efficient products and processes.

   The operating costs, for example, of an aircraft like the 707, designed when fuel was 12 cents a gallon, are affected so strongly by rising fuel costs that it will soon be economically impractical for a major airline to operate such equipment.

   Motors are another case where energy conservation is going to drive innovation. Motors presently consume 60 percent of the electrical energy produced in the United States. And losses from them represent the equivalent of one million barrels of oil per day, roughly 12 percent of oil imports. Reducing this waste is a major technological challenge.

New technologies are also going to be developed which reduce the waste of critical and increasingly expensive materials. In GE's aircraft engine business, for example, which must use such expensive materials as nickel, chrome, and cobalt, the alloy is now produced in powdered form, then squeezed under high pressure into "near net shape," then machined, a process employing far less material than does traditional forging.

3. *Changing world demographics, resulting in rapidly shifting international division of labor.* This movement is perhaps the most complex and far reaching. Changes in size and composition of the labor force in both the developed and developing countries portend more rapid growth in the levels of:
   a. Sourcing in the less developed countries (LDCs).
   b. Low- and medium-complexity manufacturing in the newly industrialized countries (NICs).
   c. More and more emphasis in the United States on highly automated, high-technology industry. Shifting U.S. domestic resources into the highest value-added segments, that is, high technology—doing more of what we do best—could be a prime productivity strategy.

The key demographic changes are the rapidly increasing labor force in the developing countries compared to the decline in growth in the developed nations. But while the number of people available for work in traditional manufacturing jobs in countries like the United States may be declining, we are also seeing an increase here in the education levels of the entering work force, and therefore a dramatic change in the kind of work for which the nation is equipped. Before 1940, only one out of 20 Americans between 25 and 29 had earned a bachelor's degree. By 1976, the ratio was one out of four.

Internationally, we are seeing rapid economic development, with nations which were formerly merely exporters of raw commodities now doing some manufacturing, and nations which formerly did some manufacturing now doing more sophisticated manufacturing.

Despite all the recent talk that developing nations are rejecting industrial society, the evidence suggests that they want it desperately. "The inhabitants of the Third World want more industry in their countries by ratios exceeding 20 to 1," George Gallup reported in a public opinion survey of nearly 70 nations several years ago.[4] The Organization for Economic Cooperation and Development (OECD) predicts that "The Third World (China included) might account for 23 to 25 percent of world industrial production by the end of the century."[5]

Where does that leave the United States? Several years ago General Electric commissioned a study which found that high-technology industries had double the productivity improvement of low-technology ones. That strongly suggests that if we have the resources—the work force, technology, capital, management—then high technology is where we ought to be.

Differentiated allocation of resources, placing their bets where their highest talents lie, is one of the key long-range strategies of some major U.S. companies, including General Electric. But what about the U.S. economy overall? Will we be able to shift the mix of businesses in the United States in favor of the high-technology companies, which have the highest productivity and growth? I will return to this critical question shortly.

But in the meantime, no discussion of driving forces in the 1980s would be complete without mentioning inflation, which is a powerful force *blocking* investment in productivity and innovation. A manager contemplating a new plant must feel some assurance that the return will justify the investment. The "hurdle rate"—the minimum predictable return at which the decision to go ahead will be made—has been going up as inflation raises the cost of capital and the risks involved. Under the pressure of inflation (and taxes on reported rather than real profits), real return on investment has been declining for the past 15 years. New public policies are needed to stem unacceptably high rates of inflation.

NEW POLICIES NEEDED

In fact, a *variety* of new public policies will be needed to make our technological renaissance a reality. To begin with, we need articulation at the highest levels of government of a U.S. strategy to *do more of what we do best*.

This means a coherent, consistent set of policies to encourage the development of markets worldwide for our high-technology, high-productivity industries. We should rethink policies protecting non-competitive "sunset" industries which keep workers and capital locked into low-productivity enterprises.

We don't need policies which "plan" the economy but, rather, policies which are consistent and positive in their approach to unleashing the highest productive energies of our economy on a global scale.

Consider our global economic policies, or what passes for global economic policies, today. We have a punitive relationship between government and business, which weakens the U.S. competitive edge in high-technology world markets. Our government seems intent on discouraging the growth of U.S. companies that operate on a world scale. The spectacle of the Department of Justice locked in mortal combat with IBM, one of our best sources of income and economic respect abroad, must be almost unbelievable in other countries.

Another major obstacle to technological innovation is excessive government regulation of industry and technology, regulation that has been imposed without any visible effort to determine whether the benefits justify the enormous costs. According to Professor Murray Weidenbaum: "Each dollar that Congress appropriates for regulation results in an additional $20 of costs imposed on the private sector of our economy."[6] Naturally, resources diverted from the productive private sector are resources which cannot be used to create innovation, new plant and equipment, and new products.

Running down the agenda of needed policy reform, I am reminded of columnist Louis Rukeyser's satirical economic forecast. Among other events, he predicts that: "The West Germans and the Japanese will propose a new Marshall Schmidt Plan to rebuild the devastated American economy. The Plan calls for the United States to announce that it really lost World War II and is anxious to learn from its conquerors. Lessons will include emphasis on private enterprise, savings, investment, hard work, and productivity, all ideas long regarded as alien to the cherished American way of life." Many a truth is spoken in jest!

AGENDA FOR BUSINESS

The seriousness of this drift needs to be explained to the American people, their representatives in Congress, and to government officials. It is not self-evident. It requires vigorous communications efforts, and business people will have to take the lead.

Business people also have other tasks on their agenda. Revitalizing our technological infrastructure means doing the right kind of strategic planning. Our businesses must develop comprehensive technical strategies, tightly integrated with their business strategies, to assure an accelerated flow of technological innovation with significant potential.

And we'll have to play for the long term. That means increasing expenditures on the right kind of research and development. In recent years, perhaps as a result of inflation-driven uncertainty, too much of our precious R&D has gone toward low-risk, small-scale projects with quick payoff and only modest improvement in existing products. Too little has gone toward long-term innovation that could mean the start of *new* businesses. We have to reverse this trend.

Will America revitalize its technological infrastructure? The question is not only one of economic vitality and international competition. The question really is, what kind of country do we want to be? Do we want to continue in our tradition of being a pioneering technological society? Do we have the courage and the energy to want to continue to lead, to grow? Or would we rather relinquish that demanding and challenging role to nations other than our own?

NOTES

1. Society of Manufacturing Engineers/University of Michigan, *Delphi Forecasts of Assembly Technology* (Dearborn, Mich.: Society of Manufacturing Engineers, 1978), p. 39.
2. Ibid., p. 31.
3. Society of Manufacturing Engineers/University of Michigan, *Delphi Forecasts of Manufacturing Management* (Dearborn, Mich.: Society of Manufacturing Engineers, 1978), p. 26.
4. George H. Gallup, "What Mankind Thinks about Itself," *The Reader's Digest*, October 1976, pp. 132–136.

5. Organization for Economic Cooperation and Development, *Facing the Future* (Paris: Organization for Economic Cooperation and Development, 1979), p. 409.
6. "Business Beat," *The Daily News,* October 29, 1979. Quotation from a lecture by Professor Murray Weidenbaum at New York University.

9.
Increasing Office Productivity through Information Technology

John Diebold
Chairman, The Diebold Group, Inc.

OVERVIEW

So imperceptibly that we have yet to recognize the full implications of the transition, our society has entered "the age of information." For the business sector, the new environment means changes in the services offered and in the ways business is conducted. A wide spectrum of government activities is affected, ranging from defense to the use of information technology to manage its own affairs and the affairs of those it regulates. The public at large is in turn affected; few aspects of our daily lives have not been altered by the new technology.

It is difficult to imagine how our institutions could have coped with the enormous demands of an ever more complex society without the information tools developed by an industry that was virtually nonexistent 25 years ago. How could banks have coped with the volume of checks? Or airlines with the surge in passenger volume? And how could the business community have dealt with the proliferation of paperwork that has characterized the past decade or two?

Today, we stand on the threshold of a society that will be significantly computerized—a "wired" nation. Already, information technology plays an important role in our daily lives—determining how we work, how we use our spare time, how we do business. In the years ahead, as computers become more and more capable of communicating with one another, geography will become far less important a factor than it is today. With smaller, cheaper, and more efficient intelligent terminals, the physical location of a worker (or, for that matter, a consumer) becomes less important. Instant shopping, instant credit, instant access to information—all in the process of being achieved—will alter the economic patterns familiar to consumer and merchant alike.

In much the same way, traditional office operations and procedures will be transformed. Part of the impetus will come merely because the technology is made available. But the major driving force will be the intensifying need to improve productivity in the office environment. Competitive pressures at home and abroad, increased record-keeping requirements, and changing worker needs and attitudes all will combine to place a premium on efficient and effective office operations.

In fact, since it is likely that small differentials in office productivity may mean the difference between profit and loss for the typical business, the willingness of an organization to embrace the new technology and make effective use of it may well prove to be a key determinant of its continued success. One has only to examine the failure rate of stock brokerage firms over the past decade due to their inability to handle the "back office" paperwork to test the validity of this contention.

The purpose of this chapter, then, is twofold: first, to analyze the rationale for what we shall call "office automation," and second, to review both the state of the art in office automation technology and the directions in which that technology is headed.

THE NEED FOR INFORMATION TECHNOLOGY IN THE OFFICE

Increasing productivity has long been a key management goal in industrial enterprises. The Industrial Revolution concept of interchangeability of parts and the later notion of the assembly line were important steps forward in achieving greater output per employee. Today, these approaches have evolved into aggressive programs for the installation of labor-saving devices in the factory, many of them utilizing data-processing capability in one form or another.

It is no surprise that the primary focus of past productivity efforts has been on blue-collar work, the area with the greatest potential for improvement. With the steady growth of the white-collar sector, however, there is now a much wider recognition of the productivity-improvement potential of the office environment. Two factors have contributed. By the end of the 1970s, white-collar workers accounted for more than half of the labor force in the United States. Moreover, white-collar productivity has actually declined in recent years. (This is in contrast to productivity across all of industry, which has grown, but at a slower rate in the past decade than in the post-World War II period.)

Together with the steep rise in labor costs as the inflation rate reached double-digit proportions, these factors have served to open management's eyes to the potential for white-collar productivity gains. In particular, there is increasing awareness of the potential for improvement in the style, level, and quality of office work.

The contribution of data processing to selected areas of corporate enterprise over the past two-and-a-half decades has helped focus management attention on the feasibility of using information systems to enhance productivity in the office. Despite the great success of business data processing, however, to date there have been few opportunities for directly connecting the computer to the administrative or clerical processes of the business.

Advances in computer technology, spurred by a tremendous decline in the cost of electronic components for computer hardware, seem to offer the opportunity to utilize office automation as a cost-effective answer to the productivity problem. Office automation is defined by the Diebold Automated Office Program, an operation of the Diebold Group, Inc., as "the utilization of computer-based systems to enhance the effectiveness and productivity of personnel working in an operational or administrative office." The term is not synonymous with small-scale data processing, nor is it another name for what is called "word processing."

Office automation gradually emerged during the 1970s with the introduction of sophisticated office and communications capability. Perhaps the first widely accepted device that was a direct precursor of office automation hardware was IBM's magnetic-tape Selectric typewriter, which provided for the first time the capability for automated production of letters and other documents after they had been typed initially and corrected. A parallel development (which would prove to be extremely important to the evolution of office automation *systems*) was the acceptance of message-oriented communications services such as Telex/TWX and Mailgram.

The fact that the definition of office automation specifies "computer-based" systems is central to the concept—and to their ultimate value in the office environment. Increasingly, such systems will also contain communications capability as well. Despite their family resemblance to traditional data-processing devices, however, office automation systems will be different in a number of key respects. Conceptually, it is more accurate to compare them with factory-automation systems than with conventional business data-processing installations.

However, as office automation systems grow in size, capability, and complexity, the lines of distinction between office automation and conventional data processing will gradually blur, and perhaps even disappear. In fact, for a selected group of applications, this has already occurred, a point that will be explored in greater detail later in this chapter.

The convergence of conventional data-processing capability on the one hand and communications capability on the other will serve to accelerate the value and acceptance of office automation. For example, typewriters that can "converse" with compatible machines in other locations open up a broad potential for business applications that simply did not exist previously. This could sever the physical links that traditionally have bound workers to specific work locations.

Cost is another factor that has helped accelerate the transition to office automation. The semiconductor devices that are the heart of contemporary data processing and much communications hardware have dropped 99.9 percent in cost in 20 years—the equivalent of a $10,000 automobile being reduced to just $10. Since semiconductors are not the only component of these devices, the overall decline in price has not been nearly so great, but it has been sufficient to make it economically feasible to justify their use by a majority of a corporation's white-collar work force. That this has yet to occur is more a function of management perspective than cost.

It is increasingly recognized that comprehensive information processing will be a critical path for a corporation to travel if it is to prosper in the 1980s and beyond. Technology constantly provides new opportunities for collecting, processing, storing, and accessing large quantities of information. In some operating areas, the lines between office and traditional business data processing, also known familiarly as management information systems/sciences (MIS), have already disappeared. In other functional areas, the potential exists for greater convergence at the management level.

However, it must also be recognized that there is a countervailing trend toward greater decentralization and autonomy of operating authority. It is feasible to generate structural entities in which *information* is managed on a centralized basis and *businesses* are managed on a distributed or decentralized basis. A corporation is not forced to manage operating components centrally merely because information is a corporate resource; communications capabilities made possible by advances in technology have effectively removed any such barriers.

The hardware currently used as the backbone of contemporary office automation began as stand-alone units with little or no connection to other units—electric typewriters, Telex machines, mimeograph units, tabletop calculators, and switchboards. None could communicate with each other, nor was there any need for such communications. In the 1970s, however, new pressures became increasingly evident. The deterioration of postal services forced corporations to develop alternative methods of communicating paper-based information. Labor costs began to rise dramatically (at a minimum rate of 8 percent per year); and few productivity increases were realized to justify the higher wage structures.

Perhaps most important, corporations no longer had the luxury of weeks, months, or even years to respond to competition or the demands of an increasingly "activist" government. In many industries, and especially for the most responsive businesses within those industries, reaction times have shortened to days or even hours.

As the 1970s drew to a close, technology had begun to make it feasible to integrate various office functions and the equipment with which to perform those functions. Steady reductions in the cost of components drove equipment costs down to levels where added functional capability produced only minor price rises. More significantly, the new technology (best exemplified by small business computers known as "minicomputers") had a universality and flexibility previously unknown.

Today, there is still a considerable amount of stand-alone equipment in offices, much of it conceptually a part of the new wave of office automation: word processors, copiers, computerized typesetters, facsimile transceivers, and even small computers. Communications are largely separated into voice and data functions. Different data communications networks are in use for different transmission media. Data formats are often incompatible. Work keyed (entered) on one machine often is not readable on another.

Technologically, it is increasingly clear that it is possible to build a "total" office system utilizing one or possibly two input methods plus storage, communications, and output technology. Such systems have been designed and parts of them have already been constructed. This integration of various discrete components is occurring despite the fact that it makes many users of the technology uncomfortable.

From a manufacturing point of view, it makes sense, for example, to merge access to Telex, word processing input to computerized typesetting, and computer data entry. All are input functions based on operator keying. Similarly, the output from facsimile transmission and document copying are much the same.

In the final analysis, the most important consideration is that the various system elements or components all deal with *information.* Keeping the pieces apart is therefore not in the best interests of the organization. Data that cannot be "read" because it is incompatible with available processing devices is of little use. Similarly, information stored in Chicago that cannot be obtained in New York is of less value. A major benefit to the information-based organization will be its ability to access information in standard forms, using standard methods. Multifunction systems will be a major step in this direction, and they are now beginning to receive the attention they deserve.

The remaining issue—perhaps one that will be harder to resolve—is the development and implementation of master plans for automating selected office functions and especially for integrating the systems into day-to-day operations. To date, there has been little analytic work to enable a corporate manager to better understand the processes within an office or administrative unit. The flow of information, the interrelations with other organizational entities (usually called "interfaces" in the parlance of the information technologist), the way in which internal interactions occur, and the delicate balance between people and equipment all are comparatively unstudied.

The balance of this chapter examines the tools of office automation at the present state of the art, the evolution of office automation systems, and the progress being made in addressing the organizational and other human considerations that ultimately will be as much (or more) a determinant of system effectiveness as the technology itself.

OFFICE AUTOMATION: THE STATE OF THE ART

As indicated earlier, office automation has emerged as a direct response to the demonstrated need for greater productivity. It has been made possible not so much by the introduction of new technology as by the adoption of new uses for technology previously existing outside the office environment. The technology in question—such advances as semiconductors, digital transmission, and laser recording—is itself relatively recent in vintage; most of it did not exist (except in the laboratory) as recently as a decade ago. It is the maturation of these technologies, with a simultaneous decline in cost, that has made their utilization in the office environment feasible.

This discussion is not intended to be a technical discourse on the electronic characteristics of various types of office-automation hardware. However, to fully understand the capabilities and potential of office automation systems, it is useful to understand the basic functions the equipment performs. These functions are direct parallels to existing office functions, but few executives or office workers will have considered their jobs in these terms, which are more familiar to the data-processing expert.

In their most simplified form, the functions are as follows:

- *Input.* The gathering of raw data and its entry into the office–work process.
- *Communications.* The movement of the raw data from various stages of the work flow to others.
- *Processing.* The transformation of raw data from its original form into a different form.
- *Storage.* The process of retaining data for future reference.

- *Retrieval.* The ability to access stored data when (and where) needed.
- *Output.* The generation of data in a form specified by its eventual user.

These categories are, of course, arbitrary. They frequently overlap. In some instances, the function is transparent (invisible) to the user, as in the case of data transmission. But each has its direct parallel or analog in the traditional office environment. For example, the most common input device is the typewriter. Telex is a typical communications link. A memory typewriter fits the definition of "processor." A filing cabinet, while rudimentary, is a storage medium, and a search of that cabinet for a specified file is the retrieval process. And finally, output is typified by a typed document, Telex message, or even photocopy.

The fact that these functional parallels exist does not in and of itself make every office a rudimentary office automation center. The missing elements are twofold. First, the various devices at each stage must contain at least a degree of electronic sophistication. And second, there must be a degree of interconnection between the various functions, at least to the extent that their characteristics are altered to provide a better interface with the others. (For example, from the broad perspective of productivity, the automated production of correspondence makes little sense if that correspondence is subsequently to be entrusted to the postal system for delivery. Similarly, a manual filing system can defeat the purpose of even a well-designed data-entry and processing system.)

The six functional categories discussed here have remained fundamentally unchanged across the entire history of business, but it has not been until the last decade or two that the devices to provide the capabilities have changed dramatically. Undoubtedly, they will change at an accelerating pace with improvements in technology and growing user sophistication.

Rather than discuss in any detail the various individual tools that are used in office automation, emphasis will be placed on automation systems. At present, and in most offices now using this technology, each of the various pieces of equipment is used as a "stand-alone," with no particular reference to any other. This is generally true across organizational lines, as well: different departments, divisions, or other organizational entities may have developed various office automation capabilities independently without regard to (or even knowledge of) the possibility of parallel developments elsewhere in the organization.

Thus, it is not unusual to find overlapping, redundant, and/or incompatible capabilities within a given organization, which is a compelling reason to consider office automation as a system, rather than as a series of potentially interlinked components.

In the pages that follow, a variety of different office automation systems will be examined, each designed to perform a minimum of two of the six functions previously discussed. These systems share the common characteristic that all are available currently. Although there may be "kinks"—isolated technical problems—in each of the systems, by and large they have been perfected and are suitable for day-to-day operations in a business environment. This is a critical consideration, for few, if any, organizations can afford to rely on any equipment, electronic or mechanical, that does not have a high level of reliability. It is even more true of office automation systems whose reliability is as yet something of an unanswered question.

The office environment is different from that in which the traditional data-processing expert has operated. Office employees are not usually technically oriented, and they are rarely technically trained. Thus, they have little interest in how a system works; it is sufficient that the system *does* work. For this reason, office workers will not shrug off system failures, memorize complex and sometimes barely intelligible instructions, decipher cryptic comments from the system, or adjust their own behavioral patterns to fit systems whose purpose is to make their jobs easier.

This points up the necessity of designing systems around the needs and capabilities of the user, a challenge that admittedly is easier to resolve on paper than in the actual operating environment. On balance, it seems probable that office automation systems will not succeed until a human-centered design approach, focused on real or perceived needs, has been adopted. This does not imply that the technology is unimportant, but rather that those who design and implement the systems need to recognize its ultimate use and especially the obstacles to that use.

The stress on user-centered systems is important, if only because it has largely been neglected to date. Manufacturers have taken good technology and connected it in ways best suited to the hardware and operating characteristics of the system. In the process, systems of high capability but low usability often have resulted; such systems are focused on *doing* things rather than *supporting* managers or office workers in their attempts to accomplish tasks. Not surprisingly, such systems have generated little enthusiasm in the marketplace.

Fortunately, this trend seems to be reversing itself. The systems discussed here are not necessarily devoid of this problem, but the designers of office automation systems, and especially the market experts, have gradually come to an awareness that knowledge of office processes and interactions is a central rather than peripheral concern.

Computing/Word Processing Systems

The term "word processing" is generally disliked by most office automation experts. Although defined as the processing, storage, and output of text, it has come to be viewed primarily as a means for obtaining higher productivity from secretarial employees. This is a shortsighted view that overlooks the essential capabilities of most word processors.

Estimates of the time a secretary spends typing vary sharply from industry to industry. It may be as low as 10 percent in support of a top executive to as high as 50 percent in a pool operation in a law firm. The key question is the value (added profit or return on equity) that accrues to the enterprise if typing productivity is improved. If, for example, a word processor can improve productivity by 30 percent in terms of pages typed, but the average time spent typing is only 20 percent, then the overall productivity improvement is just 6 percent, which may be insufficient to cost-justify the system.

Indeed, the key to improvement in office productivity lies in recognizing that many office systems exist to support managerial decision making. Managers spend as much as 60 percent of their time communicating with superiors and subordinates. In this context, the effort to automate should be based not on typing productivity, but instead on smoothing communications, permitting greater access to more information, and providing systems to support managerial functions. In fact, the office automation industry has come to view the automation of the typing function as merely a preliminary step toward the larger goal of aiding executive decision making.

The concept of an office automation system as a replacement for (or supplement to) an executive's desk is more complex than it may seem on the surface. Executives rarely perform only one task at a time, following it through from initiation to completion. This suggests that a "computerized" desk must serve many functions simultaneously.

Although word processing may be little more than a transitional stage, it represents the most common introduction of new users into the office automation movement. Word processors come in a variety of configurations, with long lists of standard and optional features that range from the necessary to the exotic. Within this broad spectrum, there are four basic categories:

- *Nondisplay* units are stand-alone machines based on conventional typewriters with the addition of memory and some form of removable media for storage. To most typists, the machines look familiar, and they can be used with little specialized training, for the most part. The units may be equipped with communications capability to permit transmission to compatible remote units. Although some feature one-line display, one major disadvantage of these machines is the difficulty of viewing document status to correct errors except by printing the entire document.
- *Stand-alone display* equipment utilizes the best features of nondisplay systems, replacing the paper orientation of the typewriter with a cathode ray tube (CRT) screen. Printing is moved to an auxiliary device. The use of the display unit permits the operator to make all possible changes in the text: character, word, sentence, paragraph, or entire document. Because of the stand-alone characteristic of the equipment, there are inherent problems with large-scale storage and with complex communications capability. They also have limited processing power, which makes it difficult to handle multilevel sorting or complex arithmetic problems.
- *Shared logic* systems are based on the concept of centralizing selected essential system resources, rather than reserving them

for the use of a single operator (or individual machine). Most commonly, the resources shared are memory, communications, high-speed printers, computational capacities, and/or optical character recognition (OCR) readers. These are selected for sharing because each is expensive, but rarely needs to be used by more than one work station at a time.

- *Main frame word processing* utilizes a conventional large-scale general-purpose computer that has been programmed to provide word-processing capability, although the operator will be unaware of whether the system is being controlled within the individual work station or in the central computer. This provides the word-processing work station with capabilities commonplace in the data processing environment—computational capacity, communications, and large-scale memory being among the most important.

Office computational capacity has become increasingly necessary to fulfilling ordinary business needs. Typically, it involves such functions as pricing, inventory, account status, and budgeting. These functions previously have been performed manually or on centralized computers, although the rapid growth of minicomputers and small business systems have changed the ground rules significantly in the past five years. What was once economically and technically necessary has now become not only feasible, but in many instances essential.

An office can be provided with computational power in a variety of ways, but the merger of computational power into word processing systems is a fairly recent, but very significant, development. Part of the difficulty has been the understandable unwillingness of data-processing users to unplug existing computational capability in favor of integrated systems with a new set of users.

Vendors are addressing this problem through modularization. An installation may move up from existing word processing to incorporate limited data-processing functions, on the one hand, or add word-processing capability to existing computational capacity on the other. Either approach appears to be economically superior to the introduction of totally new integrated computational/word processing systems, but the addition of word processing to data processing is qualitatively different, as most office personnel have not the preparation associated with the data-processing functions. On paper, an integrated system can easily be designed, but in the real world, it is still viewed as both a luxury and a risk.

Past experience with word processing suggests that the systems must have several characteristics if they are to achieve wide acceptance:

1. The user must be permitted to access data-processing files that are fundamental to his or her business.
2. The word-processing user needs certain data-processing capabilities, such as sorting and mathematical routines.
3. The user will not take advantage of the system's capabilities unless it is both easy to use and reliable.
4. The system must function locally, so that its utilization is determined solely by the user.

Given these requirements, it now seems likely that future word-processing systems will not be stand-alone units, but instead subsystems of more generalized information-processing systems. Although they may be connected to large processors for file storage, computational functions, and communications, they will function in a seemingly independent mode. In this way, they will come closest to meeting the other requirement—that they be user oriented.

Printing/Copying/Communications

In the context of office automation, the merger of electronic-communications capability with traditional office functions, such as document generation and reproduction, is important for two reasons. First, it vastly increases the capability of an executive to collect and utilize data from remote locations without first having to change its format. By the same token, it also gives the user the capability to disseminate material to remote locations, again without the necessity of re-formatting the material.

It is critical that no format changes be required; it will become even more so in the future as the capabilities of such systems are fully exploited. Most conventional "hard copy" communications services require message transcription on at least the sending end of the communications chain. A Telex message or telegram, for example, must be manually converted from hard copy to electronic signals and then back again to hard copy at the receiving location. For certain documents, such as reports or contracts, it may also be necessary for the receiver to take the additional step of retranscribing the message into a more acceptable format.

The new systems bypass at least one of these steps by permitting the reproduction of the transmitted document at the receiving location in precisely the format desired. At the option of the user(s), the document could be completely indistinguishable from the original. For example, a memorandum or report can be generated at company headquarters and subsequently be reproduced automatically in remote company offices or those of customers or suppliers. Eventually, the capability will be extended to the point that virtually all routine business correspondence will be transmitted electronically rather than physically, a concept that has been given the name "electronic mail."

In a narrow sense, this capability has existed for a number of years in the form of facsimile transmission. But "fax" has several inherent disadvantages that have impeded its growth, with poor quality of the transmitted document heading the list. In addition, it is relatively slow and requires an operator on at least one end (and usually both ends) of the transmission.

These problems will be avoided with the new systems that permit a typewriter in one location to "talk" directly with a similar device at another site. With such capability, an executive can produce a document or other message that ultimately will be typed by a central printer at another work location or even at the addressee's own desk or that of his or her secretary. Since the "message" will be identical to the original, multiple reproduction (copying) will also be facilitated. Also, there is no theoretical limit on the number of remote sites to which the document might be transmitted. The only practical limits will be the availability of compatible receivers and the transmission costs.

Although the future will undoubtedly see the introduction of far more sophisticated devices with greater flexibility, more features, and lower cost, much of the basic hardware is commercially available today. The least complex are electronic typewriters with communications capability that can be controlled from remote sites. Using such a device, secretary "A" prepares a document, corrects errors, and obtains approval to transmit. It can then be typed automatically on secretary "B's" compatible machine with no human intervention except for the insertion of appropriate paper (letterhead, formatted report stock, preprinted forms, and so on).

More complex and sophisticated are high-speed stand-alone printers with integral communications capability. Such devices are more suitable for use on an office-to-office basis than individual desk-to-desk communications because they can serve the function of an electronic mailroom by servicing many users, consecutively or simultaneously. Only the final link in the process—the delivery of the message from the remote printer to the ultimate recipient—need be a manual operation.

Facsimile/Message-Switching Systems

As indicated previously, the use of facsimile transmission has been limited by a number of factors. Similarly, the message switchers that are a familiar and routine data-processing capability have also had limitations. The standard "store-and-forward" technique required that computer terminals deliver messages to a central facility (generally a large computer) where they were stored for retransmission to receiving locations. If the receiver were out of service for any reason, the message could be stored for later transmission, readdressed to another recipient, or rerouted to its original destination by an alternative communications path. But the message format would not necessarily be that selected by the sender.

The marriage of these two concepts—facsimile transmission and message switching—is a recent and potentially very significant development, although the cost is comparatively high at present and few users have yet to see the need for this capability. Ultimately, as the message switcher becomes large and sophisticated enough to handle transmissions from any input device and to convert them to output on the remote printer, it can assume the characteristics of a facsimile device, providing this capability at low cost and with message (document) quality far superior to that of conventional facsimile systems. In a few years, the use of facsimile-type printing could increase dramatically as such devices become more readily attachable to corporate communications networks and broad-based communications become more feasible.

Message Switching/Computing

As the hardware used in communications devices and data processing have merged, the potential for merging *applications* has become clearer. Already, the lines of demarcation between the two have become so blurred that it is increasingly difficult to categorize some of the newer systems as clearly belonging to one category rather than another.

The heart of these systems are small (micro or mini) computers that perform message-switching functions, data as well as voice. Thus, in addition to normal telephone communications, these devices can handle a variety of data-processing peripheral devices, such as CRT terminals and remote printers. Because they have the added capability of being programmable, they can also perform selected data-processing or computing functions.

The key link in the communications setup of any business will be the Private Automatic Branch Exchange (PABX) that connects transmission and destination stations. The microcomputers central to such systems permit features such as inbound and outbound queuing, least-cost routing, conference calls, and detail billing, all at no significant increase in cost. For these and other technical and economic reasons, the electronic PABX is rapidly moving into common usage. All-electronic PABXs will do much to insure easy interconnections between various office automation devices, including the addition of expanded computational power into the PABX.

The PABX itself is destined to be the key link in the office, acting not only as the connection between individual devices, but also as the access path to the external world. Obviously, the "smarter" the PABX, the more that can be done to link and especially to merge various functional activities of the business.

Word Processing/OCR/Photocomposition

The previous section on word processing dealt exclusively with its use as an extension of the secretary's capability. The term is also used in a somewhat different, albeit parallel, context relating to computer-based printing. In fact, this is undoubtedly the most common word-processing application today. Many corporations have adopted this technology to establish, modernize, and/or expand in-house printing capability for documents that previously were sent to an outside vendor or were distributed in conventional typewriter format.

Cost, reduced turn-around time, and confidentiality are the three primary reasons for the success of these systems, and their popularity will continue to grow as these factors become even more significant considerations for the business community.

In this application, the word-processing system servcs all the functions of a commercial compositor, generating high-quality documents that can be reproduced by photo offset or even conventional Xerox machines. Even extensive alterations in the text are comparatively easy to make, and there is wide flexibility as to format, type font, and other physical characteristics.

Moreover, when the proper type font is utilized, the material generated can be read by an optical character recognition (OCR) device, which subsequently can convert it into a format suitable for electronic transmission.

Far more sophisticated capabilities are enjoyed by the commercial printers who have embraced this technology, as well as a small handful of corporations that have adopted it as an alternative to commercial printing services. Computerized photocomposition devices offer the graphic designer great flexibility in terms of type font and size, and can also provide electronic page layout, chart and/or slide composition, among other features.

Other Systems

The office automation systems described to this point are only a sampling of the possibilities that are either already commercially available or will be in the near future. The definition of the term "system" is so loose that virtually any combination of devices theoretically might qualify. And users and vendors alike are constantly experimenting with various combinations and linkages to achieve specific objectives. For example, a commercial facsimile service is now available that permits a user to transmit a facsimile message at high speed through the vendor's communications network. Among other benefits, it permits facsimile units that otherwise could not converse to communicate with each other.

The U.S. Postal Service, anticipating the potential for electronic mail services, is currently experimenting with an electronic message system to provide a wide range of functions for high-volume, computerized customers.

Communicating word processors, which presently represent only about 15 percent of the total units in daily operation, are expected to become increasingly popular, especially when there is broader recognition of the fact that they can be used as direct substitutes for conventional Telex or comparable services.

Digital voice recording is a technology still in the development stage, but when perfected, it offers the promise of adding considerable sophistication to existing systems. For example, it could lead to usable dictations systems that eliminate the need for a stenographer.

Video conferencing, already in limited use, is another promising avenue for development, especially as travel costs increase. This technology has a variety of useful features, including the possibility of inexpensive storage of meeting proceedings for archival purposes or future reference.

Finally, there is the possibility of mating word-processing units with microfilm systems, so that the need for long-term archival storage can be met automatically with the generation and/or transmission of a document.

THE FUTURE OF OFFICE AUTOMATION

The Real Productivity Challenge

It is clear that for the majority of organizations, office-automation technology is evolving far more rapidly than it is being assimilated into routine office operations, much less being applied to a broad new spectrum of applications representing changes in traditional business patterns. This, however, is a situation that can be expected to reverse itself—initially, to achieve gains in white-collar productivity, and ultimately to provide management with an arsenal of new working tools.

As discussed in this chapter, modern office automation systems represent a convergence of three technologies: computers, communications, and traditional stand-alone office machines. This convergence has been gradual and evolutionary, and future progress is likely to be even more so. Radical or revolutionary changes will be felt in terms of the ways in which the systems are utilized.

In this regard, The Diebold Group, Inc., believes that the major thrust of automating office functions should be to improve executive and managerial performance in decision making. If the productivity of clerical or other white-collar workers is improved in the process, it should be considered an additional benefit.

For the executive, information access is critical. But this implies many things: timeliness, obviously, and accuracy, of course. Equally important is selectivity—the ability to access only the information that is needed, without having to sort through unnecessary data. Finally, the retention and security of information is implicit in the concept of information access.

These objectives can, of course, be realized with conventional office tools, such as electric typewriters, copying machines, facsimile transmission, Telex/TWX, and microfilm or microfiche. The problem is that each of these functions must operate independently, and the links between the various stages are almost by definition the weak links in the chain. The new era of office-automation systems bypasses this problem, either by virtue of combining functions within a single component or by directly interconnecting various components.

When these links are formed, the result is a system that has the built-in capability to change many of the ways in which executives function—not only what they do during business and nonbusiness hours alike, but also where and even when they work.

There is some research to suggest that a typical executive spends upwards of 60 percent of the time communicating with superiors, peers, and subordinates. Generally, the higher up the ladder the executive is, the greater the percentage of time devoted to communicating. Given the importance of the communications function, it is logical that this is the area where the most significant gains from the new systems can be anticipated.

On a purely physical basis, the new systems must have the capability to keep track of time: schedules, dates, and deadlines. They must also contain certain intrinsic reminders of information distribution, location of employees in transit, how people can be reached and where, and even the way in which specific individuals prefer to be addressed. In addition to these fundamental capabilities, the systems must also be designed to replace (in function, if not in form) most of the familiar components of the office environment—

electronically. One observer has suggested that the technology will include areas such as "bookshelves," "filing cabinets," "desk drawers," and so forth, each of which would function in the same capacity as their traditional counterparts. For example, from a console or terminal at a desk, the executive could research a point electronically just as one would use an encyclopedia, dictionary, or atlas. The executive could also store and reference files and even personal notes and memos that might otherwise be kept in a desk drawer.

The processing of both incoming and outgoing mail is another invaluable function. Incoming mail, for example, could be held and even indexed by subject, date, or sender for examination at the addressee's convenience, which might not necessarily be during formal office hours, or even at a normal work location. It is entirely conceivable, for instance, that an executive could, via terminal, review incoming mail at the breakfast table before going to the office. Similarly, there would be no technological barrier to performing the same activity while on a business trip virtually anywhere in the world.

Future Systems: Some Scenarios

In conjunction with its ongoing research into maximizing the potential of the new technology and overcoming some of the obstacles to its efficient introduction, The Diebold Group, Inc., has developed a set of scenarios relating to specific changes in office operations that can be anticipated during the balance of this century. Some of the more provocative of these scenarios are summarized below:

- *The Entrepreneurial Work Force.* Information technology opens the door for the individual "knowledge worker" to be highly selective about the work he or she performs. Many such workers will choose to follow their entrepreneurial instincts, perhaps by becoming consultants or subcontractors to their previous employers. This will give these individuals the flexibility to perform their functions at their own convenience, in many instances off the premises of the employer.
- *The Office Communications Center.* Increasingly, each individual white-collar work station will become a computer/commu-

nications center, complete with its own terminal and communications capability. Through this center, the worker can receive and send information and instructions and perform many of the usual tasks. However, the nature of many of these tasks will change as a result of the new capability. For example, in a transcontinental meeting via television, a team of executives could consider the wording of a report or letter, make the desired changes in text on a CRT terminal, and then immediately have the text typed (or printed) in their own offices or in the offices of the desired recipients. Access to data bases will create the capability for the executive to call up historical data, industry statistics, and current operating information as needed, make modeling ("what if?") analyses, and conveniently perform a variety of data manipulations without ever leaving the office.

- *The Business Office in the Home.* Information technology will move many office functions into the worker's home, dramatically changing the work environment. As communications capabilities become more sophisticated and human/machine interface becomes easier, it will become less and less necessary for workers and executives alike to be physically located at work centers. Managers as well as clerical workers could spend several days a week at a remote work center near or even in their homes, as opposed to commuting to offices in central business district cores or suburban areas. The use of time- and geography-independent systems could lead to widespread decentralization of many office functions. People previously unable to travel to central work sites (homemakers, the physically handicapped, and so on) could become part of an office work force who work in their homes and electronically transfer the final product wherever it is needed.

The above are just a handful of the many possibilities that will emerge. Information technology will also play a major role in addressing a problem for which it is partly responsible: the rapidly deteriorating value of a worker's knowledge due to new discoveries and other advances in any particular field of expertise. Direct training or retraining of workers in the home through interactive television will help alleviate this problem, as will remote access libraries and technical information services. These sources of information will also help in making the problem less significant because a worker can easily become as current as he or she wishes in virtually any area of expertise or knowledge.

CONCLUSION

The potential for computer-based office automation is tremendous, provided we are willing to recognize the fact that the technology will extend far beyond our conventional definition of the office environment. The "office" need not be a specific room in a given building in a designated community; it can be anywhere with the proper equipment and adequate communications capability.

Furthermore, it is increasingly clear that the most important benefits to be gained from the adoption of this technology will not come in the area of clerical productivity, but rather in terms of improvements in the decision-making process within the business organization. These will be realized through improvements in the communication of business information, and through the linkage of the various elements of an executive's job to eliminate the tedious and often error-prone intermediate stages in the collection, processing, transfer, and/or storage of information.

There are, of course, many obstacles to the widespread adoption of this technology but, for the most part, they are psychological rather than technical or even economic. Executives who have worked 20 years or more with secretaries, filing cabinets, and other traditional methods will not immediately be comfortable with the electronic equivalent of a desk. By the same token, however, there is a generation of younger executives who have grown up in the computer generation and who can be expected to take a different view of the technology when they reach the top levels of management. These individuals take electronics as a matter of course—especially those who must routinely utilize conventional computers in their work.

With patience and common sense, the psychological barriers to office automation will gradually be eliminated. Accelerating this trend will be a recognition on the part of potential users that by not adopting it, they are unnecessarily placing themselves at a severe competitive disadvantage, that their costs are unnecessarily high, that they are unresponsive to changes in the external environment, and that the decisions they are making are not made by utilizing all the requisite information and, hence, are not the best possible decisions under the circumstance.

In the final analysis, to reiterate a point made in the opening paragraphs of this chapter, the willingness of an organization to embrace this technology, and make effective use of it, may well prove to be a key determinant of its continued success. To put it more succinctly, we anticipate that the business organizations that are most successful in decades to come will also be those that have discovered that office automation is to their administrative activities what automation has been to the factory—a giant step into a new era of efficiency and profitability that has benefited employee, consumer, and business owner alike.

10.
Labor Looks at New Technology

Thomas Donahue
Secretary-Treasurer, AFL-CIO

The changes that new technology makes in the way goods and services are produced and distributed provide potential benefits, but they can also have destructive effects on workers and their jobs. Therefore workers and their unions have a vital interest in making sure that new technology is introduced in the workplace in such a way that human values prevail.

New technology often involves labor-saving operations—increased production with the same number or fewer workers—which may displace existing jobs. Of course, new jobs may also be created, but the impact of technology may be to eliminate some jobs, change the job content of others, change skill requirements, and change the flow of work.

New technology often causes changes in industry location—shutdowns of departments and entire plants and shifts to new locations in suburban or outlying areas, and sometimes overseas. No industry is immune to such changes, which are constantly shifting the structure of skills, occupations, jobs, and earnings of American workers.

Labor's concern is people and what this new technology does *to* people, because the scientific community has more than enough resources to trumpet what technology does *for* people.

There are countless benefits of technology, benefits which can be shared by all. Assuring that all share in these benefits is a responsibility trade unionists can't meet just by posturing like ostriches, with their heads in the sand until the last moment. At the same time, it is incumbent upon labor to point out the results of technology and its impact on workers. What has technology brought?

It has brought about 1,100 known carcinogens in the workplace—new ways for workers to die from the benefits of new technology. Approximately 600 new chemicals are introduced each year, many with harmful side effects for the workers who produce them and the consumers who use them.

Technology has brought the new health hazards of stress and stress-related illnesses unheard of during previous industrial revolutions. Amazingly little is known about stress. For all that was written about Lordstown and the "rebellion" of younger workers against assembly-line speedups—as if the young were discovering something their parents didn't know existed in the industrial world—scant attention was paid to the stress factor.

Similarly, much of the literature on stress relates it to middle managers—the stress of success, or the workaholic syndrome—and little if any is devoted to white- and blue-collar workers. For example, forced overtime can also create stress both for workers and their families.

Another cause of stress among workers stems from increased reliance on professional managers as supervisors, rather than on the more traditional approach of training supervisors from the ranks of the work force. This means that front-line management often views workers as machines, because the supervisors lack work experience. The stopwatch mentality replaces reason; programs to control workers' absenteeism replace interesting work; and Muzak is piped in to soothe the blue-collar blues. The end result is pressure, stress.

Technology has meant a misallocation of the work force, with resultant morale problems on the job and a growing disaffection for work.

According to a recent survey,[1] an alarming 32 percent of the 1,515 workers surveyed consider themselves overeducated for their work. And 36 percent believe their skills are "underutilized." These figures accompany the first significant decline in job satisfaction in 30 years. This means human talents and resources are being wasted.

But the figures are not surprising when you consider that the number of college graduates in the work force now totals 17 percent of the total labor force. In 1940, college graduates were comparatively rare in the labor force—in fact, the ratio was one college graduate per every 22 workers. "Train people for the new technology," society is told, and we train, train, train. But when the training is done, the needed skills have been replaced by a machine and the jobs are gone.

Concomitant with technological change has been the transformation of the U.S. economy from a production base to a service base. Where formerly technological change was having its major impact on manufacturing, it is in the service economy that such change is likely to accelerate in the near future.

The implications of such a transformation are frightening, especially in contemplation of who—or what—will produce the goods people will sell one another, or how much attention and effort to ease the impact of technological change will be directed at the manufacturing sector. Currently, attention to manufacturing is still dominant even though there are many more workers in the service sector. And the service sector, even with its omnipresent computer, is largely untouched by technological change. The adjustment that will face these service workers is likely to be more abrupt and harsher than in the industrial sector, which can look back on past experience with automation.

There are the giggles: the robot internal mail delivery system which replaces the young man or woman pushing the mail cart. And machines capable of typing a letter from the spoken word; reproducing it in vast quantities; and addressing, folding, stuffing the letters into envelopes, and affixing postage—without a human hand. In Washington, legislators have computers to answer letters from prewritten paragraphs. But the laughing stops when the people these machines replace reach the unemployment line.

EASING THE HUMAN COSTS OF TECHNOLOGY

By that time, of course, it is too late, except for palliatives like unemployment insurance. The time is now to develop a strategy for dealing with technological change in a creative manner that minimizes injury, and maximizes the accommodation of technology to people and people to technology, while providing the benefits of technological advances to a better world for all people.

The creative tool which trade unions bring to this process is collective bargaining. Through negotiation, employers and employees can develop those approaches that humanize both the workplace and the work itself, and minimize the impact of innovation and new technology on workers' jobs, earnings, and futures.

If employers are willing to sit down with the unions representing their employees, then they will find a partner. If employers recognize that the labor movement does not oppose technology, but that unions oppose throwing people on a scrap heap, they will find understanding.

If employers are frank and open and willing to listen, they will hear ideas, not bombast. But if employers refuse to view worker-adjustment costs as part of the cost of industrial innovation, they will find resistance. This resistance may only delay the inevitable, but the price in bitterness and confrontation is likely to be costly.

One method to ease the human costs of industrial innovation is to assure advance information to workers and their unions about management plans for future innovation which will affect workers with job loss or other serious problems.

Major innovations result from management decisions taken long before the innovation is actually introduced. The recent shutdown of the Youngstown, Ohio, steel plant involved corporate decisions made years earlier. Certainly there should be long advance notice before a plant initiates any innovation or technological change that results in layoffs or plant shutdowns, or even in less serious disarrangement or rearrangement of people and of functions.

An "early warning system" of advance notice makes it possible to begin to meet the problems of affected workers. Such "early warning" provisions have long been standard in many union contracts. With advance notice and labor–management cooperation, workers can look for or train for a new job, perhaps with the same employer in the same plant or at another location. Employer-paid retraining is an important part of any adjustment-to-innovation program.

There are other methods and techniques for labor–management cooperation to cushion adverse effects from industrial innovation and changing technology. These include income maintenance with guarantees of work or pay or both.

One way is through "no-layoffs" attrition to reduce the work force by natural turnover, deaths, retirements, and voluntary quits, thus protecting the jobs and earnings of those workers who remain with the company. Of course, attrition alone is not an adequate solution. "Red circle" earnings protection for workers downgraded through no fault of their own attaches a wage rate to an individual instead of to the job itself, and thus protects workers against loss of income which might result from innovation-induced downgrading.

Seniority is a key principle in protecting workers against layoffs and downgradings. Early retirement is an option that older workers should have available when innovation or major technological change wipes out their jobs. But the option should be available as a free choice, not as a requirement.

Transfer and relocation rights and mobility assistance to workers are other ways to provide job and income protection. Within-plant and interplant transfers, relocation assistance, severance pay, pension rights, seniority protection, and supplemental unemployment benefits can all help cushion adverse effects on workers and their families when industrial innovation occurs.

More information is needed on the effects of industrial innovation and new technology on workers. Federal action is needed to set up a clearinghouse to gather information on a continuing basis on innovation and technological change and its effects on the welfare of the American people—on jobs, skills, training needs, and industry location. With more and better information, public and private adjustment programs can better avoid needless human hardship and suffering, which too often result from the disruptive impact of changing technology and innovation.

Through this clearinghouse, the federal government could provide unions and employers with comprehensive information and service, upon request, to help the parties develop labor-management solutions for the complex problems related to the impact of innovation and technological change at the workplace.

Innovation-caused economic dislocation and other kinds of dislocation—including plant shutdowns caused by technological change, job loss from trade policies, and production shifts away from defense-related industry—require cooperative labor-management efforts and also national programs to deal with these complex problems. Further exploration is needed of a variety of such programs, including proposals dealing with plant shutdowns and plant relocation and with reconversion of defense-related industry.

RESTRICTING THE EXPORT OF TECHNOLOGY

Export of technology is another potential problem area. Because it may well be that technology will be America's most important asset, it is necessary to take a serious look at the indiscriminate and unnecessary transfer of that technology abroad—most often by the multinational corporation for reasons of profit alone. Increasingly in recent years, the operations of multinational firms—not only through direct investment but also through licensing of patents and equipment and through trade transactions, which include "turnkey" operations that export managerial know-how as well as sophisticated equipment and skills—have transferred technology to other nations. The result is to discourage innovation at home and to stimulate innovation abroad. It is important to develop a measure of the desirability of such transfers from the standpoint not only of their effect on profits, but also of their effect on jobs and on the American people and their communities.

USING TECHNOLOGY TO PROTECT PEOPLE

Industrial innovation should not conflict with laws and regulations to protect the safety and health and environment of American people as workers, consumers, or citizens. Of course, some so-called "technological improvements," such as the "hot-wire chassis" for TV and radio sets, may be shortsighted, dangerous cost-cutting which poses safety threats to both workers and consumers—but such problems must be regarded as challenges and opportunities for more safety-oriented innovation. This has occurred in the United States in the past and will continue.

There is no quarrel with efforts to reduce uncertainty regarding the timing and direction of future regulatory actions, nor with efforts to reduce the lead time associated with the introduction of new products or processes. Efforts to reorient research and development (R&D) budgets from improved process efficiency and product development to environmental controls should be encouraged, as should federal programs to help develop environmental and health and safety technologies.

But what must be opposed are the persistent efforts of business, big and small, to undermine and to weaken the laws and the regulations aimed at protecting consumers, at getting greater protection of workers' health and safety on the job, and at protection of the environment for all Americans. The drive for so-called "voluntary standards" is one part of this campaign.

Unfortunately, from the day the Occupational Safety and Health Act was signed into law, supposedly respectable business organizations, joined by far right-wing groups, have tried to weaken, to undermine, and ultimately to destroy the law. As part of its all-out attack on OSHA, the business community continues to fight OSHA inspectors' access to the workplace and to fund a series of legal actions against nearly every OSHA standard.

Likewise, the business community—the U.S. Chamber of Commerce, the Business Roundtable, and the National Association of Manufacturers—waged an intensive and successful war against passage by the 95th Congress of legislation to set up a federal Consumer Protection Agency.

Dollar trade-offs are not acceptable when it comes to the lives and well-being of workers, consumers, and citizens generally. Ignoring environmental, occupational safety and health, and consumer product hazards is far more costly to the economy and to society than any possible immediate corrective costs. Looking at the problem in dollars is simple—and simple-minded. Economists can take up the costs of cleaning up the environment and the workplace, but they cannot say what the long-range cost of failure to eliminate life and health hazards will be in dollar terms or in human terms.

"Technology-forcing" standards should be imposed to reduce toxic materials in the workplace, with the intention of forcing regulated employers to innovate—to develop technology which will achieve the health objectives of the standards.

In fact, there is an urgent need to increase the OSHA compliance force to at least 3,000 federal inspectors and industrial hygienists, and there should be additional manpower available for standards development, statistics, education, and training. Vigorous OSHA enforcement will spur innovation by business in putting occupational safety and health measures into effect.

To stimulate further innovation in occupational safety and health, the National Institute for Occupational Safety and Health (NIOSH) must get substantial increases in funding and manpower for training personnel in the health professions to alleviate the serious nationwide shortage of qualified workers in this field and to perform scientific research and to develop health-effects criteria for human exposure to toxic materials. In this connection, more adequate safety and health protection is needed for agricultural workers who have a high injury rate and high exposure to toxic pesticides and herbicides.

Environmental requirements, consumer product-safety requirements, and worker safety and health requirements can be reconciled with the needs of the national economy without sacrificing either the environment or a healthy economy. Advancing technology makes possible development of clean energy sources and realization of the nation's environmental objectives. In those rare cases where there is an equally important but conflicting objective, such as energy production, any stretch-out in timetables to achieve environmental goals should be kept to an absolute minimum. This must be an adjustment of timetables, not goals.

ENCOURAGING RESEARCH AND DEVELOPMENT

Federal procurement policies should be encouraged which will result in "strengthening of interagency coordination of procurement through planning, standards, and the development of information systems which relate government demand to civilian innovation; enhancing programs designed to promote civilian impact of government purchasing for defense and aerospace systems; developing, implementing, and evaluating new methods for anticipating and responding to differences in civilian and government needs and markets; and designing particular procurement practices which will directly pull innovations," as one federal report stated it.[2]

Where patents have clear social benefits in terms of protecting the public interest in the environment and the safety and health of workers, the public interest should take priority over protection of private rights. This does not mean that private rights in such patents would be ignored or nullified, but rather that there would be assured utilization of patents with clear social benefits. One possible approach would be the compulsory licensing of such patents with fair compensation to the patent holder. Licensing of such patents should maximize the opportunities for social benefits and avoid nonutilization of such patents.

However, there is a great potential for channeling procurement and R&D funds to the largest corporations and thus further fostering monopoly and waste and adversely affecting the geographic location of facilities. The impact on the nation's economic and social institutions can be profound. Scientific and technological progress must be sought for urban, environmental, and social problems as well as for military and aerospace needs.

The federal government, through its procurement policy, has a clear and acceptable power to create an assured big market—a planned government market pull—to promote socially desirable innovation, such as solar-powered batteries and other innovative items.

Furthermore, patents created by private business with U.S. taxpayers' dollars must not become the private proprietary rights of private business. Title to such patents should be held by the United States and should be placed in the public domain under royalty-free cross-licensing provisions.

New legislation should prohibit requirements by private industry that employees waive to their private employer their rights to inventions they may accomplish while employed by that employer. And any efforts to raise patent-filing fees should be opposed.

Workers in private industry—whether in scientific, professional, technical, or other capacities—should have more incentives, more rewards for inventive or innovative creation that goes beyond their normal duties and responsibilities. They need and deserve the incentives and the recognition that stimulate extra, creative efforts. Therefore, the proper approach is legislation to establish the rights of employees in certain inventions that are closely derived from the employee's job or that can reasonably be connected to the job and to establish the employer's duty to compensate the employee when the employee's invention goes beyond the ordinary boundaries of the job. Of course, any other invention that is produced by the worker on the worker's own time or is unrelated to the job should be the property of that worker.

REGULATING THE FLOW OF TECHNICAL INFORMATION

Every effort should be made to improve the availability of information that affects technological innovation, in order to facilitate additional innovation by the private sector. But guidelines should be developed on international flows of information to stop what is essentially a one-way flow of scientific and technological information—out of the United States to foreign nations, including the Soviet Union and Soviet bloc nations.

A serious problem exists in terms of the deliberate export of innovation-stimulating knowledge and processes and equipment. Short-term profits and short-term balance-of-payments problems are wrongly used to justify a long-term undermining of the U.S. competitive position in the world economy.

It is also a matter of concern that access to U.S.-developed scientific and technical information, much of it with national security implications, is so available to other nations, including nations hostile to American society and to the American form of government.

Too often a simple slogan about "free trade in ideas" is used as a substitute for serious consideration of the one-way nature of the diffusion of America's scientific and technical information through a wide variety of publications and computerized information sources. In a free society there are no simple solutions to this problem, but certainly there must be some better answers. At the very least, the United States should insist on a quid pro quo exchange with foreign nations of information on innovations as well as of scientific, technical, and other innovation-stimulating data.

LABOR'S AGENDA

At present, U.S. research and development is highly concentrated in the private sector. One hundred large companies account for 80 percent of industry R&D. Eight account for 35 percent: General Motors, IBM, Rockwell International, Ford, Lockheed, AT&T, General Electric, United Technologies.

And yet, innovation in America may depend far more on the health of smaller high-technology companies than on the well-financed, highly organized operations of the corporate giants which dominate the U.S. economy to an extraordinary degree.

Unfortunately, comprehensive information on the structure and operations of these giant corporations is woefully lacking. Much more adequate public disclosure of basic economic information about these quasi-public private corporations must be forthcoming, going far beyond the quarterly line-of-business reports required by the Federal Trade Commission and the reports required by the Securities and Exchange Commission.

A full-scale congressional examination of the American economy is urgently needed to provide Congress and the public with facts on innovation and the role of big business in advancing and/or retarding innovation in the United States. There are precedents for such congressional investigation in the 1930s studies by the Temporary National Economic Committee (TNEC) and in the congressional investigations conducted by the late Senators Estes Kefauver (D-Tenn.) and Philip Hart (D-Mich.).

A new congressional investigation should develop the facts on such economic developments as business mergers, interlocking relationships among giant corporations and banks, their domination of key parts of the national economy, their effects on prices and America's position in the world economy, and their impact on American communities and democratic institutions.

Some business mergers have been aimed at acquisition of innovation—others at suppressing innovation. And some mergers generate inflation as acquiring corporations raise prices to justify inflated (i.e., watered) stock prices. The nation needs facts on such corporate activities.

In the larger sense, not alone in terms of technology-induced change, but in terms of all change and growth in America's corporations, it's time that America's corporations are judged not on their bottom-line profit figures alone, but rather on their responsibility toward their workers and the communities in which they operate. Why can't the XYZ Corporation be judged to have had a bad year in 1978 because it ended the year with fewer employees than the year before, that it provided a livelihood to fewer people than the year before? Why can't the Apex Corporation be judged to have had a bad year because it closed its plant in Akron or Columbus and left 200 or 300 people without jobs? That's surely a greater failure than a drop of one or two cents in the dividends for that year.

Furthermore, an intelligent measure of total U.S. output should recognize the social benefits derived from protecting the environment and protecting health and safety. Recognition must be afforded output gains and productivity gains in the service sector and in the government sector; the output and productivity gains taken in the form of increased leisure and better quality of life; and the need for public investment and public innovation in social goods and services as well as the need for private investment and private innovation.

Such social measures won't solve the questions of adjusting to new technology or even of adjusting to the age-old problem of greed, but they will help broaden the forms of the debate to include the social aspects of life.

Collective bargaining has a key role in meeting the human challenges of innovation and technological progress at the workplace—and this role must be expanded and strengthened.

At the same time, national full-employment programs must assure an economic climate in which collective bargaining can flourish. And these national programs must help solve the social and human adjustment problems created by new and innovative technology which lie outside the scope of collective bargaining.

If the economy is healthy and expanding, new work opportunities will develop and the benefits of technology can be enjoyed by all. Indeed, with full employment, business would be encouraged to innovate and to introduce new technology, since there would be a market for its products.

In the absence of full employment, however, rapid and thoughtless technological change can only exacerbate social problems, especially through the displacement of workers—particularly minorities and women who are just beginning to achieve job levels which permit them to enjoy the benefits of technology.

Attention, then, needs to be focused on people and accommodating technology to people and making it serve people. A strategy needs to be developed that looks at technology's dangers and develops a means to deal with its inexorable growth. More needs to be done than to concentrate on fear of its negative potential.

There is immense potential for using technology to make work processes more interesting (not less), and to make work more challenging and more satisfying (not less).

There is immense potential for using technology to reduce the workweek, to encourage educational and self-development opportunities, to enlarge interest horizons, and to improve the opportunity to enhance the human spirit.

There is immense potential for using technology to improve the environment, the safety and health of workers, and consumer product safety. The potential for misusing technology is equally immense.

Clearly, technology is itself neutral and the only question is how it is put to use. If applied badly, it is a savage beast. If it is put to use with a meanness of spirit and with an intent to enlarge profits and to further enrich those already abundantly well off, all will suffer its consequences.

If technology is applied with a soaring spirit, if it makes possible the enrichment not of the few but of the many, if it creates the opportunities finally to help the least, the left-out, and the lost, then people will be able to look back in 50 years and say we did well taming the savage beast.

NOTES

1. Graham L. Staines, and Robert P. Quinn, "American Workers Evaluate the Quality of Their Jobs," *Monthly Labor Review*, January 1979, pp. 3–12.
2. U.S. Commerce Department, Advisory Committee on Industrial Innovation, *Work Plan of the Domestic Policy Review of Industrial Innovation* (interim report), p. 7. *Final Report* (Springfield, Va.: National Technical Information Services, 1979).

11.
Making Research and Development Work

Robert M. Ranftl
Corporate Director, Engineering/Design Management
Hughes Aircraft Company

Through technology the broadest base of world population has achieved the highest standard of living known throughout history. Technology—the product of organized research and development (R&D) efforts—has clearly become the mainspring of our economy. And, with due respect to technology's impact to date, mankind has so far experienced only a hint of its ultimate potential.

Increased technological productivity enables each generation to pass on a better world to the next generation: superior concepts, materials, and methods are developed; new resources are enlisted; and existing resources are more effectively utilized—thereby endowing future generations with a greater heritage and a higher quality of life.

The direct socioeconomic impact of technology is clearly evident; our daily lives are spent in constant contact with, and are virtually dependent upon, its countless products. Correspondingly, technology fulfills an equally important indirect role in providing the indispensable technological aids so vital to achieving high productivity and competitive prices in all sectors of the economy. In essence, technology constitutes the key link in the entire productivity chain.

From a business standpoint, increased technological productivity enables organizations to give customers more product value per dollar; utilize available resources more effectively; improve internal operations; realize a greater return on capital investment; compete more effectively in the marketplace; and increase sales volume and profits.

From the individual viewpoint, productive work is rewarding, both psychologically and financially, and affords an expanded sense of personal satisfaction and self-esteem while simultaneously opening new avenues for personal growth, advancement, and higher earnings.

In a real sense, therefore, increasing technological productivity creates a "win/win" situation in which everyone gains—nations, present and future populations, stockholders, management, and employees.

Today, however, we are at an economic crossroads in our quest for achieving a higher quality of life through technology. There is serious concern about excessive inflation, energy shortages, trade imbalances, and unstable exchange rates. Already, living standards show signs of serious erosion. Only through greater productivity—particularly technological productivity—can these problems be dealt with effectively, thereby permitting an even broader base of current and future world population to achieve a higher standard of living.

THE HUGHES PRODUCTIVITY STUDY

Until recently, relatively little direct research has been done on technological productivity. An extensive productivity study was undertaken by Hughes Aircraft Company in January 1973. The objective of this study was to identify useful techniques for optimizing productivity in technology-based organizations. The study encompassed not only traditional research and development (R&D) efforts, but also key interfacing activities—marketing, contracts, finance, procurement, manufacturing information systems, support, and services. To date, the study has involved the active participation of 59 organizations in industry, government, and education; the services of 28 consultants; surveys of more than 3,500 R&D managers; and an extensive literature search.[1] In addition, valuable source data has been derived from 40 Hughes in-house management courses in operational, managerial, and personal productivity.

A report, *R&D Productivity—An Investigation of Ways to Evaluate and Improve Productivity in Technology-Based Organizations*, was published in 1974, and a comprehensive second edition was published in 1978. The report represents a consensus of the study participants, the consultants, and the authors researched in the literature. It is designed to serve a broad spectrum of managers at all levels—today's managers as well as the managers of tomorrow.

Findings of the Hughes study show that productivity improvement in virtually all organizations is "there for the asking." There are significant untapped and underutilized resources in every individual and organization; all have the potential for improvement. Furthermore, productivity improvement is warranted in profitable organizations as well as unprofitable ones, and in good times as well as bad. In practice, productivity improvement should be an integral part of the daily way of life of every individual and every organization.

Study findings show, further, that the specific approach to improving productivity is unique to each individual and to each organization; there is no universal formula. However, there are certain basic principles and techniques which encompass productivity improvement and generally apply to all organizations. The primary purpose of the study report is to identify these basic factors.

In the following sections, excerpts from the report highlight some of the study's more significant findings on how to improve operational, managerial, and employee productivity.

IMPROVING OPERATIONAL PRODUCTIVITY

Key operational functions of an enterprise—investing, organizing, staffing, planning, and control—play a critical role in the success of the enterprise and require competent and diligent attention. Each of these functions must be effectively executed by management for maximum productivity.

Investment in R&D

Prudent investment in R&D operations is basic to industrial survival and success. Since, by its nature, R&D is a long-term, ongoing process which builds on itself, it cannot be approached in a start/stop manner. Therefore, it is necessary that an organization (1) develop and maintain an effective, competently staffed, and adequately equipped R&D capability, (2) invest continually in independent R&D efforts, and (3) keep R&D plant facilities and equipment current with the state of the art through an effective updating program.

In addition, the ever-expanding use of technological aids continually adds new potential for R&D productivity improvement. Of all these aids, computers and computer-based information systems have created the greatest impact. Examples include:

- Access to scientific computers via remote and on-site time-sharing terminals.
- Interactive graphics.
- Computer augmentation of such functions as analysis, design, drafting, manufacturing, testing, cost estimating, and report preparation.
- Electronic calculators.
- Computer-output microfilm.
- Information-retrieval systems.
- Management information systems that facilitate visibility and control of operations.

It should be emphasized, however, that computers must be carefully selected and skillfully applied if their advantages are to be fully realized. Improperly applied, they can be a costly drain on productivity. Therefore, selecting computer applications for optimal productivity is a particularly important managerial responsibility.

Productive Organizations

Regardless of the organizational structure used, the following characteristics were identified in the study as common to many organizations that exhibit high productivity:

Effective Grouping of Functions. Organization structure should represent the most effective grouping of functions to achieve the organization's objectives. It should never be an end in itself, but should be viewed simply as a means of achieving the best possible use of available resources. Many managers interviewed during the study stressed the importance of organizing with clear identification of responsibility, decision making, authority, and performance accountability in mind. They further stressed the need to keep organization structures simple, flexible, and adaptive to change.

A Minimum Number of Management Levels Consistent with Effective Operation. Such an organizational structure enhances direction, provides less fragmented responsibilities, commits fewer top technical people to managerial roles while at the same time giving those in supervisory roles enough responsibility to personally develop and grow, minimizes proliferation of overhead activities, and helps prevent employees from feeling buried under excessive layers of organization.

If there are too many levels of management, the jobs at each level suffer dilution. Responsibilities that could have been carried out by those below are absorbed by the levels above. This is particularly unfortunate, since carrying out challenging responsibility is the most important single element in individual development. Furthermore, since many managers—especially middle managers—are grossly underutilized in an overexpanded organization, they frequently become bored and insecure. This situation—commonly referred to as "middle-management syndrome"—is a prime cause of low productivity.

An Optimum Level of Service and Support. The number and size of service and support activities must be carefully regulated to ensure adequate support of the R&D effort without excessive cost. Also, management should closely monitor all such activities to see that they are oriented directly toward assisting program and product-line organizations, that is, that they contribute directly to the mainstream of operations.

Titles Based on Need. Title inflation should be avoided, since it can lead to a top-heavy organization, increased overhead costs, and reduced organizational flexibility. Title inflation can be prevented by basing all titles strictly on organizational needs, and not using them as rewards or substitutes for money. Furthermore, standards for titles must be high, and titles must be awarded equitably. Titles have value only when (1) there are relatively few of them, (2) they are awarded with consistency, and (3) they are clearly based on the merits of the positions and individuals involved.

Productive Staffing

Since the performance of an R&D organization is dependent far more heavily upon its people than on any other resource, effective staffing is critically important. Participants in the study concurred that selecting the right people is the key to achieving the balance of technological and managerial capability, creativity, experience, and so on, most conducive to high productivity. To maintain this balance, they point out the need for continually introducing "new blood" into the organization. New, talented people—especially those knowledgeable in new technology—act as a stimulus to the organization and often lead directly to some of the most valuable innovations.

Selecting managers and key technical personnel is cited as the most critical staffing task. Since the overall productivity of an R&D organization is heavily dependent on the performance of its management personnel and the top 5 percent of its technical staff, standards for these positions must be particularly high. If these positions are filled by competent people, other competent people will be drawn to the organization. If, however, less competent people are selected for key roles, they usually attract similar people to positions below them.

Participants in the study offered the following recommendations on staffing for increased productivity:

- Stress quality not quantity—adding more people does not necessarily result in increased output. Before hiring new people, ensure that present people are performing to capacity.
- Don't overhire in times of expansion. The optimal staffing level appears to be about 90 percent of apparent needs; individual output seems to drop off both above and below that level. Overtime can be judiciously applied to meet temporary peak demands.
- Maintain an effective transfer policy to permit employees to move to assignments where they can be most productive.
- Delay, when feasible, replacing personnel lost through normal attrition (retirement, voluntary termination, and so on). Allow the responsibilities and workload of the remaining individuals

to increase until an optimal level is reached. In this manner retirement and attrition frequently open the way for effective job enrichment.

Productive Planning

The study indicates that effective planning improves operational productivity by (1) helping ensure the best possible use of resources—personnel, machines, materials, facilities, capital, and time; (2) integrating all aspects of a program into an efficient unified effort; (3) providing a baseline for evaluating performance and improving productivity; and (4) better preparing for future risks and contingencies. It is important to note that when the employees who will ultimately do the work being planned actually participate in developing the plans, they acquire a personal sense of involvement and a vested interest that strengthens their commitment to perform in accordance with those plans. Furthermore, planning makes employees aware of organizational goals and helps them establish a productive relationship between those goals and their personal objectives. Following are effective planning practices identified during the course of the study:

- Quantize plans whenever possible, dividing large plans into smaller units.
- Examine all pertinent trade-offs.
- Eliminate all unnecessary items and avoid excessive detail.
- Ensure realistic cost and schedule parameters.
- Optimally time-phase all important elements of a plan.
- Assure that planned budgets adequately represent the realities of effective operation.
- Examine ("debug") plans critically before implementing them.
- Develop contingency plans well in advance of potential events that may have a negative effect on the effort.
- Recognize that plans can succeed only if they are communicated effectively, are understood, and are properly carried out.
- Assign specific responsibilities for adhering to plans—stress accountability.
- Avoid overplanning.

Productive Control

Participants in the study singled out control as one of the more important but difficult problems of R&D management. They cite specifically the difficulty of establishing and meeting realistic milestones and schedules when working at the forefront of technology. Furthermore, they stress the delicate balance required in the implementation of control systems. All agreed that, if improperly applied, control systems have tremendous potential for counterproductivity among scientists and engineers. Conversely, if control is effective, it can contribute significantly to improving productivity.

Effective control systems, in essence, measure progress against plans, detect deviations, pinpoint responsibilities, indicate corrective action, and assure that all "out-of-tolerance" performance is improved.

As study participants point out, the existence of a control system does not guarantee that control exists, nor does adding more controls necessarily result in better control. It is the quality, not the quantity, of control systems that is important. Therefore, control systems must be frequently and critically appraised to ensure that they remain effective. Following are control techniques identified during the study as being particularly effective in R&D activities:

- Involve the users of a control system in the system's design.
- Control an operation at its most critical point—where the work is accomplished and the impact is greatest.
- Keep controls reasonable—do not permit too many or overly tight controls that restrict creativity, innovation, and intelligent risk taking.
- Be especially cautious about imposing any system of control across the board, or from outside the organization directly involved.
- Ensure that the control system is forward looking, so that deviations can be forecast or detected in time to make corrections before major problems arise.
- Ensure that the control system is not too time consuming or burdensome to employees.
- Keep a balance of control between tangibles and intangibles; don't overcontrol tangibles and undercontrol intangibles.

- Apply controls judiciously—ensure they are valid, simple, objective, and cost effective.
- Conduct operations reviews to maintain visibility over key operational factors.
- Conduct program reviews, system reviews, and design reviews to assess progress toward meeting milestones, and to detect and take timely action to correct problems.
- Review all control systems regularly—obtain feedback on their effectiveness from users and modify accordingly.
- Avoid overcontrol—continually monitor the "watcher" to "doer" ratio.

IMPROVING MANAGERIAL PRODUCTIVITY

Study findings clearly stress that skilled, responsible management and superior productivity are inseparable. We are entering a far more demanding era requiring greater professionalism in R&D management. Tomorrow's R&D manager—in addition to being technically qualified—must be a respected, people-oriented leader skilled in the latest techniques of behavioral science and sound business practice. Following are some specific study findings on productive management.

Leadership in Management

Of all factors, managerial leadership has the greatest leverage on productivity. Ultimately, the destiny of any organization hinges on the quality of its leadership; true leaders bring out the best in people and organizations. This is largely because leaders elicit strong, positive emotional reactions, and people tend to fulfill their needs and grow under effective leadership. Such leaders have an uncanny knack for cutting through complexity, providing practical solutions to difficult problems, successfully communicating these solutions to others, and instilling enthusiasm and a "can-do" attitude. However, while leadership is readily recognizable, it is difficult to define. No two leadership styles are the same—each style is, and should remain, unique to each individual. Furthermore, a good leader in one situation may not be a good leader in a different situation. Also, the type of leader needed depends specifically on the group to be led. Yet even the same group may require a different kind of leadership at different times in its evolution.

Most managers have some leadership ability, but unfortunately very few are outstanding leaders. Although much attention over the years has been given to developing leaders, the study showed little support for the concept of providing specialized training in leadership as an entity in itself. Rather, development of a true leader appears to be a lifelong process heavily influenced by early childhood environment. It is important, however, that while an organization cannot create leadership, it can be catalytic in enhancing the leadership potential already present.

A point particularly emphasized in the study: since leadership is basically a self-development process, it is important that top management (1) select for advancement to key managerial positions those who show leadership promise, and (2) provide the appropriate climate, opportunity, challenge, and incentive for those selected individuals to further develop their leadership skills.

Management Attention to Productivity

The approaches taken and the techniques practiced by management have tremendous potential for either stimulating or depressing productivity. Management's attitudes, actions, and personal example pervade the organization and directly affect employee attitudes, motivation, and actions. Since employees take their cues from management and respond to the perceived reward system, it is particularly important that management clearly convey (1) its feelings about the importance of productivity, (2) its strong desire to see active productivity improvement efforts throughout the organization, and (3) its intention to equitably reward increased productivity.

Management must create a proper climate for high productivity—an open, performance-oriented, professional climate where (1) organizational objectives and performance goals are clearly identified, (2) high standards prevail, (3) effective communication and technology exchange are emphasized, (4) politics and gamesmanship are minimized, (5) a high degree of personal job freedom is advocated, (6) equity prevails, and (7) producers are rewarded at the expense of nonproducers.

Effective Direction of the Work Force

While the approaches taken by management have great impact on productivity, any given management approach or technique cannot be expected to stimulate all employees or apply to all situations in the same way. Therefore, productive managers must exercise acute awareness and perception, continually picking up and interpreting cues and tailoring their approaches and techniques as appropriate for each situation.

Study participants were asked to identify specific managerial objectives that had, in their experience, led to high productivity. The following objectives were frequently cited:

- Establish high performance standards and promote personnel and product excellence.
- Optimize the use of all available resources and be alert for unused and underutilized resources strive; particularly for total involvement of the entire work force.
- Develop a sense of entrepreneurship throughout the organization, ensuring that everyone is performance-oriented.
- Delegate authority, responsibility, decision making, control, and accountability as far down the organization as practical.
- Manage time effectively by setting priorities and deadlines and by stopping nonproductive efforts as soon as possible.
- Invest in future technology through sound basic and applied research and development programs.
- Be open-minded and imaginative, quick to see the potential of new concepts and ideas.
- Always search for more productive ways of doing things; encourage technological innovation and the use of the latest technological aids.
- Be alert for, and correct, counterproductive factors within the organization.
- Strive for preventive rather than corrective action.
- Encourage an effective working relationship between R&D and all other related company and customer activities.
- Assure that no individual or facet of the organization gets shortchanged or overemphasized.
- Minimize organization politics and gamesmanship; avoid the connotation of "insiders" and "outsiders."

- Maintain effective, equitable compensation and promotion policies.

Study results stress that to supervise effectively, managers must exhibit a genuine interest in and concern for employees. When employees feel that their abilities are respected and that proper recognition and reward are given for their efforts, they will normally perform effectively and measure up to management's expectations. Only when management gives employees proper attention will employees give management proper attention.

Throughout the study, participants were asked to identify the specific supervisory techniques of an R&D manager that they felt would lead to high productivity. The following were frequently mentioned:

- Make a genuine effort to understand subordinates; know their strengths and weaknesses, their primary sources of motivation, their career goals, and so on.
- Effectively integrate the abilities of all individuals within the organization.
- Match individuals to the jobs for which they are best suited.
- Involve subordinates in planning, goal setting, and decisions that affect them.
- Let employees demonstrate their capabilities and grow professionally; help subordinates prepare themselves for jobs to which they aspire.
- Manage by expectation; set high standards and high expectations, and encourage subordinates to achieve them.
- Be available to subordinates through an open-door policy.
- Provide subordinates with feedback on their performance; recognize and reward achievement; cite mistakes fairly and tactfully.
- Represent equitably all subordinates and their work to higher management—whenever possible, have the person who originated a unique idea or did an outstanding job be the one to brief management.
- Be sensitive to factors that cause employee dissatisfaction and frustration; get to the root of such factors and resolve conflicts in a timely manner.

- Serve as a buffer to protect subordinates from many of the daily administrative and operational frustrations.
- Maintain an effective flow of two-way communication.
- Serve as a catalyst to ensure effective technology exchange within the organization.
- Avoid imposing personal standards on subordinates and "over-supervising."

IMPROVING EMPLOYEE PRODUCTIVITY

The performance of an R&D organization is determined almost entirely by the integrated performance of its people. Study participants consistently pointed out that among individuals and organizations, most differences in performance are attributed to variations in employee attitudes and motivation. The key to improving employee productivity, therefore, is for management to (1) be aware of and understand employee attitudes, and (2) be a catalyst for an environment in which the level of motivation of each employee is maximized. This requires strong "people orientation" on the part of management.

Following are some key study findings on personnel administration.

Job Assignments

When assigning work, much can be done to help assure that the ensuing effort will be productive. Most important, people must know what is expected of them. A common study finding was that lack of sufficient direction and definition when assigning work often results in gross inefficiencies and wasted effort—a major drain on R&D productivity.

Before an assignment is started, a discussion should be held between the supervisor and subordinate and agreement reached on three basic factors: (1) work to be done, standards to be adhered to, and goals to be achieved; (2) budget and schedule constraints; and (3) criteria for evaluation of performance. Furthermore, care should be taken not to fragment responsibility; people normally are more productive when they are responsible for a total, clearly identifiable task.

Subsequently, people should be allowed to plan their own work; this gives them a vested interest in the job and a strong incentive to meet their own commitments. Within broad but practical limits, they should be permitted to do the job their own way.

Reassignment of a person part way through an effort should be avoided unless it is absolutely necessary. This is not only frequently demotivating to the individual, but a replacement may need considerable time to become familiar with the assignment—usually a period of decreased productivity.

A new employee's firm work assignment within the organization can be very important, according to study participants, in establishing a pattern of high productivity. Unfortunately, a new employee often suffers early disillusionment and demotivation by being given an inadequate work assignment or being asked to temporarily fill in time doing a "make-work" project. Prompt assignment to a well-chosen job can do much to get the new employee started performing productively. Also of significance, the first assignment introduces the new employee to responsibilities, people, and paths of communication that can significantly influence his or her long-term effectiveness and ultimate position in the organization.

Study participants were asked to identify specific practices for enhancing the productivity of job assignments. Following are frequently mentioned practices:

- Provide assignments that lead to a feeling of accomplishment and a sense of contributing and belonging.
- Ensure that assignments are important to the organization's overall objectives and have management's active interest and support.
- Assign work in keeping with individual capabilities. Avoid misemployment, and never get employees "in over their heads."
- Ensure that assignments make effective use of employees' skills and talents while, at the same time, affording them an opportunity to develop new skills and grow.
- Keep assignments from being overspecialized—jobs should not be divided too finely.
- Ensure that assignments are clearly defined and involve specific responsibility; avoid open-ended assignments whenever possible.

- Focus on end results (technical performance, costs, schedules, and so on), giving the employee as much freedom as possible for work planning and decision making.
- Make schedules tight but realistic; permit adequate time to do the job effectively.
- Provide employees with the necessary resources to do the job properly.
- Minimize the amount of nonengineering work done by engineers.
- Strive for equity of work load among employees; don't overload good people just because they "always come through."
- Change or expand employee assignments periodically; don't destroy capable people by trapping them in "indispensable" functions that lead nowhere.
- Maintain an adequate backlog of work. The productivity of people waiting for new assignments is usually relatively low, and existing projects tend to overrun if there are no new assignments in sight.

Misemployment

Study participants feel that misemployment is a particularly important but frequently overlooked factor in reduced productivity. Many employees who are underproductive in their present jobs could be more productive in other jobs. In some cases, employees may actually be in the wrong type of work; in other cases, they may be overqualified for their jobs, a situation frequently resulting in severe demotivation and lowered productivity.

The most common misemployment problem—the one that represents the greatest drain on overall productivity—is "moderate misemployment." In this case the employee performs satisfactorily but is not "turned on" by the job. Thus, the employee works far below his or her potential level of productivity, viewing the work merely as a "job with a pay check" rather than as a challenging segment of a rewarding career. Frequently, only a change in assignment is necessary to reverse this condition. Since the potential productivity gain is significant, study participants recommend constant concern by management to place employees in the right jobs.

Equitable Parallel Promotion Ladders

Parallel ladders of advancement—managerial and technical—are used by most organizations that participated in the study. Technical ladders help prevent scientists and engineers who are outstanding in a technical field from being needlessly drawn into management where their performance may be poor and their careers eventually imperiled—a classic case of misemployment. The following observations regarding parallel ladders were made by study participants:

- Parallel ladders can and should be developed for all specialty fields (e.g., marketing, contracts, finance, material, manufacturing, support, and so on), not just for scientific fields.
- Parallel ladders within any given field should have similar salary scales, benefits, and status symbols. Ideally, except at the very top, there should be the same number of "rungs" on each ladder.
- To preclude premature selection of a career ladder, the first level or two of parallel ladders can be common, converting the ladders into "Y-shaped" structures.
- Parallel ladders are frequently not properly emphasized or implemented; there is a tendency to overemphasize the managerial ladder.
- The parallel scientific ladder of advancement should never be used as a "burial ground" for individuals who do not perform adequately on the managerial ladder.

Technological Obsolescence

An important problem in R&D associated with low productivity is that of technological obsolescence. According to the study, this "falling behind in one's field" does not seem a major threat to R&D efforts as a whole, but unfortunately it does affect adversely a number of individuals. The primary causes of technological obsolescence cited in the study are: (1) lack of desire to keep up and learn to do new things—frequently the employee's fault, and (2) lack of job challenge—frequently management's fault. Lack of basic ability seems to be a minor factor; conversely, lack of stimulation, challenge, or motivation appears to be a major factor.

Technological obsolescence tends to beget itself, that is, a negative syndrome ensues, wherein loss of motivation, lack of vitality, and lowered self-confidence feed on one another, all spiraling downward. In extreme cases, employees may simply "retire in position."

Although older employees are more likely to become technologically obsolete, no consistent correlation was found between age and technological obsolescence. Study findings indicate that a great many scientists and engineers maintain creative output and high performance until retirement age and far beyond, and frequently are considerably more productive than their younger counterparts. Scientists engaged in basic research appear less likely than engineers to become technologically obsolete; by the nature of their daily work, they tend to be more stimulated to keep up in their fields. Also, particularly creative people are less likely to become obsolete, since they live closer to the forefront of technology and tend to be more challenged by, and adaptable to, changing times and technologies.

Formalized efforts to reduce technological obsolescence, the study finds, must be skillfully planned if they are to be beneficial. Programs for updating technologically obsolescent personnel are most effective when they are voluntarily pursued at the initiation of the individual. The primary role of the organization is to be catalytic: it should assign employees stimulating, challenging work; encourage them and keep their expectations high; reward them for increased ability and improved performance; and reimburse them for outside training expenses. Formal training programs that are imposed and directed by the organization tend to be of less value. Employee rotation programs, an important exception, can be very effective in reducing technological obsolescence.

Management should give special attention to keeping expectations high in all employees, but particularly in older employees. Age, along with many years on the job, often tends to condition people into lowering their expectations; the challenge to keep up and grow diminishes. Older employees need renewed confidence that management considers them important to the organization, and that recognition and reward will, in fact, result from high productivity on their part.

In the case of individuals who do not respond to the need to overcome technological obsolescence, both the organization and the individual can usually benefit if such employees are channeled into jobs where they can be more effective. Employees who can no longer work at the forefront of technology may very likely be productive in other types of assignments. Such employees usually have considerable knowledge and experience that they have amassed over the years. If this knowledge and experience is effectively channeled and utilized, the value of these employees need not be lost to the organization. Unfortunately, all too frequently such employees are pushed aside and "written off" as liabilities.

Incentive and Reward Systems

In the R&D environment, the selection of incentives that stimulate employee productivity is a particularly important task. Study participants offered the following basic observations concerning such incentives:

- Every job should provide an adequate psychological reward as well as an adequate monetary reward.
- Equity is fundamental to the successful application of incentives.
- Management must maintain a continual overview of the equity of salaries, titles, status symbols, and so on.
- Wage and salary policies should be kept flexible, so that compensation can "track" significant swings in productivity levels.
- There should be a clear relationship between performance and reward. Rewards should be scaled to contribution.
- Simplicity should be rewarded over complexity, when simplicity does the job just as well.
- Fringe benefits should be kept within scope, since they have little relationship to productivity and employees tend to regard them as "rights." (However, although such benefits have little motivational value, below-average benefits can be demotivating. Therefore, from a practical point of view, benefits should be comparable to those offered by other organizations that compete in the same labor market.)

Periodic salary reviews are of great importance in providing employees with "bottom-line" feedback on management's appraisal of their work performance. However, the motivational effects of a salary review are, unfortunately, usually short-lived; the motivational boost tends to wear off within a few weeks or, at best, several months. This is why it is highly advantageous to conduct separate performance reviews six months prior to salary reviews: the employee is much more likely to improve and sustain performance after the performance review in anticipation of the salary review.

PRODUCTIVITY EVALUATION

Due to the abstract and complex nature of research and development efforts, productivity evaluation presents a unique and difficult problem. Following are study observations on this subject:

- There are two basic approaches to evaluating productivity: (1) quantitative measurement, and (2) qualitative assessment. Highly structured, repetitive tasks tend to be suited to quantitative measurement; creative, abstract, nonrepetitive tasks tend to be better suited to qualitative assessment. Between these two extremes there is a mix of quantitative and qualitative factors.
- In R&D work, qualitative assessment is often more practical and meaningful than quantitative measurement, primarily because of the nature of the work. R&D work tends to be creative and complex, dealing predominantly with concepts and ideas. Frequently, something entirely new and different is developed, and great uncertainty is involved. Also, the ultimate results of R&D efforts are often not evident until long after the completion of those efforts. An additional complication is created by the fact that R&D technology is constantly evolving. Tasks that have been traditionally unmeasurable may, in time, become measurable—only to be replaced by more advanced unmeasurable tasks.
- A universally applicable evaluation system is not feasible. Rather, R&D productivity evaluation is unique to each organization and to the specific work involved, that is, evaluation must be tailored to each application. Furthermore, work should be evaluated at the point where the work is done. The farther away from this point the evaluation takes place, the more obscure and less meaningful the results become.
- Evaluation is best conducted by responsible line managers within their own organizations. The line manager knows what

information is most relevant in determining the productivity of the organization and is best equipped to devise and operate the evaluation system, judge results, and implement improvement. Farther down in each of these organizations, first-line supervision—with proper skill and experience—can be very effective in evaluating individual employee productivity. Close association with the employees and their work makes the first-line supervisor uniquely qualified for this task. Day-to-day informal assessment, interpreted with sound judgment and integrated over an adequate period of time, is particularly desirable and useful.

- In R&D work, the most effective level of evaluation often involves a group of people working in a common effort. Their output can typically be evaluated in terms of (1) design performance achieved compared to requirements, (2) actual cost and schedule of completed designs compared to the planned cost and schedule, and (3) overall success of the product in the hands of the customer compared to customer expectations.
- Any attempt to evaluate productivity should take into account employee response to that evaluation. Most employees are apprehensive about having their output formally and critically evaluated. In such situations, employees may take fewer risks, be less innovative, and tend to play it safe by working on "sure things"—factors all counter to creative, productive R&D. Also, where employees know what specific factors are being measured, they are prone to give more attention to those factors and less to others that are not being measured. Such action will likely be counter to the best interests of the organization and can completely invalidate the results of any evaluation system.
- Various basic techniques can be enlisted to evaluate R&D productivity. Such techniques include:
    1. The establishment and monitoring of valid quantitative productivity indicators, as for example, profit per R&D payroll dollar, profit generated per R&D dollar spent, and so on.
    2. The establishment and monitoring of valid qualitative productivity indicators, as for example, the quality and usefulness of ideas generated, product performance through its life cycle, and so on.

3. Work sampling.
4. The tracking of meaningful ratios and trends.
5. The observation of performance patterns.

- When evaluating productivity, one should critically differentiate between work and valuable work (always ask whether the work is necessary in the first place). Avoid confusing activity with results, efficiency with effectiveness, and working hard with working "smart."

PRODUCTIVITY PROFILES

Because quantitative measurement of R&D productivity is difficult, many managers have developed, through their experience, informal guidelines or indicators for identifying productive individuals and organizations. During the study, executives, managers, scientists, engineers, educators, and consultants were asked what indicators they use most to identify highly productive individuals and organizations. In addition, the literature search revealed a number of such observations. While the inputs from all of these sources were expressed in a variety of ways, they focused on a few basic characteristics. The profiles identified in figures 1-4 (pages 226–238) present these characteristics, with typical observations under each.

A NEED FOR ACTION

Currently, the United States is the world leader in technology, but time and technology are moving swiftly; we cannot afford to rest on our laurels. The portents of economic change signal the need for immediate action: greater technological productivity is needed right now. Clearly, technological productivity constitutes the key link in the entire productivity chain and, as such, is the most important challenge facing today's technologist, whether in management, research, applied technology, or support.

The potential gains from increased productivity for any individual, organization, or nation are great. Such gains, however, can be realized only if positive steps are taken to improve productivity. Fundamentally, each of us has an inherent responsibility to apply, in the most effective manner possible, the resources with which we are endowed or entrusted. We must always seek a better way and try

(text continued on p. 239)

PROFILE OF A PRODUCTIVE EMPLOYEE

Since R&D productivity focuses on people, it is important to be able to readily identify high producers. Many study participants felt that while no two individuals are alike, an envelope might be developed to include common characteristics of particularly productive employees. Key characteristics contained within this envelope are listed below. Typical observations follow each characteristic.

Is well qualified for the job. Job qualification was considered basic to R&D productivity. Without the proper job qualifications, high productivity was considered out of the question.

Typical observations:

- Is intelligent and learns quickly.
- Is professionally/technically competent—keeps abreast of his/her field.
- Is creative and innovative—exhibits ingenuity and versatility.
- Knows the job thoroughly.
- Works "smart"—uses common sense—organizes work efficiently—uses time effectively—doesn't get bogged down.
- Is consistently concerned with design performance, quality, reliability, maintainability, safety, producibility, productivity, cost, and schedules.
- Looks for improvement, but knows when to stop perfecting.
- Is considered valuable by supervision.
- Has a record of successful achievement.
- Continuously develops self.

Is highly motivated. Motivation was termed a critical factor—a "turned-on" employee is well on the road to high productivity.

Typical observations:

- Is self-motivated—takes initiative—is a self-starter and self-driver—has a strong sense of commitment.

Figure 11.1.

- Is persevering—productively works on an assignment until it is properly completed—gets the job done in spite of obstacles.
- Has a strong will to work—keeps busy.
- Works effectively with little or no supervision.
- Sees things to be done and takes appropriate action.
- Likes challenge—likes to have abilities tested—enjoys solving problems.
- Has a questioning mind—demonstrates a high degree of intellectual curiosity.
- Displays constructive discontent—"thinks" improvement into everything.
- Is goal-/achievement-/results-oriented.
- Has a strong sense of urgency and timing.
- Has a high energy level and directs that energy effectively.
- Gets satisfaction from a job well done.
- Believes in a fair day's work for a fair day's pay.
- Contributes beyond what is expected.

Has a positive job orientation. A person's attitude toward work assignments greatly affects his/her performance. A positive attitude was cited as a major factor in employee productivity.

Typical observations:

- Enjoys the job and is proud of it—looks to it as the primary source of need satisfaction.
- Sets high standards.
- Has good work habits.
- Becomes engrossed in the work.
- Is accurate, reliable, and consistent.
- Respects management and its objectives.

Figure 11.1. *(continued)*

- Has good rapport with management.
- Takes direction well—readily accepts challenges and new assignments.
- Is flexible and adaptive to change.

Is mature. Maturity is a personal attribute rated important by study participants. A mature employee displays consistent performance and requires minimal supervision.

Typical observations:

- Has high integrity—is genuine/honest/sincere.
- Has a strong sense of responsibility.
- Knows his/her personal strengths and weaknesses.
- Is self-reliant, self-disciplined, and self-confident.
- Has deserved self-respect.
- Lives in the "real" world—deals effectively with the environment.
- Is emotionally stable and secure.
- Performs effectively under pressure.
- Learns from experience.
- Has healthy ambition—wants to grow professionally.

Interfaces effectively. The ability to establish positive interpersonal relationships is an asset that does much to enhance productivity.

Typical observations:

- Exhibits social intelligence.
- Is personable—is accepted by and interfaces effectively with superiors and colleagues.
- Communicates effectively—expresses thoughts well—is clear and concise—is open to suggestions—is a good listener.
- Works productively in team efforts—is cooperative—shares ideas—helps colleagues.
- Exhibits a positive attitude and displays enthusiasm.

Figure 11.1. *(continued)*

PROFILE OF A PRODUCTIVE MANAGER

The characteristics cited above, used to identify productive employees, are also applicable to managers. However, since management plays such a key role in organizational productivity, the study also sought special *additional* indicators which identify productive managers. These indicators are listed below, with typical observations included under each.

Is competent at staffing. If an organization is to be productive, its manager must ensure that it is staffed with capable personnel.

Typical observations:

- Has high recruiting standards.
- Is skilled at recognizing talent.
- Attracts and holds capable, productive people.
- Is not afraid to hire top people—does not feel personally threatened by them.
- Maintains an optimal balance of the talents and capabilities needed to achieve the objectives of the organization.
- Continually introduces "new blood" into the organization.

Directs the organization's efforts effectively. Skillful direction has great potential for increasing productivity.

Typical observations:

- Responds to the organization's current and long-range needs.
- Applies sound, practical technical and administrative judgment.
- Exhibits conceptual skills—keeps everything in proper perspective.
- Integrates and synchronizes the application of available resources.
- Is results-oriented.

Figure 11.2.

- Supplies goals and keeps work properly focused.
- Delegates effectively—clearly defines assignments, responsibilities, and commensurate authority—tries not to second-guess subordinates.
- Is competent in dealing with people—is candid and straightforward—skillfully influences others to work effectively.
- Always keeps things under control—continually monitors performance, e.g., technical progress, schedules, and costs.
- Knows when to stop work on a project.
- Continually assesses productivity and strives to improve it.
- Manages effectively in good times or bad.
- Consistently sets a good example.
- Is willing to be held accountable for stewardship.

Is competent at handling complexities and problems and in dealing with new concepts. The problems encountered by an R&D organization typically involve trade-offs among a wide variety of known and unknown parameters. Skill in handling these complex entities is an important asset for achieving high productivity.

Typical observations:

- Has a good understanding of the work and problems involved.
- Does the job with full consideration for all associated limitations and trade-offs—keeps realities in perspective—adapts strategies accordingly.
- Recognizes good ideas and accurately senses their intrinsic value.
- Skillfully identifies potential new technologies and product lines.
- Is not easily misled—sees things in their true light—readily detects inconsistencies, inaccuracies, and inefficiencies.

Figure 11.2. *(continued)*

- Is skilled at improvising—effectively identifies and removes roadblocks and bottlenecks.
- Effectively develops and applies preventive and corrective measures—considers contingencies and is prepared.
- Pinpoints problems quickly—digs into problems, distills them down to their simplest terms, asks pertinent questions, gets critical information, considers all alternatives, makes necessary assumptions and trade-offs, and arrives at effective decisions.
- Is willing to take calculated risks.
- Handles emergencies decisively—is not prone to "crisis management."

Is a skillful communicator. Productivity in the R&D environment depends heavily on effective interfaces between individuals and groups whose areas of specialization often have a minimum of common ground. The manager frequently must provide that common ground.

Typical observations:

- Interfaces effectively with superiors, peers, and subordinates.
- Keeps superiors, peers, and subordinates properly informed.
- Maintains an effective flow of two-way communication.
- Is readily accessible—maintains an open-door policy.
- Encourages effective exchange of technical and administrative information within the organization.
- Is skillful at oral and written communication—conveys ideas clearly, concisely, and persuasively—makes effective presentations.
- Conducts meetings skillfully—sets proper tone and pace—maintains focus, draws out and clarifies relevant points, and channels discussion effectively toward productive conclusions and actions.

Figure 11.2. *(continued)*

Supports and guides subordinates in their work performance and encourages their full participation in the work environment. The manager of a productive R&D organization helps subordinates optimize their job performance and achieve their career goals.

Typical observations:

- Knows subordinates, their capabilities, and their aspirations.
- Respects subordinates and their individual differences—is sensitive to their feelings—earns their respect.
- Makes everyone involved a party to the action—involves employees in decisions that affect them—makes all members feel they are important to the team effort.
- Provides effective assignments and background information necessary for performance of those assignments.
- Holds subordinates responsible for performance—requires thorough and timely completion of assignments.
- Provides effective feedback—appraises performance skillfully.
- Helps subordinates in their personal development and career pursuits.
- Serves an ego-building role with respect to subordinates—supplies necessary motivational reinforcement.
- Gives appropriate credit—rewards fairly—praises publicly (criticizes privately).
- Is receptive to employees' concerns, ideas, and suggestions—is empathetic and a good listener.
- Gets involved when subordinates have problems—helps them and backs them up—promptly corrects employee grievances.
- Serves as a buffer to protect subordinates from many of the daily administrative and operational frustrations.

Figure 11.2. *(continued)*

PROFILE OF AN OUTSTANDING LEADER

Leadership is an elusive quality which in R&D, as in other fields, is an asset with great potential for stimulating productivity. Although many managers have distinct leadership abilities in certain aspects of their jobs, very few qualify as outstanding leaders. The few who do are unusually competent, dynamic, confident individuals who somehow "have it all together." Such leaders are not only vitally needed today but will be needed in greater numbers to meet the complex challenges of tomorrow's R&D world.

Study participants identified the following as distinctive qualities of an outstanding leader:

Sets a particularly positive example as a person. The outstanding leader exhibits characteristics that stamp him/her as a "person of note."

Typical observations:

- Is unusually competent.
- Has quality and quickness of mind.
- Is particularly creative, innovative, and nontraditional—a unique individualist.
- Is highly self-motivated, self-confident, and self-directing.
- Has extremely high integrity, values, and standards—stands above organizational politics and gamesmanship.
- Has unusually high motives—is dedicated—has a firm sense of purpose and commitment—is never self-serving.
- Has a strong positive orientation.
- Displays total self-command.
- Has a high level of deserved self-respect and self-esteem.
- Accepts the role of leader with appropriate humility—enjoys the role and is clearly accepted as a leader.

Figure 11.3.

- Is willing to work harder than other members of the team.
- Has particularly high vitality, stamina, and reserve energy.
- Is continually searching/learning/developing/expanding/evolving.
- Is a "winner."

Takes a dynamic approach to activities. The outstanding leader approaches tasks with verve and enthusiasm, is always oriented toward improvement.

Typical observations:

- Is action-oriented—has a compelling drive to accomplish and achieve.
- Is quick to size up the merit of people, ideas, and opportunities.
- Uses a persuasive personality rather than force of power to get things done.
- Is tenacious—perseveres in the face of obstacles—always sees things through to successful completion.
- Is always willing to "stand up and be counted"—makes necessary decisions and does what has to be done, even though such action may be unpopular and result in adverse criticism.
- Continually seeks new and better ways.
- Is a visionary—is unusually skilled at predicting future technological and operational needs and applications.
- Always sees new challenges and new fields to conquer.

Brings out the best in people. Getting people to do their best and to work together effectively is a special talent of the outstanding leader.

Typical observations:

- Is strongly people-oriented.
- Exhibits great respect for human dignity.

Figure 11.3. *(continued)*

- Is particularly skilled in motivational processes and in dealing with people.
- Has well-defined, meaningful goals and successfully inspires associates to help achieve them.
- Has confidence in people and effectively communicates that confidence.
- Brings about dynamic synergism within groups.
- Is stimulating and catalytic—instills enthusiasm—maintains an exciting organizational climate—communicates a "can-do" attitude in all actions.
- Helps subordinates achieve their full potential.

Demonstrates great skill in directing day-to-day operations. The outstanding leader exhibits unusual ability in dynamically directing operations for maximum results.

Typical observations:

- Conceptually integrates all facets of the operation.
- Has a strong sense of timing and limits—accurately senses "when" and "how much" in each situation.
- Has an uncanny knack for cutting through complexity—effectively sorts out irrelevancies and identifies the real driving factors—provides practical solutions to difficult problems and successfully communicates these solutions to others.
- Senses what might go wrong and develops contingency plans.
- Maintains control of all situations, performing with relative ease during times of stress.
- Displays an "elegant" simplicity in all actions.

Figure 11.3. *(continued)*

PROFILE OF A PRODUCTIVE ORGANIZATION

Organizations as well as individuals should be evaluated for productivity. The study revealed that managers responsible for R&D organizations use, formally or informally, indicators similar to those used in identifying productive individuals. The most commonly used indicators focus on the basic characteristics identified below. Typical observations follow each characteristic.

The organization is effectively staffed and is people-oriented. Without these qualities it has virtually no chance of achieving high productivity.

Typical observations:

- Has effective and respected management/leadership.
- Has outstanding personnel in key positions.
- Uses people to the best of their abilities—matches the assignment to the individual.
- Provides the proper opportunities and performance feedback necessary for personal growth and advancement.
- Respects employees and their individual differences.
- Is sensitive and responsive to employee concerns.
- Keeps employees informed.
- Has an effective system for recognizing and rewarding achievement.

The organization has high standards. A reputation for high technical and managerial ethics is the hallmark of a productive R&D organization.

Typical observations:

- Stresses managerial, employee, operational, and product integrity.
- Is performance-/quality-/reliability-/safety-/cost-conscious.

Figure 11.4.

- Maintains justice and equity in all operations—discourages politics and gamesmanship.
- Continually strives to improve operations.

The organization operates in a sound, competitive manner. Prudent business operation and a readiness to perform and compete are necessary for productive enterprise.

Typical observations:

- Is responsive to the customer/market.
- Has clearly established, worthwhile goals.
- Meets its goals/commitments—consistently gives timely responses—can be counted on.
- Is profitable—a strong business sense prevails.
- Maintains a balanced capability which is sufficiently broad in scope to assure stability.
- Is always current with the state of the art.
- Is totally committed.
- Keeps costs under control—lives within budgets.
- Requires accountability.
- Maintains a sound business backlog—consistently gets an adequate share of business in its field.
- Affords reasonable organizational growth, or at least relative stability.
- Responds quickly and effectively to emergencies.

The organization has a creative and productive atmosphere. In the R&D environment, factors that are conducive to creativity correspondingly stimulate productivity.

Typical observations:

- Provides an open, creative, professional work environment.
- Encourages innovation and the taking of calculated risks.

Figure 11.4. *(continued)*

- Furnishes a continual flow of meaningful and challenging assignments.
- Maintains effective communication and technology exchange.
- Provides up-to-date facilities, equipment, and technological aids.
- Effectively recognizes, channels, and manages creative ideas.
- Consistently conceives, promotes, and successfully conducts independent research and development programs.
- Successfully selects and develops new areas of product expansion —is willing to invest in embryonic concepts of significant ultimate potential.
- Dares to be different—is not satisfied with merely matching the competition.
- Is leading the way to the future and advancing the state of the art.

The organization has a "can-do" attitude and high esprit de corps. The enthusiasm, dedication, and teamwork of the people in an organization can never be underestimated as key factors in achieving optimal productivity.

Typical observations:

- Employees exhibit high vitality, a genuine sense of commitment, and a determination to perform.
- Employees show mature confidence in the face of difficult situations.
- Employees have a strong team spirit—they enjoy their jobs and are proud of their contribution to the team.
- Team members depend on each other rather than compete with each other—they exhibit strong interpersonal trust.
- Employees have confidence that management fully supports them and their efforts.
- Employees have strong organizational loyalty.

Figure 11.4. *(continued)*

to leave things better than we found them. Improved productivity requires awareness, commitment, ingenuity, action, and perseverance. The opportunity is there—what we do with it depends upon ourselves.

NOTES

1. Productivity study participants: Air Force Flight Dynamics Laboratory; Air Force Rocket Propulsion Laboratory; Air Force Systems Command; Aluminum Company of America; Army Electronics Command; Army Missile Command; Bell Laboratories; Bethlehem Steel Corp.; Boeing Aerospace Co.; Burroughs Corp.; California Institute of Technology; Celanese Corp.; Chrysler Corp.; Collins Radio Group (Rockwell); Cornell University; Corning Glass Works; Dow Chemical Co.; Eastman Kodak Co.; E. I. du Pont de Nemours and Co.; Exxon Corp.; Federal Aviation Administration; Fiber Industries, Inc.; Firestone Tire & Rubber Co.; General Motors Corp.; Goddard Space Flight Center; Goodyear Tire & Rubber Co.; Harvard University; Hughes Aircraft Co.; Lockheed Missiles & Space Co.; LTV Aerospace Corp.; Massachusetts Institute of Technology; Merck and Co., Inc.; Minnesota Mining & Manufacturing Co.; Miramar Naval Air Station; Motorola, Inc.; National Bureau of Standards; National Science Foundation; Naval Air Systems Command; Naval Electronics Laboratory Center; New York University; Northwestern University; Philco-Ford Corp.; Princeton University; Rand Corp.; RCA Corp.; Rockwell International; Sperry Rand Corp.; Stanford Research Institute; Stanford University; Texaco, Inc.; TRW, Inc.; United States Steel Corp.; United Technologies Corp.; University of California, Los Angeles; University of Michigan; University of Minnesota; University of Pennsylvania; University of Southern California; Xerox Corp.

III.
HUMAN FACTORS

12.
Productivity and People

Jerome M. Rosow
President, Work in America Institute, Inc.

The rate of productivity growth in the United States has been declining in recent years. Productivity has been dropping in other industrial countries, too, but the decline in the United States started earlier and lasted longer, offering more cause for alarm.

Although economists have advanced a variety of theories to account for the decline of the productivity rate, there is general agreement that productivity gains in the 1980s will depend in large part on four factors: the availability of capital; the rate of interest on capital; the introduction of new technology; and, not least of all, the productive quality of the work force. Which of these factors will assume the most importance depends to some degree on inflation.

Inflation, which soared to new heights at the beginning of the eighties, has acted as a disincentive to some methods of achieving productivity gains and as an incentive to others. While runaway interest rates have placed a serious damper on capital investment, the high cost of wages and benefits has encouraged organizations to manage their work forces more efficiently for greater productivity. Coming full circle, productivity is acknowledged to be a prime weapon in the battle against inflation, thus placing further emphasis on the enlightened use of human resources in every occupation and at every level of the organization.

For example, early in 1980, the chief executive of one of America's largest steelmaking corporations asked permission to send a delegation of senior managers to Work in America Institute for advice on how to improve productivity. When the Institute offered to discuss problems of technological change, he pointed out that his primary interest was in the human element—that the corporation could no longer afford to invest in major technological change or capital investment. It had to raise productivity through its employees. As it becomes apparent that the surest route to higher productivity is through people, more companies will follow suit.

The purpose of this chapter is to examine the role of people in improving productivity and how organizations and society can tap this valuable resource for productivity gains. Initially, it discusses the background of productivity problems, describes the work force of the 1980s and its potential, reviews the forces that spur productivity through people and those that oppose it, and offers some practical options to organizations for improving productivity through the better utilization of the human resource.

U.S. PRODUCTIVITY IN PERSPECTIVE

Traditional Causes of Decline

In the past, economists related the decline in the rate of productivity growth primarily to two classic factors: investment and research and development (R&D). The President's Council of Economic Advisers has evaluated these factors and others in probing the causes for the slower growth of productivity in recent years in the *Economic Report of the President,* transmitted to the Congress in January 1980.[1] The council drew the following conclusions:

Capital Investment. The slowdown in the growth of the capital–labor ratio may have contributed about one-fourth of a percentage point to the decline, although some estimates are higher. Recent Bureau of Labor Statistics data show that the capital-labor ratio has deteriorated since 1973 and has reflected a growth rate of less than 1 percent per year.

Government Regulation. The diversion of resources to comply with government regulations may have accounted for as much as three-tenths of a percentage point of the decline, although the impact has not been so large in recent years. The council points out that many of these regulations have also improved the quality of the environment and the health and safety of workers and consumers, and that these benefits are not reflected in business output and productivity statistics.

Research and Development. The relevance of spending for R&D in explaining the decline of productivity is controversial. The real volume of resources devoted to R&D fell by 7 percent between 1968 and 1975, but since the latter date, it has increased steadily. As a percentage of the gross national product (GNP), R&D spending declined from 3 percent in 1964 to 2.2 percent in 1979. However, in private industry, where the links between productivity and research and development are more firmly established, real expenditures have increased steadily over the last two decades and have remained relatively stable as a share of the GNP.

Other factors. Sudden changes in energy prices or the impact of inflation on decisions by business and individuals affect productivity in ways not yet understood. Available evidence does not suggest that these represent a major source of decline since 1973.

The Council of Economic Advisers believes that since it is difficult to identify a single cause for the slowdown in productivity growth, the immediate prospects for a dramatic improvement are not good.

Two other nonstatistical factors have been cited by many experts: (1) the movement of large numbers of youth and women into the labor force, and (2) the so-called decline in the American work ethic. As a result of the post-World War II baby boom, a tremendous number of younger people poured into the labor market during the 1970s. There is no hard evidence, however, that these young people have been less productive than other workers, although there is a popular myth that relates this factor to the decline in the productivity growth rate. Nor has the rapid influx of women into the labor force in the 1970s had an adverse effect on productivity. The movement was unusual by any standard, but there is hardly any evidence that these millions of women were less qualified, less capable—or less productive—than other workers.

The decline in the American work ethic has also been widely touted as responsible for the drop in the productivity rate, but there is no real evidence that the work ethic has actually declined. In fact, the theory is contradicted by the increased knowledge, education, and skills of the American work force. What *is* evident is a greater gap between the capacity of American workers and the utilization of their potential in the workplace.

Whose Responsibility: Management's or Labor's?

A Gallup Poll in September 1979 surveyed American public opinion on the productivity issue in order to find some answers.[2] While corporate officials blame government regulations for the decline in U.S. productivity, American labor blames itself, the Gallup organization found.

A majority (70 percent) of 1,000 top executives from across the country blamed the federal government and the expanding burden of federal regulations and interventions for this productivity decline. Some 48 percent of this group also felt that the poor attitudes of workers and the ease of obtaining public assistance of varying kinds had caused the decline.

Surprisingly, when American workers were asked the same series of questions, 64 percent blamed themselves and the poor attitudes of fellow workers for the drop in American productivity. Workers also blamed poor management (45 percent), government regulations (42 percent), and failure by their employers to invest in new capital equipment (23 percent).

The contrast between the responses of executives and workers is significant. The fact that corporate executives tended to place the blame primarily on external forces—that is, the government—means that corporate executives are not looking inside the organization for causes and solutions. Their attitude reflects a lack of attention to the problem, and the assumption of little responsibility for taking direct action and control. American workers, on the other hand, are more self-critical and seem to reveal higher expectations for themselves and their co-workers. They also expect better leadership from their own management.

A similar reaction by management was demonstrated in a recent seminar of 100 top managers of a multi-billion-dollar corporation. Meeting in small groups of about 20, they were asked to consider the productivity of their own company. The first question was: "Consider and rate your own productivity as a manager on a scale of 1 to 100. Then place the number on a blank sheet of paper, fold it, and pass it forward." Averaging the self-ratings of all the executives present produced a rate of about 65 percent productivity. The results were announced to the group.

The second question was, "Considering your own productivity, how much time, effort, or initiative would you be willing to take to increase your productivity as a manager on a scale of 1 to 5, with 5 representing the maximum?" These answers, which were also submitted anonymously, averaged out at 2.5, but 20 percent of the executives indicated their effort at zero. Obviously the low-average and the negative responses reflected certain disincentives in the system. The managers were either overworked already, considered that increased personal effort would not be advantageous to their careers, or possibly felt that the effort would be wasted.

Finally, the group was asked to enumerate the most serious problems facing the organization in the present and near future. After a full discussion, the consensus of opinion was that the company had five major and universal problems. Then the group was asked the following question: "What can we do to deal with these problems?" The response was a dead silence. The question was repeated. There was still no response. The leader of the seminar then said, "If you people can't deal with these problems, who can? It was my impression that this was the top management of this company and that the people in this room are essentially in control of the overall business decisions."

After some murmuring and discussion, the group agreed that it should take more responsibility for the solution of these problems, but no course of action was clear at that time.

It would be unfair to suggest that this incident mirrors the situation in corporate management generally, but the fact that this particular group manages one of the leading corporations in America is thought provoking.

The Role of Labor Unions

American labor unions are wary of the word "productivity," which they commonly associate with the substitution of capital for labor or with a speedup of the processes of production.

It is true that in the short run the search for productivity has sometimes created job insecurity and unemployment in particular industries; in the long run, however, it has resulted in more jobs, better wages, and improved working conditions for all Americans.

Many employers blame productivity problems on the labor contract or on restrictions imposed by a collective agreement. This may be true in particular instances, but it is certainly not a valid generalization. American labor unions are unique in their strong support for the free enterprise system, they believe in capitalism and profits, and they have no desire to change the economic or political system.

Despite their reluctance to endorse productivity in the conventional sense, American labor unions are sophisticated enough to know and understand that productivity is critical in controlling inflation, meeting foreign competition, and encouraging economic growth. Thus, they have shown increasing interest in cooperating with management at plant level to improve quality output and to control costs. Still, their adversarial role effectively removes them from any operational authority or control and continues to place the primary responsibility for improved productivity on management.

Leadership Attitudes

American leadership exhibits growing concern about innovation and productivity. Six out of ten government officials in 1979 indicated a belief that our pace of technological development was lagging behind that of other nations, and one out of two saw the lack of productivity growth as a cause of continuing inflation.

According to Yankelovich, Skelly and White's *Corporate Priorities, 1979*, "While government officials clearly linked the issues of technological innovation and productivity (and gave moderate support to tax reform to encourage research and development and technological change), they indicated a belief that 'labor relations and employee relations' represented more fundamental causes of the productivity problem than did either capital formation or lagging research and development. Indeed, these officials tended to see 'innovative employee relations programs' as the most promising solution to the productivity problem."[3]

Their viewpoint has not been commonly held. Labor has been seen generally as a cost in the process of production, rather than as a critical factor in the productive outcome. This attitude tends to be a negative rather than a positive one and narrows the options for action with and through people.

The human factor in productivity is subtle and usually underestimated, if not ignored. Productivity studies show, in fact, that the human factor contributes between 10 percent and 25 percent to productivity growth. People account for 50 percent or more of controllable costs; in labor-intensive service and government, they account for 70 to 85 percent of all costs. So managers who ignore the human side of the enterprise do so at their own peril.

THE WORK FORCE OF THE 1980s

Since conventional wisdom cannot explain the decline in productivity growth, it is necessary to look more closely at the human factor in the productivity equation. The human factor is not limited to blue-collar workers on the production line. It includes, rather, everyone in the American economy who is working for wages or salaries, including corporate executives; middle managers and supervisors; professional, scientific, and technical workers; the clerical staff; retail sales personnel; and service workers in all sectors of the economy—private, public, and not for profit—and in every occupation.

The work force of the 1980s will grow at a slower rate than the work force of the 1970s and will reflect a different and richer mixture of skills. Understanding the nature of the work force, in general, and the nature of the internal work force of each organization, in particular, is the starting point for the effective utilization of people in work organizations.

Higher Educational Level

The American work force is the best educated in the world. Since World War II there has been an education explosion. Presently over 3,000 colleges and universities in the United States are educating more than 11 million people. The proportion of high school graduates entering college is about 50 percent, the highest of any industrialized nation in the world. (Typically, in Western Europe, only about 10 percent of high school graduates have access to higher education.) Further, of the 50 percent of American high school students who go on to college, at least half complete their education. The accessibility of education, combined with the growth in population during the last thirty years, has resulted in an enriched labor force.

For example, more than one-third of the American work force age 18 and over has completed at least one year of college, the Bureau of Labor Statistics reports as of March 1979. As recently as 1970 only one worker in four had completed a year of college.

Although college-educated workers are heavily concentrated in white-collar work, many are also now found in blue-collar, service, and farm jobs. The percentage of both men and women age 25 and over in these occupations who have completed one or more years of college has doubled during the 1970s—from 7 percent to 16 percent for blue-collar workers, from 8 percent to 18 percent for service workers, and from 9 percent to 18 percent for farmers and farm workers. The percentage of white-collar workers with some college rose from 45 percent in 1970 to 57 percent in 1979.

During 1979 women received nearly half of the master's and doctoral degrees and about a fifth of the medical, legal, and theological professional degrees. As the proportion of women in the labor force with advanced degrees continues to grow—as it has for women under age 35—women will be better able to pursue careers requiring higher levels of education.[4]

Greater Heterogeneity

The work force is much more diverse. It is comprised of a higher proportion of women and minorities and, increasingly, a higher proportion of older workers. This heterogeneity increases the difficulty of supervision and management but also enriches the work force with a variety of talents.

The changing mix and variety of workers will continue to intensify during the 1980s. Although the proportion of youth entering the work force will decline, it will be offset by more women, more minorities, and more older workers who opt to extend their working lives beyond 60 or 65. The underlying social and economic forces that impel more women and more minorities into the labor force, and that encourage older workers to continue working, initially present obstacles to management in achieving high productivity. In fact, this changed mix will demand greater skill, sensitivity, and attention from employers than ever before.

Shift in Occupations

The occupational shift to white-collar, professional, scientific, and managerial work during the 1970s gives every indication of continuing during the 1980s. This shift reflects the fact that a greater portion of the work force is no longer engaged in direct production activities that lend themselves to quantitative measures of output, but in a variety of jobs that call for self-direction and individual effort. Because the output in these jobs is not easily measured, more subtle and more individual kinds of motivation are required in order to encourage greater productivity.

Rising Expectations

In view of the enriched educational preparation and change in occupational mix, it should not be surprising that the American worker has a new set of expectations regarding employment. A recent Gallup Poll, for example, reports that 68 percent of American workers say that "the most important aspect of a job is the opportunity to develop individual abilities."[5]

This is a new breed of worker, one who expects to be treated fairly, who wants a more interesting job, and who would like an opportunity to develop his or her capabilities to the fullest; it is also a worker who believes that work is simply part of the total pattern of life and not the most important source of satisfaction.

Thus, American workers in the 1980s have both higher expectations and a sense of entitlement to good pay, decent working conditions, employee benefits, and reasonably enlightened supervision. These workers are no longer prepared to follow orders blindly. They require an understanding of *why* as well as *how* things should be done in the organization.

Managers and supervisors do not generally accept these new values and tend to behave according to the norms of at least ten years ago, an attitude that leads to conflict between the goals of management and workers, lagging interest on the part of workers, dissatisfaction, and, finally, a drop in productivity.

Changing Composition

One of the most likely changes in the work force of the 1980s will be an enormous increase in the number of prime-age workers, accompanied by a shortage of youth. In his study "The Work Force of the Future: An Overview," Professor Richard B. Freeman cites these as "the two most important potential labor-force changes in the decade ahead." Especially significant are the predicted changes in the number of workers in the 25–44 promotion-age category during the period 1975–1990.[6]

The bulge of prime-age workers will emerge as the product of a number of interactive labor-market and demographic forces: first, the degree to which the organizational age mix reflects the age of people in the general population; second, increased longevity and the extension of working life; third, the possible reversal of early retirement trends that have resulted in the sharp withdrawal of men aged 55–64 from the labor force; fourth, the equal-employment agenda, with its growing political and legal backing; and finally, the increased educational qualifications and occupational expectations of Americans.

The demographic bunching in the 25–44 prime-age group is remarkable by any standard. The absolute numbers will jump from 39 million to 60.5 million—an extraordinary rise of 55 percent. Furthermore, as the figures indicate, the composition of the total civilian labor force will shift considerably. The share of youth will decline by 6 percent, whereas the share of prime-age workers will increase by 10 percent. Fierce competition for promotions among these groups is generally predictable, but the severity, timing, and character of the conflict will vary among and within different organizations.

Professor Arnold Weber probes the pressures in this prime-age bulge and notes that the outlook is not very comforting for those in the 25–44 age bracket. In his study "Conflict and Compression: The Labor-Market Environment of the 1980s," he predicts that "competition to move up the organizational ladder will be sharpened further by the secondary effects of the antidiscrimination laws, which have brought women and minorities into the privileged corners of the occupational structure from which they were excluded in the past. Whereas in 1975 there may have been ten workers competing for a middle-management position, there will now be 13—and to this total you can probably add three women and three members of minority groups."[7]

The Internal Work Force

National data provide a broad view of the labor force of the 1980s. The degree to which these may reflect the internal data in any organization is at best a rough guess. But these data are the source of trend forecasts that are sufficiently alarming to cause planners to carefully examine their own organizational situation.

Computer technology has advanced the information art. Yet the application of software technology to extract all of the critical knowledge in this area has lagged. Now is the time to develop a simple but effective program to report annual data on intraorganizational demographics by function; by business or product line and geographical area; and by occupation, age, sex, service, performance, and potential. The supply side can make sense only in these specific terms. Such ongoing analysis and reanalysis are basic and essential not only to fulfill government requirements in the broad area of equal-employment opportunity, but to satisfy the organization's own needs to know and understand its own personnel complement. The facts are there, but it will take work and top-management decisions to make them available for intelligent policy making.

THE HUMAN FACTOR IN THE PRODUCTIVITY EQUATION: AN OVERVIEW

Two forces make it imperative for management to secure a better return on the human investment: (1) a work force that has changing values toward work, and (2) the rising cost of wages and benefits, exacerbated by rampant inflation. What management is seeking, in short, is improved productivity. Progressive managers realize they can no longer afford to rely on old methods and old assumptions.

The failure of management to adopt new approaches in managing people can only result in a continuation of, or perhaps an increase in, the negative and unproductive behaviors of workers that have plagued many organizations in the past. These negative behaviors include:

- Absenteeism, which is disruptive to work scheduling and output
- Turnover, which necessitates replacement and training costs
- Grievances, accompanied by stress, anxiety, and interpersonal friction
- Defiance of rules, policies, or authority
- Militant union activity, resulting in slowdowns, stoppages, or extended strikes
- Sabotage of equipment, materials, or product
- Theft or dishonesty in dealings with fellow workers or customers
- Accidents and work-related injuries
- Wastage of materials, supplies, equipment, space, or energy
- Interpersonal conflict with co-workers or supervisors
- Poor quality of work output
- Hostility or disinterest toward the goals of the organization
- Malingering or killing time on the job
- Poor quality of service and poor customer relations

Practical, innovative work-design programs already carried out in many organizations demonstrate that these negative behaviors can be reversed, with substantial improvements in productivity. The potential benefits for policy makers in the 1980s include:

- Better communications and information sharing
- Improved quality of service
- Optimum output in quantity and quality of product
- More human and effective management and management style
- Improved safety and health in the workplace
- Better accommodation to technical change
- Development of new problem-solving capabilities
- Regained employee allegiance and loyalty
- Greater involvement of employees in the company and union
- Reduction of unnecessary supervision
- Reduction of waste of energy, materials, supplies, equipment, and space
- Diminished counterproductive behaviors, reduction of grievances, work stoppages, strikes, and industrial sabotage
- Increased job satisfaction
- Human growth and development
- Better competitive positions—domestically and abroad

In the past, organizations have focused more on the economics of work than on its psychosocial aspects. This preoccupation tended to detract from quality-of-working-life issues, which, in the long run, may prove to offer more permanent solutions to the problem of work-force productivity.

There are many signs that a growing number of U.S. managements are no longer going to let the working environment just happen. Successful companies are managing that sector of their business as deliberately as they manage markets, finance, costs, and assets. They have discovered how large a multiplier effect a turned-on, released, and cooperative work force can have on production.

As a first step, employers must recognize the new realities within which they will function. The issue then becomes the degree to which management can successfully identify, anticipate, and address these changing values as they surface in their own organizations. Properly managed, many of these changing values can have a positive effect on productivity; others may have a negative effect and will require more skillful management.

In order to compete profitably in the market of the 1980s, it will be essential to have a stable, productive, dedicated, and committed work force, free of the resentments which fester and grow in a poor working environment. The goal for management is to make positive use of new and surfacing employee values, rather than to temporize and be forced to take reactive and resistive postures.

The Positive Side of the Equation: Spurs to Productivity through People

A series of forces, both economic and social, provide incentives for organizations to improve productivity through the human factor.

Qualitative Improvements in the Work Force. The real challenge to management is to achieve optimum utilization of the talent, time, and commitment of its own employees. As a result of the education explosion, the work force will be stronger and provide better potential for productivity gains. The new expectations of men and women in the work force will be strongly oriented toward achievement, and the workplace will provide the most natural outlet for their ambitions. A better-prepared and more highly motivated work force in the eighties will provide a high potential for performance irrespective of new capital investment or a major change in product or service.

Demographic Forces. The demographic bunching of over 30 million people in the 25–44 prime-age group will be not so much a bottlenecking of talent as a potential talent boom. The coming shortage of youth in the eighties will also shift the focus of attention to this prime-age category. In dealing with both the external and internal labor markets, organizations have a great opportunity to draw the 25- to 44-year-olds into the mainstream of their productivity programs and, in so doing, to benefit from their contributions.

New Awareness of the Human Factor. A number of economic factors have created a new awareness of the human factor in the productivity equation: inflation, the high cost of money, slow economic growth, high energy costs, and increased foreign competition have all served to broaden our perspective. Although in the past top management has tended to downgrade or minimize the importance of the human factor, there is a new awareness of its significance today. A national opinion survey of leadership in the United States in 1979 revealed that government leaders considered improved employee relations to be one of the principal avenues of productivity improvement. Increasing awareness by the chief executive officers in American industry of this source of productivity will also focus corporate attention on more innovative programs within the workplace.

Using the Organization's Full Potential. In national reports on plant utilization, it is not unusual to find that the American physical plant is operating at 85 percent or 80 percent of capacity. The nation has no such statistics with regard to the utilization of the organization, apart from the physical plant. But if these statistics were available, it is clear that the unused capacity with regard to all of the resources of the organization, especially human, would be substantially greater than 15 percent or 20 percent, particularly since many organizations staff for peak loads. In fact, many chief executive officers in major companies have estimated that their work force is working at about

60 percent of its potential. It would be radical and startling to speak of "half-time America," as an associate did of "half-time Britain" in the mid-sixties, but the label would certainly fit many organizations.

This is a negative condition only if it is allowed to persist and grow without remedy. A positive reaction to the real facts about the underutilization of human talent within work organizations would unleash a great burst of productivity. Unfortunately it cannot be turned on by throwing a switch or even by having the best of intentions. Nevertheless, it is there and waiting.

Most of the people in an organization who are functioning below their optimum ability are anxious and ready to be engaged in a more productive manner. Just as top management holds the key to the full use of its plant and equipment, so does it hold the key to a greater level of use of its own people.

Mature Union–Management Relations. Although American labor unions take an adversarial position in relation to business, they are not counterproductive to the efficiency of the organization. Unions are fully supportive of the free market system and recognize the value of efficiency, growth, and profitability. There is a growing awareness among union members of the job security issue. No one can expect unions to take the initiative in improving productivity, but the management that assumes that the union represents opposition carved in granite is missing the point: namely, that management must lead and unions will follow, assuming that there are reasonable trade-offs and options for full cooperation and understanding.

Inflation as an Incentive. Record-breaking levels of inflation make improved productivity imperative. The new urgency points directly to the need to utilize all resources better—especially people. People represent an attractive option because they are in place, they do not involve a new investment, and they do not require any fundamental changes in technology. What is involved is a fundamental change in the way they are managed, motivated, and rewarded within the existing employment system. During periods of high inflation, people cost more individually. Since their cost is a factor in the total cost equation, it constitutes an additional incentive to the organization to fully utilize their talents. These opportunities are present in relation to employees and managers alike.

Shift to the Sun Belt. The forecast of employment growth in the eighties continues to point to the Sun Belt cities. A recent nationwide job-growth forecast for the period 1979–1990 released by Chase Econometrics indicates that all of the top twenty areas are in the southern tier of the country—particularly in the Southwest. The average annual growth rate in the United States is projected at 1.7 percent. By contrast, the average annual employment growth rate in the top ten cities will exceed 3 percent, or about double the national rate. Tucson, Arizona; Fort Lauderdale/Hollywood, Florida; Houston, Texas; and Las Vegas, Nevada, are projected to have rates in excess of 4 percent a year.[8]

This continuation of the shift to the Sun Belt is a long-term plus in the human equation because it will continue to redistribute and balance the human and natural resources across a broader spectrum of the economy. Further, it has meaningful productivity potential because new plants and technological investments will be created, optimizing the productivity of these organizations.

The potential increase in the employment of older workers who would like to relocate in the Sun Belt will be an added spur to productivity.

The Negative Side of the Equation: Obstacles to Productivity through People

A series of factors are operating today which create obstacles to the improvement of productivity. Certain of these factors stem from societal change and others from the economic climate.

Inflation Psychology. Inflation can act as an incentive to companies to improve productivity, but it can also act as a disincentive for individual workers.

The volatility of the economy has changed personal expectations and increased uncertainty; it has also accelerated a change in values and behavior, as evidenced by the reduced incentive to save and conserve.

Inversely, inflation has increased the incentive for people to secure credit, finance debt, and borrow against the future. With the erosion of real purchasing power, their incentive to work is sharply reduced and, as a result, productivity suffers.

Since motivation through money is much more difficult in an economy where real wages are declining at about 4 percent to 5 percent a year, American management must be increasingly attentive to the question of incentives. It must also devote attention to the impact of taxes and the cost of living on real take-home pay.

Job Insecurity. A concerned worker, uncertain of the future, is less likely to be highly productive than a secure employee. A high and persistent level of unemployment and the threat of economic recession may be basic to a shake-out of inflation, but it also creates new resistance to change by workers, unions, and managers.

Technology as an answer to the productivity lag is resisted and feared since it represents a threat to jobs in the short run. The increase in plant closures in the industrial heartland of the country, the economic squeeze, and the pressure of inflation also add up to job insecurity—and thus, lowered productivity.

The Lag between Society and the Workplace. Changes in Western society have been more rapid and penetrating than have been changes within the workplace. Society's changing attitudes toward legal abortions, youth, divorce, the use of drugs, women's rights, civil rights for minorities, and more casual sexual mores present an imposing agenda of sweeping social change. By contrast, conditions have remained relatively static in the workplace. The large bureaucracies of government, industry, the church, universities, and the military all remain relatively resistant to change. Authoritarian rules and customs are deeply embedded and keep these organizations sheltered and secure from the outside environment.

Many large organizations are almost self-contained societies. They are relatively immune to external social forces and continue to respond best to the internal sounds of the cloistered world in which they work. Slow to act, corporate leadership views social change as an unwelcome disruption of the relative tranquility of the past and as a constant threat to efficiency. Thus, the institutional lag persists.

Executive leadership in these vital organizations needs to reduce this time lag and bring organizations into a more harmonious relationship with society and its current values.

The Gap between Management and the Employee. The gap between management and worker and between management and middle management has widened. The pressure on managers to perform in a slow-growth, high-inflation economy tends to divert their attention from the immediate workplace and the need to increase the productivity of the total organization, to external matters, such as finance, marketing, government relations, tax policies, and competition. Thus, organizations become more impersonal and less communicative—and the social and physical distance between management and the worker becomes even more difficult to bridge.

Technological Pressures. Productivity in the eighties will be influenced substantially by new and radically different developments in technology itself. In the past it has been common to consider the introduction of equipment and process technology as separate from the development of human resources.

New technology leads, in fact, to a new work environment where factory and office workers, supervisors, and managers alike react with new perceptions and new expectations. In this environment every dimension of work is affected: the content of individual jobs, pay, the role of managers and staff experts, and even organizational structures and decision-making processes. Whenever management has imposed such a change without prior and continuing consultation, resistance has been the most prevalent and pervasive reaction.

Unfortunately all current indications are that technological change will not be preceded by planning to assure an adequate interface with the people affected by the new machines. As long as past practices prevail, friction will increase between men and machines, and productivity will lag. The more sophisticated, complicated, and costly the technology, the more serious will be the adverse effects of human resistance to the technology.

Aging of the Work Force. The aging of the population will inevitably result in the aging of the work force, yet productive society remains wedded to the youth culture. The raising of the mandatory retirement age to 70 and the extension of legislation to eradicate age discrimination in employment are creating a new legal environment which broadens the entitlement of older workers to extend their working life to 70. Three other forces will also motivate older workers to extend their careers: better health, increased longevity and, finally, the economic pressure of inflation.

The potential reversal of the trend to early retirement in the past two decades is not anticipated in current work force planning. Work organizations, operating under the prevailing stereotypes, have negative attitudes toward older workers and continue to discriminate against them, despite federal law. To the extent that these negative practices continue, organizations will undermine the potential productivity of their own employees.

Secrecy and Privileged Information. Many organizations continue to favor the so-called "need to know" theory of information. The theory is rooted in privilege and assumes that information is a benefit and an advantage to the employee or the manager and not a necessity. The result is that many employees' groups and many levels in the organization are excluded from knowing about important ongoing activities in the organization. Some secrecy may be justified, but much of it is counterproductive.

In the 1977 Quality of Employment Survey conducted in the United States by the University of Michigan, more than half of American workers stated that they did not receive sufficient information to perform their jobs.[9] This is certainly a warning flag of productivity failure. Normally most employees in an organization do not have access to critical cost information that will enable them to understand the options for cost reduction. Certainly, people can't cut costs if they don't know what the costs are. Insofar as an organization hoards information and surrounds it with secrecy and privilege, it deprives itself of the active participation and commitment of its own people.

The closed books of many organizations need to be opened in order to involve more people in a better-managed business. If secrecy is more important than success, then it may be necessary to redesign the goals of the organization.

TARGETS OF OPPORTUNITY FOR IMPROVING PRODUCTIVITY

Despite obstacles, various organizations have taken advantage of the opportunities that exist to improve productivity through the human factor. Their experiences illustrate the avenues that are available to other organizations in solving the productivity problem.

Reduction of Absenteeism and Tardiness

Absenteeism is a symptom, not a cause, of poor performance. Overall, American statistics do not paint a serious or growing problem of absenteeism. When absenteeism is a serious problem in particular industries or companies, companies tend to conceal the information from the public, the shareholders, and even their own unions. Surprisingly, many organizations do not measure absenteeism on a regular basis. Nor are the different forms of voluntary and involuntary absences recorded. Companies also have different standards for absenteeism and tardiness in different occupational groups and social classes in the work force. The system may be very rigid and inelastic on the shop floor in plants and factories, but highly elastic, informal, and even lax in executive and managerial staff offices.

In Sweden and the Netherlands, absenteeism is reaching levels as high as 20 percent. Both countries have reported this as a growing problem and have been unable to find a national solution, largely because the social insurance program almost fully compensates workers absent from work. Because the United States has not emulated these social programs, the opportunity to improve productivity by reducing absenteeism is still open.

Several companies have been particularly successful in reducing absenteeism.

- As a result of the introduction of full-scale quality-of-working-life programs in over 60 General Motors plants, substantial improvements in attendance have taken place. In a new plant in Georgia, the absenteeism level has been reduced to 1 percent, whereas in some of the plants in the industrial Midwest, absenteeism is 12 percent.
- In the Eaton Corporation, where quality-of-working-life programs that are sensitive in their approach to supervision and

personal relationships have been introduced, factory absenteeism has declined from 12 percent to below 3 percent.

- Cummins Engine introduced an entirely different and improved method of managing a new plant in Charleston, South Carolina, and later adapted some of these methods to its other facilities, both new and old. Worker participation, job redesign, and teamwork resulted in a reduction in absenteeism to below 1 percent in Charleston. In fact, many workers appear on the weekend without formal assignments to complete critical projects at their own initiative.
- At the Con-Vel plant of the Spicer Universal Joint Company in Detroit, a Dana Corporation facility, hourly paid workers were put on a salary, and clocking in and out was eliminated. Absenteeism has dropped from 5.5 percent to 3.5 percent at this plant, and productive time, previously only three-and-a-half to four hours per eight-hour shift due to the need to set up machines, is now almost six hours. The company, which attributes the success of the program to its treatment of employees as responsible people, is making the experimental program a permanent one.
- A worker at the Fisher Body plant of General Motors in Grand Rapids, Michigan, has described the transformation brought about by a quality-of-working-life program at the plant. If the worker arrived at work late before the program was instituted, her supervisor assumed that she was at fault and she was penalized. Under such circumstances, it was common for workers who were unavoidably delayed to remain out of work for the entire day rather than to accept discipline. Thus tardiness was converted into an unnecessary absence.

The changes brought about by the quality-of-working-life program were dramatic, recounts the same worker. The assumption now is that the worker is trustworthy and conscientious. When she recently arrived two hours late as the result of a family crisis, her supervisor acknowledged that she had been delayed by a personal problem and thanked her for staying out only the necessary time. "We need you in your unit," he added. Workers respond to the new climate of trust by making every effort to get to work, and to get there on time.

A contrasting and totally different philosophy of handling absenteeism is demonstrated by a family-owned factory in South America. Despite the remoteness of the area, the poor public transportation, and the low wage level, the manager/owner requires that the workers be at the work site by 7 a.m. If they arrive late, the gates are locked and they are sent home without pay. Here, tardiness is translated into a penalty for both workers and the organization, with negative effects on both parties.

The need for a reduction of absenteeism, tardiness, and voluntary absences from work is pressing. However, it is understandable that this behavior is a function of many factors: working conditions, supervision, the rewards and penalty structure, hours of work, location of the plant or office, social and family pressures, and the increase in multi-earner families, with responsibility for child care shared by mothers and fathers. The best answer to absenteeism, thus, is a level of motivation and worker involvement which impels people to appear in the workplace of their own volition because work serves their own psychic, economic, and social needs. Sympathetic, intelligent, and forceful supervision, and schedules flexible enough to fit family needs can reinforce these goals.

Reduction of Waste and Pilferage

A great many examples of employee waste and pilferage have been attributed to a change in ethics and values and to a deliberate action by employees to break the moral code. This may be true in some cases, but in the main, the opportunity for waste is great and attention to its reduction or elimination is small.

Both employees and managers have the opportunity to waste space, materials, and supplies; abuse equipment; and waste energy. They can also waste the costly and valuable time of their co-workers, managers, and supervisors and their own time. Much of the waste is hidden or subtle and freqently not intentional. However, when the waste or pilferage is overt and obvious, it is a serious factor in the cost of operations and, in some cases, can actually place an organization in jeopardy. Yet organizations have not paid sufficient attention in the past to the need for measures to reduce waste and pilferage.

A case for closer scrutiny by employers of dishonest activities by employees was made in a recent study by the American Management Association and the University of Minnesota. The report states that organizations with low theft rates have a clearly defined policy on theft, have rules and procedures to detect crime, and hire selectively. Conversely, theft takes place more frequently in organizations where there has been a failure to address the problem; where security forces are more concerned with thefts by outsiders; and where the integrity, fairness, and ethical quality of the organization itself is questioned.[10]

A few flagrant examples of waste and pilferage follow:

- In a major midwestern hospital, it was reported by the staff that all of the IBM typewriters were taken from the hospital by a group of employees during one night shift. When the question arose as to how this was accomplished, fellow workers pointed out that the typewriters were loaded in laundry baskets, covered with dirty linens, and taken to the parking lot to be transported away in several station wagons. There was no overt reaction by the management of the hospital, and the affair was passed off without any feedback or change in policy.
- In a major corporation allowance is made for the waste of office supplies and equipment, especially portable supplies that can be carried home. There is no policy of attempting to control this waste, which has become an accepted practice in the company.
- As a result of the energy crisis, the DuPont Company's engineering consulting service has increased its assistance to other companies in reducing the waste of energy. According to these consultants, a simple walkthrough inspection of a typical American factory could result in energy savings of 30 percent without cutting production. The savings are largely related to the standards of power and heat, which produce a much higher level of steam than is necessary to operate the plant.

Now that the ability to transfer the cost of such waste to the consumer is being reduced by inflation and competition, organizations are beginning to pay more attention to the problem. Certainly the options for reducing waste and pilferage are legion. The responsibility rests first and foremost with management, but it must be reinforced by employees' behavior at all levels. It can also be strengthened by peer pressure and by a level of loyalty and character within the work force which does not condone such behavior. With respect to the more indirect and costly forms of waste, program control and standards are needed which aim directly at these issues.

Improvement of Quality Control

One disturbing finding in the 1977 Quality of Employment Survey is the startling revelation that 28 percent of American workers feel that their consciences are violated by the services they are required to perform or the products they make.[11]

Quality of product or service assumes new importance in an inflation economy, for if buyers are forced to pay what they consider an inordinately high price for a product, they will insist on equally high quality. In addition, the consumer movement has created a new awareness in business and government of the need for consumer protection, which is, essentially, quality control imposed by the buyer or the government. For instance:

- In an era of scarcity, consumers want long-term use of expensive equipment and other hard goods. They are rapidly moving away from the planned obsolescence and high turnover of these products as well as of clothing and other less durable goods.
- Companies can only deal with warranty losses, a decline in market shares, the influx of foreign products, class-action suits, dealer-service problems, a decline in customer loyalty, and reduced profit margins if they insist on quality controls.
- Managers and consumers alike may complain about the decline of worker commitment to high quality, but the responsibility lies first and foremost with *leadership*—with the management of an organization.

The problem is that quality control has not been a priority. Management goals have been directed toward output quotas, fast delivery, turnover, and marketing and styling, instead of toward quality. Also, cost controls, production standards, and the separation of inspection and quality control from production weakens the quality of the product.

Productivity may be measured in output per worker-hour—but without quality control it can be a hollow measure. The Japanese have become the world's model in quality production just as they are in productivity growth. Norihiko Nakayama, president of Fujitsu America, Inc., and a director of the Amdahl Corporation, feels that Japanese methods, which directly involve employees in problem solving, can be transferred to production in the United States. In an address at the Japan Society in 1980 he described an effort to improve the quality of a subassembly made by Fujitsu America for Amdahl:

"I conducted a meeting once every week and had the American managers discuss their work openly," said Nakayama. "I encouraged everyone to think through problems together to an eventual solution. Working together, we found these problems: carelessness, poor handling of delicate parts, inaccurate testing equipment, improper placement of parts to be tested, and, most important, failure of managers to act on the foregoing.

"In due course, the employees discovered that management had no intention of punishing them. The objective was to identify mistakes and correct them. As a result, our Fujitsu America product became equal to—or even better than—the one made in Japan.

"Quality control is not just a little room adjacent to the factory floor, whose occupants make a nuisance of themselves to everyone else," Nakayama concluded. "Quality control is—or should be—a state of mind. It must permeate the entire operation, from the president to the production trainee."

Providing Better Service

In the postindustrial society of the eighties, the shift to government and service industries shows no sign of decline. All organizations in the society—government, the private sector, the universities—are becoming more sensitive to customer relations. These relations depend on all levels of the organization, from top management to the salesperson or serviceperson who meets the customer face to face. The quality of service is as important a factor in the productivity equation as the quality of a product. The fact that it is more subtle, more individual, and less subject to physical quality control does not lessen its importance. If anything, the importance of service is growing. Wherever service is marginal, poor, or unacceptable, it results in a cost to the organization.

Service represents a special target of opportunity for improving productivity. The basic method is training and more training, but it needs to be augmented with goals and objectives, employee motivation, employee recognition, and employee rewards. The people who directly render the service need to feel important, need to be clear as to the standards of good and acceptable behavior, and need reinforcement of their results.

- A good example lies in the traditional practices of the telephone company. In its early training programs a generation ago, the company indoctrinated operators with the philosophy of "put a smile in your voice." More recently, as part of its highly sensitive customer relations program, operators conclude every contact with the expression "Have a good day." These are small considerations, but important to the consumer.
- The commercial airlines have responded to the issues of customer service by greatly increased attention to their service personnel, especially flight attendants. This has been obvious to many travelers on airlines that have given service high priority. The result is that passengers prefer to travel on those lines even though the price and the time in transit are the same. In fact, some passengers will make special efforts to travel on those airlines even when the schedules are less convenient.
- In the hotel industry, the more progressive companies have built a system of feedback from the customer to the hotel. This is accomplished by careful service on registration, by self-administered cards in the room, and even by periodic follow-ups with a sampling of guests to maintain a careful finger on the pulse of quality of service.

Another important opportunity for service exists among dealers' or manufacturers' representatives, or in retail outlets. These agencies employ the only people who normally deal with the customer, yet they are once or twice removed from the source of manufacture and frequently may be franchised, independent businesses. The principal organization producing the product needs to consider these people as an important adjunct to their human organization. Unless this is done, manufacturers cannot build a strong bridge from their own system of values to the customer's system of values.

Better Management of Time

The importance of the allocation of time compared with that of income (the work/leisure dichotomy) is increasing. The 1977 Quality of Employement Survey by the University of Michigan uncovered a growing problem with regard to working hours.[12] A majority of workers reported some difficulty with their working hours, and more than one-third reported a conflict between work and leisure. Another third reported insufficient time for both work and the family. A considerable number reported problems with commutation and unscheduled hours, overtime, and weekend work.

The growing friction between time and income creates conflict and stress. The result is a reduction in productivity. The rigidity of time patterns and traditional work schedules is no longer compatible with the needs and expectations of many people in our society. New patterns of work, such as flexitime, part-time jobs, shared jobs, and the compressed workweek, are clearly productivity-linked issues that have a good payout, low cost, and will serve to attract a more effective share of the labor market. These new work patterns also have a positive effect on reducing absenteeism, grievances, and turnover.

During the 1980s time-management issues will extend to a number of aspects of working hours. Among these are the following:

Unscheduled hours. More and more workers will resist the fact that they do not work regular hours and are subject to virtually an on-call work plan that can vary from day to day.

Management, supervisory, and professional overtime. Most of this time is spent without pay and without compensatory time. As the management role has increased, so has the necessity for overtime, both at the work site and at home.

Rigid work schedules versus more flexible life-styles. Although about 6 percent of the American work force is now on flexitime, 94 percent is not. Organizations are experimenting, but the rate of change is too slow and, as a result, organizations are missing an opportunity for improved productivity.

Shift work. Both in the factory and in offices shift work has been increasing. As the investment in office technology and computers increases, management seeks to secure a faster return on the investment by increasing the hours of usage. This will lead to second and third shifts in offices in a society where employees are pressing for more leisure and more flexibility of their working lives.

Multiple-worker families. The number of multiple-worker and dual-career families is growing. Three out of every five married-couple families have at least two income workers. The steepest boost in the number of women in the work force comes primarily from working wives. Since many of these families have preschool and school-age children without adequate child care, the pressures for flexible hours have increased and will grow. Further, with both parents working, there is the problem of the compatibility of their work schedules. The more rigid the arrangements in a particular workplace, the less likely it is that they will be compatible with multiple-worker family needs.

Involuntary overtime. The prolonged strike at International Harvester in 1979–1980, which endured for over 140 days, was the longest in the history of the United Auto Workers. One issue among many was the resistance of the local union to involuntary overtime. In a dramatic way this demonstrated the growing gap between the needs of management, accustomed to control of labor scheduling, and the desires of workers who want to control their own life-styles.

After the Great Depression, overtime was a privilege and frequently was assigned by seniority. We have come full circle now, and although some workers are highly attracted to the premium pay related to overtime, many others resist it and, in fact, despise it. The answer to the overtime question is a greater degree of choice and incentives, or a redesign of working hours to reduce the need for overtime.

Firestone Tire and Rubber provides an interesting case history. The company recently introduced a two-day workweek on Saturday and Sunday. This work force works a 12-hour day, two days a week, and is paid for 36 hours, i.e., time and a half. This special work force likes the compressed workweek, and the balance of the work force enjoys the fact that it is not compelled to work on weekends.

Transforming Managerial Discontent into Positive Action

The Opinion Research Corporation has collected trend data for more than 25 years, measuring the attitudes of three groups in the work force—hourly workers, clerical personnel, and managers. As recently as 1977 the data showed favorable and steady managerial attitudes. Since 1977 the data reflect a downward shift in managerial attitudes. The overall conclusion is that managerial discontent is growing and that the national data point to a frustrating scenario for today's managers. Therefore the challenge now facing organizations is to transform middle-management discontent into positive action.

The findings reflect problems in seven areas: compression of treatment; impersonality of work; loss of identity in the face of corporate growth; external pressures reducing the power to act; breakdown in communications; problems of job security and advancement opportunity; and pay problems.

Compression of treatment. Managers see that other employee groups are making significant gains, often achieved with the help of managers. The result is that managers are becoming more and more concerned that they are "losing something" in relative position.

Impersonality of work. The rapid rate of advancement of technology and automation has increased the impersonality of work and has disturbed time-honored values and traditions. These factors are still contributing to dissatisfaction among clerical and hourly employees and are now beginning to affect managers as well.

Loss of identity in the face of corporate growth. Mergers, acquisitions, diversification and growth of corporations, and multinational entities have added to corporate impersonality. Managers find it increasingly difficult to maintain a sense of identification with and commitment to the goals and mission of one particular company in such a large mass of companies.

External pressures reducing the power to act. Pressure from many external constituencies, especially the federal government, has reduced the power of middle management. In addition, managers must negotiate with labor and with new kinds of pressure groups, often foreign to their experience. These include a variety of environmentalists, consumer groups, and social-action groups.

Breakdown in communications. Strange as it may seem, managers now feel less informed than do hourly or clerical employees. The survey calls attention to the fact that the importance of managers' growing discontent with company communications must not be underestimated, because information has usually been one of the sources of power for middle management. This discontent could, over time, translate into a growing alienation of managers.

Job security and advancement opportunity. In light of the foregoing problems and pressures facing managers, it follows that their ratings of their own advancement opportunity and even their own job security are also slipping. Considering the loss of autonomy and authority, it is not surprising that the percentage of managers who question their ability to hold onto their jobs has increased; nor is it surprising that many of them feel that their advancement opportunities have diminished to some degree because of the rising age ceiling on mandatory retirement and the tendency not to fill managerial jobs vacated by attrition. One of the important current factors contributing to this decline in feelings about job security and advancement opportunity is the recent inundation of the job market by MBAs. The Opinion Research Corporation points out that ten years ago about 18,000 master's degrees in business management were granted. Recently the total has soared to nearly 50,000.

Satisfaction with pay. Only 50 percent of managers rate the company pay levels as "very good" or "good." This decline in pay satisfaction also occurs among clerical and hourly employees. In fact, Americans at all levels consider themselves to be on an economic treadmill in the face of growing inflation.

These data do not necessarily paint a picture of a broad-scale middle management malaise. Rather, they flash a series of important warning lights to alert top management to the need for an aggressive and responsive program of action. The parameters for such a program are defined by the seven items identified in the national data, but should be more carefully planned in relation to the internal situation in each organization. Top managers must address these problem areas in order to turn around the complacent or negative attitudes among middle managers. This target of opportunity should be at the top of the agenda in any program to restore and maintain productivity growth. To deal with middle-management problems in purely negative terms, or to consider the situation as irreversible, is impractical and unacceptable.

CONCLUSION

Economists have conjectured about the causes of the current productivity lag and have advanced various theories to account for the precipitous drop in the productivity rate. Since, as the President's Council of Economic Advisers points out, there is apparently no single cause, it is difficult to find a single cure.

It becomes incumbent, then, on each organization to seek its own "cure." The investment of capital and the introduction of new technology each play a part in boosting productivity, but the human resources of the organization—employees in every occupation and at every level—are clearly at the heart of any effort.

Thus, progressive management in the eighties faces the challenge of addressing the productivity lag through the improved use of *all* resources in the organization, including human talent. Although the entire organization will be involved in a productivity effort, the responsibility is primarily management's, because top management alone can stimulate and sustain the drive to make more effective use of the abilities of every member of the organization.

In trying to solve the productivity equation, certain forces will exert a negative influence, others a positive influence. An examination of the plus side of the productivity equation reveals marked qualitative improvements in the American work force, a potential talent boom in the prime-age 25–44 group, and a growing awareness of the importance of the human factor. It also demonstrates that the human resources available to American organizations have an enormous untapped potential; that union–management relations are not a serious or insurmountable obstacle to improved worker productivity; that inflation provides a strong economic incentive to press hard for improved productivity; and, finally, that the shift to the Sun Belt offers a new base of investment and opportunity for growth.

An analysis of the minus side of the equation confirms that obstacles to productivity do exist. Productivity is discouraged when employees have no real job security and fear layoffs due to plant closures and economic recession; when the real purchasing power of employees is eroded by inflation; when workplaces do not keep up with the changes in society; and when technology is so poorly introduced that it antagonizes the work force. The productivity of organizations also suffers when negative attitudes toward older workers discourage them from using their full potential and when information is hoarded to the detriment of work in progress. Yet every negative can be converted to a positive in the sense that it is a problem that has a solution. To the extent that management policies face these problems, they can transform obstacles into opportunities.

Finally, the targets of opportunity discussed here are representative of the many options to improve productivity inside the organization. They are by no means the only opportunities. Deliberate emphasis has been placed on pragmatic programs that affect both productivity and profitability: reduction of absenteeism and tardiness, reduction of waste, improved quality control, better customer service, efficient management of time, and most important of all, the transformation of managerial discontent into positive action.

It is clear then that opportunities do exist for a broad-scaled attempt in the 1980s to use *people* to advance productivity in work organizations and in the society as a whole; they are practical; and they can make a difference.

NOTES

1. Council of Economic Advisers, *Economic Report of the President* (Washington, D.C.: U.S. Government Printing Office, 1980).
2. Leonard Wood, The Gallup Organization, Inc., "Changing Attitudes and the Work Ethic," a presentation to The Third National Conference on Business Ethics, October 19, 1979, Bentley College, Waltham, Mass.
3. Yankelovich, Skelly and White, Inc., *Corporate Priorities*, 1979.

4. Bureau of National Affairs, *Daily Labor Report,* February 15, 1980.
5. Leonard Wood, The Gallup Organization, Inc., op. cit.
6. Richard B. Freeman, "The Work Force of the Future: An Overview," in *Work in America: The Decade Ahead*, edited by Clark Kerr and Jerome M. Rosow (New York: Van Nostrand Reinhold, 1979).
7. Arnold Weber, "Conflict and Compression: The Labor-Market Environment of the 1980s," in *Work in America: The Decade Ahead,* edited by Clark Kerr and Jerome M. Rosow (New York: Van Nostrand Reinhold, 1979).
8. Edward Schumacher, "Computer Study Predicts Job Loss in New York Area of 4% by 1990," *The New York Times,* March 28, 1980.
9. Robert P. Quinn, and Graham L. Staines, *The 1977 Quality of Employment Survey* (Ann Arbor, Mich.: University of Michigan, Institute for Social Research, 1979).
10. "Theft by Employees," *Industrial Relations News,* March 22, 1980.
11. Quinn and Staines, op.cit.
12. Ibid.

13.

Labor–Management Committees: Their Impact on Productivity

Wayne L. Horvitz
Director, Federal Mediation and Conciliation Service

The quick answer to the question, Do joint labor–management committees improve productivity? is yes. It's when the next question, How much? is asked that the answers become more difficult.

For a concept that has been around in its modern form for most of this century, the lack of sufficient documentation to prove the impact of labor–management committees on productivity would seem to argue that the improvement is more illusion than fact. Increasingly, however, experiences with labor–management committees are providing impressive examples of productivity gains.

These gains are difficult to measure in a manner that will provide statistical confirmation of the claim. But in an industrial society of increasing complexity, my experience of better than 30 years in this field tells me it is a given that a positive, joint labor-management approach to problem solving improves productivity. My "proof" for this assertion rests on observations throughout these years that without such an approach the resulting negative character of the relationship acts as a drag on productivity.

The Federal Mediation and Conciliation Service (FMCS) is in a unique position to see the development of this concept. It is and has been a major participant in the development and operation of many of these committees of all kinds in all parts of the country. Its role as a neutral that can and does occupy the third-party role necessary to the successful establishment and functioning of these committees gives it a special vantage point. In this capacity, the FMCS sees the kinds of topics being discussed and acted on by these joint ventures and the outcome of many of their actions. So I am going on more than faith in the assertion that productivity gains result from these arrangements.

The designation of FMCS, in the Labor–Management Cooperation Act passed by Congress in late 1978, as the agency responsible for the dissemination of grants to qualifying labor–management committees will give the FMCS an even more central role in the development of this concept. Some $2 million of the fiscal year 1981 budget, the year beginning October 1, is earmarked for these grants.

These committees, with their potential for problem solving and productivity improvement, are attracting increased attention from both unions and management. The number of joint committees, of varying makeup, size, and scope, is increasing. The auto, retail food, and construction industries have a substantial commitment to the labor–management committee concept. The major steel companies are taking a new experimental tack with in-plant groups of "participation teams" in place of the "productivity councils" provided for in the just-expired collective bargaining agreement with the union. (A major reason for their replacement was that the councils were perceived as "management-inspired.")

Corporate participants in these joint labor–management arrangements include General Motors, Bendix, Whirlpool, TRW, Kelley-Springfield Tire, U.S. Steel, Bethlehem, Rockwell, Carborundum, A&P, Kroger, Safeway, Northrup, Lockheed, and American Airlines, to name a random few. Participating unions include the Machinists, Autoworkers, Steelworkers, construction craft unions, Teamsters, and the retail food unions. These cooperative arrangements vary in form and may be, as in the case of the retail food industry, industry-wide; the steel industry arrangement does not quite fit that blanket terminology, but it is broad.

Many communities, faced with the departure of a major employer or experiencing the consequences of a poor labor–management climate, form area-wide, or community-wide labor–management committees. At present there are more than two dozen of these in existence in such locations as Evansville, Indiana; Buffalo–Erie County in New York State; Muskegon, Michigan; Green Bay, Wisconsin; Clinton County (Lock Haven), Pennsylvania; Riverside, California; and Cumberland, Maryland. These include nearly all of the major companies and unions in the area; their prime thrust is to retain industries which are threatening to move out of the area, to repair the poor labor image projected by labor–management strife over an extended period, or to rebuild a badly depleted economic base.

There are a thousand or more in-plant committees. As the designation signifies, these are confined to a single company or plant of that company—or even a division—and deal primarily with matters within that universe.

Quality control circles, which a growing number of American companies have established in their plants, copying an example which has proved successful in Japan, are a variation on this theme. These are small groups of employees who meet regularly and are trained to spot and solve production problems; companies which employ the circles include General Motors, Ford, Northrup, Rockwell International, International Harvester, and American Airlines.

The committees are now beginning to make inroads on public-sector problems. In 1978, controversy over the Massachusetts collective bargaining law and its provision for compulsory arbitration for police and fire disputes led to the creation of a unique labor–management committee. John T. Dunlop, Harvard economics professor and former secretary of labor, entered the controversy with a compromise which brought agreement to a joint labor–management committee to oversee all police and firefighter collective bargaining within the state; the committee of 13 includes Dunlop as chairman and 12 members selected by the governor, six from nominations submitted by the firefighters union and two police employee organizations, and six from nominations by a local government advisory committee. This committee uses what *Business Week* has called a "highly flexible combination of mediation, internal arbitration, and return of disputes to the parties for more bargaining. The committee has cut the time from declaration of an impasse to settlement from 15 months to three, and only four disputes have gone to outside arbitration instead of the 97 between 1975 and 1977 under the old strict compulsory arbitration law."[1]

The joint cooperation concept has been utilized in situations that involve issues outside the traditional collective bargaining setting. Both the steel and garment-industry unions have joined with employers in their industries to seek legislative and governmental relief from the impact of imports.

Reports to the FMCS on the operating results of the industry-wide, area-wide, and in-plant committees provide substantial evidence of productivity improvement.

REDEFINING PRODUCTIVITY

It is important to understand, however, that productivity in the context of labor–management committees is far broader than the textbook definition of "output per worker-hour," although that can be affected. Experience with the joint-committee approach has made it clear that there is a wide range of elements that vitally affect productivity in the broader meaning, that are not measured now. These would include fewer strikes, improved attitudes on the part of the workers, and more harmonious relations with management, to mention only a few. There is also the cost and supply of capital, the skill of the work force, and the sophistication of the new technology. Taxes and tax policy can affect productivity; so can government regulation, or the lack of it. Transportation and the warehousing of goods are, in many industries, major components of the end cost of a product to the consumer; variables in these costs affect productivity. So do the many factors in the process of getting goods from the end of the production process to the consumer. How management manages can affect productivity to as great an extent as how labor labors and under what conditions.

The turnover of capital is an essential ingredient in the ability of an industry to increase its productivity. The Japanese company Nippon Kokan (NKK) recently scrapped an entire plant and built a new one that produces 6 million tons of steel with only 8,000 workers, compared to an output record of the old mill of 5.5 million tons a year with 18,000 workers. Much of the productivity increase came from investment in the latest automated handling equipment and huge, superefficient blast furnaces. In the drive for peak efficiency, NKK was willing to scrap equipment that was less than 30 years old; some of the equipment still in use in American steel mills dates back to the early years of the century.

At the plant level, absenteeism, accidents, strikes, the general health level of the work force, and job safety affect productivity. So do theft, waste, the level of grievances, worker motivation and morale, restrictive work rules, and labor–management relations.

While it may not be possible to quantify some of these elements, there is no question that they can and do have a significant bearing on productivity. And many of these are or can be affected by a joint labor–management relationship.

Arriving at a more realistic appraisal, if not measurement, of just what productivity is has considerable current importance. There is a consensus that lack of productivity, by any measure, is at the bottom of our current crop of economic ills, chief of which is inflation. There are countless and confusing theories as to what makes productivity move up and down, and why. Edward Denison, assistant director of the Commerce Department's Bureau of Economic Analysis and a leading expert in the field, was recently quoted as admitting that "more than half of the reasons for the productivity decline are a mystery."[2]

Unfortunately, the word productivity in many circles has gotten a bad name. Labor unions react viscerally to nearly any mention of productivity, equating it with speedup, or with the introduction of the kind of technology that either totally replaces or substantially substitutes for human endeavor.

It should be pointed out here, however, to those who may view a greater reliance by management on the introduction of new technology as the chief response to the problem of productivity, that technology does not and cannot stand alone. Technology's capabilities are only as good as the institutional arrangements into which technology is fitted.

For most of the nation's industrial community, the collective bargaining agreement is the centerpiece of the institutional relationship. And if the parties don't have a working collective bargaining agreement, no amount of technology in the world is going to be good.

As one approach to redefining productivity, Dr. Michael Maccoby, of Harvard's Project on Technology, Work and Character, has proposed describing productivity in social terms. Increasing social productivity would mean improving effectiveness in the use of resources—including the work force, technology, energy, capital, and raw materials—to produce goods and services wanted by the public, but under such social constraints as to avoid harm to people in the form of pollution or other adverse effect on the consumer's or worker's health; it would not damage the mental or emotional health of workers, unduly increase social inequity and injustice, or lead to the inability of workers to find useful paid work. Social productivity could also be defined in terms of positive criteria, says Dr. Maccoby, which "would identify the goal of productivity rather than leaving that up to any producer. . . . The goal of social productivity might be to provide only those goods and services that enhance the lives and strengthen the health of workers and consumers and therefore American society as a whole. In terms of this definition, both the process of production and products must contribute positively to the healthy development of workers, managers, and consumers."[3] It would be up to the employers, the workers, and the consumers to develop this new definition through their relationships.

What is becoming apparent from this concentration on the deficiencies of the present definition of productivity is the deficiency of measurement of the human factor in any program or effort to improve productivity. This deficiency becomes more and more critical as increased evidence becomes available on the contribution the human factor can make to productivity. Productivity studies have shown that the human factor contributes from 10 percent to 25 percent to productivity growth. In labor-intensive service industries and in government human factors account for 75 percent to 80 percent of all costs.

Another developing concept is that of the job as a property right of the worker. Peter F. Drucker, in a recent writing, pointed out that "in every developed non-Communist country, jobs are rapidly turning into a kind of property. . . . The property rights in the job . . . cannot be . . . taken away from their 'rightful' owner. . . . Today, the job is the employee's means of access to social status, to personal opportunity, to achievement, and to power." Mr. Drucker speaks of the emerging "employee society."[4]

LABOR-MANAGEMENT COOPERATION AS A SPUR TO PRODUCTIVITY

International Longshoremen's and Warehousemen's Union/Pacific Maritime Association

This principle, the employee "ownership" of job rights, was a vital consideration in my early introduction to what a positive joint labor-management endeavor could produce. This was the fashioning of what is now called the mechanization and modernization agreement between Harry Bridges' International Longshoremen's and Warehousemen's union and the Pacific Maritime Association (PMA). What this agreement did, in effect, was to "buy out" the rights of the longshoremen in order to introduce a whole new technology—containerization—and reap the full benefits of that technology.

That agreement was an important example of the productivity potential of joint labor–management relations. While the mechanization and modernization agreement did not come out of a formal labor–management committee, it was the product of agreement between the parties that cooperation at top levels was vitally necessary to solve some festering problems, namely, the frequent strikes and restrictive work rules that prevented the introduction of new technology vital to the survival of the industry. The best way to solve these problems, they believed, was away from the heat of the bargaining table. The relationship of the union and management had, up to that point, been one of constant conflict. Every bargaining situation was crisis and confrontation, and the clashes that resulted adversely affected not only the industry but the entire community. This pioneering effort in the field of labor–management relations was, therefore, a dangerous thing for leaders on both sides to undertake in terms of their constituencies.

Yet, for all of the animosity shown, leaders emerged from both groups who recognized that the survival of an industry was at stake and were willing to attempt the unusual and the innovative in search of an accommodation that would bring desperately needed stability to the industry. Rising above their differences, they took a long look at the technology, the economics, and the other forces affecting the industry and the people in it, and to determine what sort of an accommodation would be needed to meet those forces.

This took people of understanding and dedication, people who would take the risks involved in facing reality. It took continuing communication and consultation, some of it under the most trying circumstances, over a long period of time. A lot of old attitudes had to be discarded. A lot of misinformation had to be cleared up. A lot of old grievances, real or fancied, had to be resolved. Leaders on both sides not only had to take unpopular and difficult positions, but they had to defend them as well. The result was the mechanization and modernization agreement. It worked, and it still is working.

In an article in the *Los Angeles Times* commemorating the signing of the agreement it had termed "revolutionary," Harry Bernstein wrote: "Since Bridges and his union removed all roadblocks to the use of containers in a historic contract 20 years ago, harbor productivity on the West Coast has jumped 483 percent, a figure apparently unmatched by any other industry. . . . It took one hour and 12 minutes to load or unload one ton of cargo in 1960, before the union and the industry agreed to unlimited use of containers. Today, it takes less than 12 minutes to handle one ton. When the famed mechanization and modernization agreement was signed by Bridges and the PMA, 16,000 longshoremen were needed to handle 19.9 million tons of cargo a year . . . mostly piece by piece. Today, just 10,000 longshoremen move nearly 64 million tons of cargo a year."[5]

General Motors/United Automobile Workers

The gains that can be reaped from greater employee participation in the production process also are demonstrated by the experiment of the United Auto Workers and General Motors in their "quality-of-working-life" program. Recently Irving Bluestone, former UAW vice-president and director of the union's General Motors Department, gave a report on the progress of some 50 of these programs in a speech before a Work in America Institute conference.

"There is ample evidence that the introduction of a QWL program has a salubrious effect upon the adversarial collective bargaining system," Mr. Bluestone said. "Simultaneously with national negotiations between the UAW and GM, the local parties negotiate with regard to local issues. These include local seniority, transfers, shift preference, equalization of overtime agreements, and so on. They concern proposals to improve working conditions, health and safety issues, grievances, and many other subjects of concern to the workers. When the National Agreement expired in 1970, only two locations had settled their local negotiations. In 1973 there were five; in 1976, eight. In 1979 there were 54. Moreover, of the first 90 local settlements in 1979, all of which were accomplished without a pending local strike threat, 44 were engaged in some stage of a QWL program. Considering there are about 50 QWL programs in GM, this represents a noteworthy achievement. I believe the figures speak for themselves."[6]

Bluestone also said that studies at locations where a QWL program has existed long enough to be meaningful show, in addition to a more constructive collective bargaining relationship and a more satisfied work force, "improved product quality, less scrap, fewer repairs, a reduction in grievance handling as problems are more frequently resolved directly as they arise on the shop floor in absenteeism, a reduction in labor turnover, and a reduction in the number of disciplinary layoffs and discharges."[7] All of these elements have a direct and substantial impact on the productivity of the work force.

Based on this experience, Bluestone says, "I am convinced more than ever that this should become the inevitable direction of the future of union–management relations in this country."[8]

Retail Food Industry/Teamsters and the United Food and Commercial Workers

From 1974 to my appointment as director of FMCS, I helped form and was the first neutral chairman of the Joint Labor–Management (JLM) Committee of the retail food industry. The committee is made up of an executive committee composed of the chief operating officers of the major supermarket chains, the heads of the major retail food industry unions (the Teamsters and the United Food and Commercial Workers), and a steering committee of management's labor-relations officers and their counterparts from the unions. The committee, with FMCS participation, meets once a month to discuss mutual industry problems, mostly related to current collective bargaining. The committee has been instrumental both in helping companies and unions in the industry avoid strikes, and in lessening the length of strikes which do occur.

While the current thrust of the JLM steering committee is consideration of involvement in the industry's collective bargaining problems—which are many—it has had for some time a productivity subcommittee. The subcommittee is required by a policy statement in the agenda of the parent committee to look at the full range of new technology waiting to be introduced in the industry and to assess its impact on productivity and manpower.

Because of the sensitivities involved in the introduction of this technology (principally the automated checkout stand) and the polarization that has taken place, committee members felt they could not safely take up the issue, and thus its productivity aspects were never frontally addressed. Indeed, the committee still has to grapple with this problem.

The JLM Committee provided an example, I believe, of the kind of labor–management relationships that can flow from the workings of the committee. In this case, the opening up of the relationship permitted the parties to deal jointly and constructively with a problem which, while it affected the relationship, was quite far removed from the bargaining table.

The problem involved the committee's fashioning of a change in a federal regulation on protective clothing. At issue was the Occupational Safety and Health Administration's attempt to enforce a federal government regulation concerning the wearing of mesh gloves and aprons by employees in retail meat departments of supermarkets. The result of the enforcement effort was a series of lawsuits, involving both the supermarkets and the unions, that dragged on interminably.

The Joint Labor–Management Committee, through its safety and health committee, undertook a series of studies of retail meat operations around the country to find out what kinds of experiences meat department employees had had with the protective clothing. On the basis of the committee's findings, it compiled a report which it took to OSHA, along with a revised regulation covering the wearing of the mesh aprons and gloves in retail meat departments. The federal agency, after considerable deliberation and consultation, agreed to the modification. The result was the immediate wiping out of a series of lawsuits that would have kept the government, the companies, and the unions involved in litigation for possibly years to come.

Unfortunately, that model of cooperative problem solving was not followed by the JLM committee on other issues concerning the relationship of government to the industry.

I believe that federal regulations which affect the productivity of industrial operations are a fertile field for exploration by joint labor–management committees.

When John Dunlop was secretary of labor in the Ford Administration, he made the point that one of the basic fallacies of the regulatory process was that the parties, who are in a sense the victims of regulation, are rarely asked, either in advance or during the formulation of regulations, their views on the practical and philosophical problems involved. Dunlop suggested that there should be not only prior consultation of the parties, but prior *joint* consultation. Regulations, he believes, should be developed by three equal partners—business, labor, and government—rather than by the government alone after the obligatory hearings for the other two parties are completed—at a stage far too early for them to participate in the actual formulation of rules.

Construction Industry

The potential for mutual gain through the formation of labor–management committees has attracted considerable interest in the construction industry. Collective bargaining agreements in St. Louis, Indianapolis, Boston, Columbus, Nevada, and Colorado provide for local labor–management councils, which concern themselves with work rules and other problems that affect productivity and competitiveness within the construction industry.

The St. Louis Council's acronym is PRIDE, Productivity and Responsibility Increases Development and Employment. PRIDE's account of its accomplishments includes changes in work rules, reduction of jurisdictional disputes, a lowering of construction costs in comparison with other areas, and improved morale and communication on the job site. Once ranked among the most expensive areas in which to build homes, St. Louis is now at the low end of the scale in home-building costs.

Health-Care Industry

Quietly, but regularly, labor and management representatives of the private health-care industry across the country have been meeting as a committee under FMCS auspices to discuss a range of issues affecting that major industry. The management members are made up of the American Hospital Association, the League of Voluntary Hospitals, Kaiser Permanente, and individuals who represent large groupings of hospitals in their geographical areas. There are representatives of seven unions on the committee: these are the Service Employees International Union; the Laborers' International Union; The American Nurses Association; the Operating Engineers; United Food and Commercial Workers; Licensed Practical Nurses; and District 1199 of the Retail, Wholesale and Department Store Union.

Of late, the committee has begun to discuss some issues of concern to both parties which, in the broadest sense, have an impact on the efficiency, and thus the productivity, of the industry. One topic under discussion is the geographical supply of and demand for nurses, the ratio of licensed practical nurses to registered nurses, and hospital cost-containment legislation in Congress.

Steel Industry

In their new collective bargaining agreement signed in mid-April, the major steel companies and the United Steel Workers union scrapped the existing productivity councils and introduced a new experiment in labor–management cooperation. This provides for the establishment of "participation teams" to deal with job-related issues during the life of the contract. The program, specifically spelled out in the agreement, authorizes the local parties at the department level to "discuss, consider, and decide upon proposed means to improve department or unit performance, employee morale and dignity, and conditions of the work site." The companies and the union describe this as a "radical departure" from previous efforts primarily because it allows the local parties to explore a full range of solutions to their problems. The agreement calls for the program to go into effect on "a pilot basis only at those plants where both the local union and the local plant management agree they want to be part of the experiment."

According to the contract, appropriate subjects for discussion by a team include: use of production facilities, quality of products and quality of the work environment, safety and environmental health, scheduling and reporting arrangements, absenteeism and overtime, incentive coverage and yield, job alignments, contracting out, and energy conservation and transportation pools. All are subjects which either bear directly on productivity or have an indirect impact on it.

Community-Wide Labor–Management Committees

Labor and management in several communities have found that cooperation on an area-wide basis has been a way of getting at severe economic problems which were damaging the positions of both parties. In Jamestown, New York, unions and companies got together under the leadership of then Mayor and now Congressman Stanley Lundine to form an effective plan which forestalled the departure of some industry with its attendant job loss.

Thriving and ongoing area labor–management committees are alive and well in both Buffalo, New York, and Evansville, Indiana. Robert Ahern, executive director of the Buffalo–Erie County Labor–Management Committee, in a recent report outlining the origins and accomplishments of the committee, described its beginnings thus:

"In 1975, Buffalo reached the bottom. Between 1970 and 1975 30,000 manufacturing jobs, 20 percent of the total, had been lost. Unemployment was approaching 11 percent. The city teetered on the brink of bankruptcy. The county was hurrying toward its own severe financial problems which would result in a crisis a year and a half later. Buffalo ranked among the top three cities in the nation in working time lost due to strikes in 1970, 1972, and 1975. Construction had virtually ground to a halt. The downtown was dotted with patches of blight. The once thriving port was moribund. It was the worst of times."[9]

In the face of these conditions, labor and management leaders sought each other out to determine what could be done to reverse the situation. A small group of representatives from both business and labor discussed the problem with the congressional delegation, the county executive, and the mayor of Buffalo in a series of private meetings. These officials decided that two glaring problems could be solved by joint union–management effort: (1) The various economic development agencies, which had been factionalized and warring bureaucracies, could be brought together under one coordinating agency headed by labor, management, and local government; and (2) the area's labor relations could be improved to reverse the city's long-standing image of being a "bad labor town."

At the end of three-and-a-half years of experience, the committee could point to these accomplishments described by Ahern:

"Since early 1976 the economic situation has been reversed. Total employment has increased 10 percent, and almost 50,000 jobs have been added. About 10,000 of those jobs are in manufacturing, and some 8,000 jobs have been added in construction. The unemployment rate is the lowest it has been in the decade. Working time lost due to strikes has fallen in each of the three years of the council's existence, and instead of ranking first, the city now ranks below the median of a sample of 33 major cities. County government is stable, and the city has a surplus. The Port of Buffalo has had more traffic this year than in the last six years put together. The downtown area is crawling with construction sites. A new convention center, new hotels, a rapid transit system, new arterial roads, industrial parks, and a growing sense of regeneration and pride have developed."[10]

A "bad" labor image and the loss of a major employer some years ago led to the formation of another currently active area labor–management committee, in Evansville, Indiana. The strike that led to the formation of the committee came at Whirlpool, the town's major employer after Chrysler moved out, and is cited by many of those who were involved in the formation of the committee as the turning point in the area's relations between labor and management.

As in the formation of several area labor–management committees and countless in-plant committees, the initial suggestion that such an arrangement might prove fruitful came from an FMCS Commissioner. The idea was picked up by the major unions and companies in the area, and with the FMCS providing the third-party guidance and counseling which is most often the necessary ingredient in the start-up of these arrangements, the committee flourished. Both sides credit the committee with fostering an improved labor–management relations climate, which has resulted in a reduction in strikes.

Some of the Evansville committee's effectiveness can be traced to the simple fact that it exists. Indeed, what these committees are proving is that by "simply existing," they are providing a forum for the parties to talk out mutual problems and to seek their solution. Their easy availability to the parties to a dispute makes it more than likely that they will be used.

One of the founding members of the committee, Jack Buttrum, has offered this explanation of the climate created by the committee:

"The committee sets high standards. Members who are on the committee try to live up to them. We got a settlement between one company and a union largely because both sides committed themselves to get one, and they didn't quit until they did. In almost any other setting, there would have been a strike."

PREVENTIVE MEDIATION

It is part of a federal mediator's bag of tools to be knowledgeable about the formation and operation of labor–management committees. It is part of the range of services FMCS can provide to the parties, although it is not as well known as mediation. Such programs, initiated as "preventive mediation," have now become part of the FMCS "technical assistance function."

In its broadest terms, preventive mediation consists of getting the parties to recognize that they have a relationship problem, getting them to sit down and jointly examine the reasons for the problem, and then devising a mechanism for getting at solutions.

Joint labor–management committees are one such mechanism. A variation of the committee is a program that FMCS has found successful over recent years called relations by objectives (RBO). The RBO is a highly structured program usually run by a team of federal mediators designed to persuade the leadership on both sides of the table to analyze what it is they are doing wrong, and then to set specific goals and timetables to eliminate the problems. A primary thrust is to cure the problem common to many relationships of time lost to strikes and grievances; both of these have a direct bearing on productivity. Among the companies which have undergone RBO programs are United Parcel Service in New York City, Whirlpool in Indiana, Georgia-Pacific, and several unions in Maine.

The RBO program, involving United Parcel and the 5,000 member Teamsters Local 804 in New York, is worth a closer look:

The program was instituted as part of an agreement that brought an end to a bitter 13-week strike that crippled package delivery in the metropolitan New York City area in 1974. The strike was the culmination of labor problems that had resulted in a strike at every contract expiration since the early 1960s, and from 3 to 12 wildcat walkouts every year.

Some 80 to 90 management and labor leaders—from the top level to the floor supervisors and plant stewards—were involved in sessions conducted over six months. The result: In 1977, a new contract was negotiated and ratified three weeks before the old contract was to expire. The vote: 2,717 to 348. There have been no wildcat strikes since the RBO programs started. Grievances and arbitration cases have been reduced by 75 percent.

And management says that productivity has increased by more than 20 percent, directly attributable to the improvement in worker morale since RBO was launched. All of the productivity increase is credited to the improved attitude among workers and supervisors, since no new automated equipment was installed during that period.

THE FUTURE OF LABOR-MANAGEMENT COOPERATION

With recorded results such as these, along with the enthusiastic testimonials of the users, the natural question is why have these arrangements not been utilized more? Unfortunately, labor and management seem to be more occupied with pointing their fingers at each other as the prime blame for inflation and a host of other economic ills, while other voices decry the lack of productivity gains from either.

It is disturbing that for all of the anguished cries that we do something about productivity, there is no discernible organized effort to provide any sort of mechanism to do anything about it. There is nothing in place to make it happen.

Despite expressions of concern from the top ranks of both labor and management about the state of productivity, there has been no major, joint effort on their part to demand such a mechanism. It is time for both labor and management to provide a bit of leadership in devising a set of steps to improve productivity rather than offering rhetoric about who is to blame for there not being any. One way to do this is for labor and management to get together at their top levels, discuss jointly what it is that needs doing, and then jointly present their program to the administration and to Congress.

A major part of the reason that this has not happened can be found in the state of the relations between labor and management generally in this country. There is no question that relations between the parties have worsened, not only at the bargaining table—and that's bad enough—but in the entire range of their relations. The rhetoric coming from both sides is strident and divisive. We seem to be heading back to the politics of confrontation. And that is bad for collective bargaining, because there is no attempt at the kind of accommodation needed in this relationship to begin solving some of the really difficult problems the parties face.

In light of this situation, one can begin to understand why joint labor–management committees have not been more widely utilized, despite their problem-solving potential. The sad fact is that these arrangements are acceptable to the parties only when outside forces have literally frightened them into the same room. The major industry is leaving town, taking thousands of jobs, for example. Or a bad labor climate that has gotten worse is scaring prospective industries away from the area. There has to be, it seems, some strong negative force in effect, pushing the parties into what they regard as this court of last resort.

The mechanization and modernization agreement in the West Coast longshoring industry came about only after 20 years of guerrilla warfare on the waterfront. A revolution in technology was occurring with the advent of containerization. Because of the restrictive work rules that had grown up in this industry, the introduction of technology enabling the Pacific maritime ports to remain competitive was blocked. The longshoremen and the port employers had the simple decision before them of whether they would continue their debilitating war or adjust. They finally chose to adjust.

What concerns me is that if the only way American labor and management can come to the utilization of labor–management committees is as a last resort, then I fear we will start to fall farther and farther behind in facing up to the growing problems confronting industry.

Management must share part of the responsibility for failing to explore the problem-solving potential of such joint arrangements as labor–management committees. I have contended for some time, and I don't see anything today which disabuses me of this view, that American management has never been willing to accept the bilateral foundation of the collective bargaining system. It will accept unions as adversaries reluctantly. Management understands the responsibilities and rights of unions under the law even if it does not agree with the law. But it rigorously avoids any step which might cast unions in the role of an equal partner.

It is not as if American management isn't able to be innovative in this field. Drucker has observed that "Europe and Japan now have the managerial edge in many of the areas which we used to consider American strengths, if not American monopolies."[11] But what he also finds is that the management practices being used—including the quality control circles now being imported from Japan—were American in origin in the fifties and sixties, and even before. A major reason why some of these techniques and practices are not being currently used by American management is that they involve degrees of shared participation and increased responsibility on the part of the work force or its representatives. This establishes the legitimacy of unions as equal partners, which management finds unacceptable.

Labor also bears a share of blame for what I believe is a missed opportunity offered by the greater utilization of labor-management committees. Organizationally unions find it difficult to recognize that American management is faced with real and sizable problems, stemming from imports and the sagging economy, and that it has a legitimate need to free its operations from some of the rigidities which have grown into the labor-management relationship. In many cases, these are no longer either applicable or defensible.

With the potential for problem solving that labor-managment committees have shown in practical application, both management and labor should be showing more positive acceptance of this concept. Such arrangements are perfectly compatible with the collective bargaining relationship, and indeed can strengthen it. What is needed to help cure some of the present ills that beset collective bargaining is to broaden the opportunities for that relationship to work and not to narrow them, as both labor and management seem to be doing. These institutional arrangements offer a survival mechanism for both labor and management. The sooner this is recognized, the better off both sectors will be.

There is no question that collective bargaining is beset by problems. It always has been and always will be, because that is the nature of the process.

What is needed is for the labor-management community to respond to these problems with some innovation and daring and some willingness to take risks in search of solutions to these problems. If it does not, we are in danger of losing an institution that has worked well for us.

If I had to single out one element that I think is crucial to this process, it is trust. It is trust that produces the kind of give and take the collective bargaining process needs to make it go. What I get out of the current confrontation rhetoric is that the parties no longer have the kind of trust that enables them, for example, to form a labor–management committee to work on the kinds of problems that involve both their interests.

I attach a great deal of importance to this element of trust and to the potential of these kinds of committees. Experience shows that they can be of considerable help in defusing problems that have become so complex that it is not possible to arrive at comprehensive, thoughtful, and constructive solutions within the present bargaining framework.

I believe we have come to the stage in our development of industrial relations where progress—perhaps even survival—ultimately depends on a shared recognition of the need for joint cooperation. The forces that obstruct the collective bargaining relationship have shaken our faith and belief in the standard economic responses for correcting the imbalances of the economy.

Because our system of industrial relations is so intertwined with economics, I believe that we are being told that the traditional labor–management attitudes and answers are no longer applicable. Our experience with the workings of labor–management committees and other cooperative arrangements still is new, but one lesson that I believe is clearly emerging is that change is more easily accommodated and sustained if reached jointly rather than unilaterally imposed by management or unwillingly extracted by labor.

I have always felt that the vast majority of Americans believe in their institutions. They are disappointed and disillusioned when that belief, that faith, is shattered by the performance of the stewards of those institutions. When failure in performance is accompanied by loss of faith on the part of the stewards themselves, we are in trouble.

The representatives of labor and management, who have the ultimate responsibility to make collective bargaining work, should be mindful of the unique quality of the institution they have created.

It is their task to keep intact the best of what has been done, create innovations, and keep the spirit of the past for the work of the future.

This is the challenge ahead for collective bargaining. I believe it is time we started work on it.

NOTES

1. "Making Arbitration Palatable," *Business Week*, March 10, 1980, p. 123.
2. Michael Harrington, "The Productivity Ploy," *The New York Times*, Op Ed page, March 21, 1980.
3. Michael Maccoby, "What is Productivity?" *Value World*, July–September 1979, p. 7.
4. Peter F. Drucker, "The Job as Property Right," *Wall Street Journal*, editorial page, March 4, 1980.
5. Harry Bernstein, "Bridges' Revolution Boosted Dock Pay, Productivity Too," *Los Angeles Times*, March 8, 1980, pt. IV, p. 1.
6. Irving Bluestone, "How to Put Quality of Work Life to Work," a paper presented at a conference on "Critical Economic and Work Force Issues," sponsored by the Work in America Institute in Washington, D.C., December 1979.
7. Ibid.
8. Ibid.
9. Robert W. Ahern, *The Area-Wide Labor–Management Committee: The Buffalo Experience* (Buffalo, N.Y.: Buffalo–Erie County Labor–Management Council, 1979).
10. Ibid.
11. "Learning from Foreign Management," *Wall Street Journal*, editorial page, June 4, 1980.

14.

Employee Participation for Productivity: A Management View

Stephen H. Fuller
Vice-President, General Motors Corporation

From its earliest days, the United States has been a grand social experiment, an experiment based on the inalienable rights of individuals and the application of democratic principles. The experiment continues today, and the momentum of 200 years is generating another revolution.

The aim of today's revolution is the guarantee of democratic ideals in *all* of our institutions—the military, the church, labor unions, and business. In the workplace the manifestation of this revolution is known as "quality of work life."

In practice, quality of work life involves a variety of interactions:

- Employee involvement on the factory floor and in the office.
- Better relationships, especially between supervisors and the people reporting to them.
- Cooperation between union and management.
- Improved integration of people and technology.

Quality of work life is all of these things and more:

- Quality of work life is a continuing process, and not something that can be turned on today and turned off tomorrow.
- It is utilizing all resources, especially human resources, better today than yesterday, and even better tomorrow.
- It is developing among all the members of an organization an awareness and understanding of the concerns and needs of

others, and a willingness to be more responsive to those concerns and needs.

- Finally, quality of work life is improving the way things get done to assure the long-term effectiveness and success of organizations.

It is important to understand what quality of work life is. It is also important to understand what it is not.

Quality of work life is not a happiness program, although happy employees may certainly be a by-product. It is not a personnel department program, although quality of work life has important implications for personnel management. It is not a subtle employee incentive program, although employees motivated to achieving the goals of the organization certainly ought to be one of the outcomes. And it is not another productivity program, although better productivity is certainly one of the important results.

Because of the wide range of benefits to the individual and the organization, at General Motors we are making a concerted effort to improve the quality of work life for all our employees. QWL projects are under way in most of our North American operations and in many of our operations overseas.

Our approach to quality of work life was not developed overnight. It has evolved from a philosophy of management, shaped by events and experiences occurring over a considerable period of time.

Our planned, organized approach began in 1969 following a series of sporadic, crippling strikes in several of our car and truck assembly plants across the country. We launched a pilot QWL program, using the resources of the Institute for Social Research of the University of Michigan.[1]

We had two major goals for this initial organizational development effort: (1) to seek long-term improvements in the human organization of General Motors, and (2) to stimulate new concepts of managing people, concepts more consistent with the changing nature of the modern work force.

Initially, four GM plants were involved in research and organization development activities. Major emphasis was placed on employee involvement, information sharing, and training. We learned that there is a close relationship between an organization's performance and how employees feel about the organization—how they feel about the work climate, the quality of management, and employee–management relationships.

The project demonstrated that we could improve performance *and* human satisfaction by creating conditions in which people can become more involved, work together, and experience personal growth and development. Since then a number of steps have been taken by General Motors to initiate and sustain a process of organizational improvement.

In 1971 a conference was held to explore the spectrum of our people-related problems. That conference has evolved into an annual executive conference on quality of work life; it has become an important vehicle for sharing ideas and encouraging further action throughout the corporation. Other means of creating understanding and support for quality-of-work-life principles also have been developed. Quality-of-work-life familiarization meetings are held regularly in the General Motors Building in Detroit. For supervisors, a program has been introduced which focuses on the relationship between quality of work life and productivity.

We also saw a need for reliable data on employee perceptions of quality of work life. A few years ago we inaugurated a survey to assess 16 different areas of work life, among them the physical work environment, economic well-being, the development and utilization of employee skills and abilities, employee involvement and influence, and supervisory and work-group relationships. Today, the survey is being used primarily with salaried employees, but we are encouraging its use among hourly employees as well. The survey is helping us evaluate our progress in improving the quality of work life and in assessing the effectiveness of specific projects. Additionally, many units are using it as a springboard for involving more people in identifying problems and in developing solutions.

Another key component of our QWL process is union participation. Quality of work life became a joint effort of General Motors and the United Automobile Workers in 1973 when we established a National Committee to Improve the Quality of Work Life. Representing the UAW on the committee are two high-level officials of the international union. The corporation is represented by the two officers responsible for personnel matters. The committee meets periodically to discuss joint activities under way in the corporation. One of its chief functions has been to educate executives of the union and the corporation in order to encourage cooperative QWL ventures at the local level.

Furthering quality of work life requires coordination and constant attention. Five minimum standards have been adopted by our units to assure that every location has the basics of a QWL effort. Each operation is expected to have:

1. A group to oversee the quality-of-work-life process.
2. A statement of long-term objectives incorporating quality of work life along with other desirable business targets.
3. Regular measurement of quality of work life.
4. Seminars and other activities to make the organization more knowledgeable about QWL concepts and techniques.
5. Adequate internal resources and skills to assure that the developmental process is moving ahead and accomplishing its objectives.

In all cases, specific approaches are optional; however, quality-of-work-life-improvement is mandatory. Let me offer a few examples of how quality of work life is being applied in General Motors.

QUALITY OF WORK LIFE AT EXISTING GM PLANTS

One of our assembly plants could have been characterized, a decade ago, as a problem plant. There was an air of hostility between management and the union. Costs were high. Performance was poor. Something had to be done. Fortunately, the local management and union were willing to take some initiatives. As both sides explored and discussed their mutual problems and concerns, an atmosphere of understanding and mutual respect began to emerge. In 1972 the plant faced a major rearrangement, and, for the first time, management took the opportunity to involve employees in planning the change. The rearrangement went well, due in part to the suggestions of hourly employees.

Then, following the lead set by the GM–UAW National Quality of Work Life Committee, plant management and the union established their own committee. In 1977 management and the union initiated a three-day training program for all employees at the plant. The program provided employees with training in team problem solving. At the same time, it was an opportunity for management and the union to tell employees about their plant and their union. The program was completely voluntary, but nearly all of the 3,600 employees participated over a period of about a year and a half.

What about the bottom line—for people and for the organization? Today, employee morale at that plant is high. Grievances are only a fraction of what they were a decade ago. While the signs point to a much-improved quality of work life, the plant also has become one of the best-performing assembly plants in General Motors.

Another GM plant abandoned the traditional organization structure a few years ago. Today the plant is organized into six business teams, each consisting of the necessary production activities and support elements: engineering, scheduling, material handling, quality control, and maintenance and accounting. The system has made support people an integral part of the plant's business operations. Support and manufacturing people together can now function better as a team. Involvement also extends to hourly employees. The quality control circle concept, which has flourished in Japan and is being introduced by a growing number of firms in this country, has been incorporated into the business team structure. The circle concept gives hourly employees the opportunity to meet regularly to work on problems affecting their work environment and the plant's performance.

These are only two of many approaches under way in established GM plants. We also are focusing a lot of attention on new plants.

QUALITY OF WORK LIFE AT NEW GM PLANTS

In contrast to existing organizations, a new plant offers a unique opportunity to design an organization from a blank sheet of paper—an organization in which the quality of work life and the effectiveness of the organization are mutually supportive. Free from the constraints of past practice and stereotyped roles, each new plant is an opportunity to introduce new approaches.

Underlying our initiatives in new plants are three important considerations:

First, there is no best system or organizational design. What is best for one plant may not be best for another plant.

Second, there is an ongoing interaction among the parts of the system. A change in one part of the system can have a significant impact on the entire system.

And third, each part of the system must reinforce consistency of operations and facilitate employee involvement.

To achieve an organizational system in which each part is congruent with the rest, careful consideration is given to the basic values, principles, and objectives held by local management. We view the development of a philosophy and goals, then, as a necessary first step in the planning process. The philosophy and goals are statements reflecting the local management's beliefs about people and work and the relationship between those beliefs and the plant's objectives (figure 14.1 is the philosophy and goals developed by one of our new plants).

A team concept is a major feature of many of our new plants. Job

It is possible to organize work to meet the personal needs for self-respect and personal improvement while still achieving the objectives of the business.

Every individual is unique and has the ability to contribute to the objectives of the organization.

When people are treated as adults, they behave as adults.

The more responsibility people have, the more responsible they become.

How the business is managed significantly affects the behavior and performance of individual members.

Just as employees have a responsibility to contribute to the objectives of the organization, they have the right to share in the organization's success.

When work is interdependent, cooperation is more effective than competition.

Social and technological innovation is necessary for organization survival.

People support what they help create.

Figure 14.1. Philosophy and Goals of a New GM Plant

rotation within the team is encouraged. Employees thus acquire broader skills which, in turn, allow for greater flexibility in performing all of the tasks within the team. This concept tends to promote employee involvement and satisfaction, and to minimize the disruptive effects of occasional absenteeism and turnover. Employees are encouraged to move from one team to another, once they have learned all of the jobs in the team. This further adds to the fulfillment of employee interests and to the expansion of experiences and achievements.

The team concept encourages a high degree of employee responsibility and involvement. For example, employees may have responsibility for:

- Training team members.
- Assessing individual team members' progress in satisfactorily performing job assignments.
- Forecasting efficiency, scrap, and work force requirements in their operating areas.
- Recommending corrective action for improper conduct of team members.
- Contributing to the selection of new employees.
- Selecting team leaders.
- Maintaining operation of tools and equipment within process standards.

Our plants are placing major emphasis on effective two-way communication, particularly face-to-face communication. It begins with the orientation, which usually includes, in addition to traditional topics, a thorough review of the plant's philosophy and goals. Periodic plant meetings and team meetings are used to discuss pertinent aspects of the business—for example, quality, schedules, scrap and rework, housekeeping, safety, employee facilities, production facilities, and customer orders. There also is ample opportunity for employees to discuss their concerns with management.

A few new plants have adopted pay systems which provide for employee compensation based on the ability to perform different jobs. An employee's rate is dependent upon the number of jobs he or she can perform. Teams normally have greater autonomy than traditional work groups. The inspection function, for example, usually is integrated into the team's overall responsibilities. In these plants there is essentially only one job classification for production employees—team member.

All our QWL efforts require a firm commitment at the top levels of the corporation to QWL principles and objectives. This high-level support, combined with a variety of successful projects, has led to the creation of a process of quality-of-work-life improvement in nearly all GM plants. I do not mean to imply that we have all the answers or that quality of work life is fully developed in General Motors. On the contrary, we recognize there is much that has to be done, but we think that we are on the right track and making progress.

We in the personnel function in General Motors are excited about our role in this effort. Specifically, our role is to facilitate the process through organizational development, consulting with management, with employees, and with their elected representatives to see that quality of work life takes hold and grows. We also recognize that quality of work life has a strong impact on the personnel function, and that there is a real need to "personnel-ize" quality of work life. Well-conceived and effectively administered personnel programs are absolutely essential for a strong quality-of-work-life effort.

One such program is a system of redress for salaried employees and those hourly employees not represented by a union. A formal open-door policy is one approach, but it must have the support of all levels of management. An effective appraisal system for all employees, including managers and executives, also is essential. Employees must know exactly where they stand in terms of their performance. The appraisal also should evaluate managers' support and implementation of quality-of-work-life principles.

Training for all employees, including lower-level salaried and hourly employees, is an absolute necessity. If employees are to be involved in the decision-making process, if they are to grow and develop, they must have the opportunity to acquire the necessary knowledge and skills.

Finally, it is necessary to have a statement of philosophy that spells out the general role people have in the organization and how they are to be treated. A statement of philosophy that represents the consensus of senior management provides a basis for encouraging managerial behavior consistent across plants and functions. The philosophy, when widely communicated, also lets employees know how they can expect to be treated.

An increasing number of GM managers and organizations, attuned to the rising expectations of a better educated work force, are questioning the percepts of scientific management and are demonstrating a willingness to experiment with new approaches.

At the same time, an important shift in union–management relations began in the decade of the 70s. Unions and management are showing a willingness to explore new alternatives and, in some instances, levels of cooperation once thought impossible are producing dramatic results.

QUALITY OF WORK LIFE IN THE EIGHTIES

In this decade employees, unions, and management together have taken a few circumspect steps toward a new world of work. What about the decade of the eighties? What is the future of quality of work life in America?

Quality of work life in the 1980s and beyond will face serious challenges. The ability of people and organizations to adapt and to change will be tested. I would like to touch on some of the challenges quality of work life must meet if the seeds of innovation of the seventies are to bear fruit in the years ahead.

As we begin the 1980s, two critical forces will have a significant impact on the future of quality of work life.

One is the changing values people bring to the workplace. An increased sense of entitlement, disregard for authority, and a general low esteem for our institutions have been major factors in the developmental years of quality of work life. The whole concept of work is being redefined by today's workers who are placing less emphasis on material achievement and more on personal fulfillment. A majority of Americans feels aspirations for self-fulfillment can no longer be wholly satisfied through conventional success.[2] A new breed of worker talks about achieving potential and personal growth and development. The value shift of Americans will significantly influence the future of quality of work life.

The other critical force is economic. While business is being challenged to respond to dramatically changing values, our country is facing economic problems. Chrysler Corporation has received a great deal of publicity. Other companies also are confronted with economic difficulties. At General Motors we are faced with extremely high capital expenditures to meet the changing needs of consumers and to comply with government regulations. At the same time, our ability to accumulate capital for reinvestment is inhibited by a declining profit margin.

These problems are not peculiar to the automotive industry; other companies find themselves in similar circumstances. The fact of the matter is, the United States is locked in a fiercely competitive economic struggle which could have either a positive or negative impact on quality of work life—positive if it leads to innovative solutions and negative if it results in simply greater emphasis on traditional approaches.

Our nation's poor productivity improvement rate is a major factor contributing to our economic ills. The problem has not come about overnight. Between 1947 and 1967 output per hour of work in the United States nearly doubled. Since 1967 output per hour worked has risen only about one-fifth. Even before the 1974–1975 recession, the rate of productivity growth had slowed—from 3.3 percent annual rate of growth before 1967 to around 2 percent for the 1967–1972 period.[3] At the time, it was thought a 2 percent productivity growth rate was disturbingly low. But things have become worse. In 1978 the United States' productivity growth rate was an alarming one-half of 1 percent, a dismal performance compared to the rate of growth of other major industrial nations, particularly Japan.[4]

In the past America has been able to compete with cheap overseas labor because of our capital investment. In 1978, however, capital investment per worker in this country amounted to less than $3,700 as compared to over $4,700 per worker in Germany and nearly $5,000 per Japanese worker.

Capital investment per worker is not the sole reason for Japan's superior productivity performance. According to Joji Arai, manager of Japan's Productivity Center, there are many factors in addition to capital investment which contribute to Japan's envious productivity growth rate.[5] Among them, he says, are government policies and programs that actively support economic expansion, technological innovation, and harmonious union–management relations.

There is a spirit of nationalism in Japan that is reflected in business, government, and labor and supported by educational institutions. The success of a Japanese business is tied to the success of government, education, and labor. In general, the adversary relationship between union and management that is characteristic of this country is far less prominent in Japan. But Japanese management also recognizes that the union has a contribution to make. Overall, the Japanese have built an extremely complex economic and social system that results in a positive climate that has been missing in this country.

There are other important factors contributing to Japan's success. One of these is a totally dedicated work force.

Group goals are far more important than individual successes in the Japanese structure. It is hard for many Western managers to appreciate the importance of this, but it is a tenet of the Japanese system and vital to the rest of their activities.

In Germany, government has given strong financial support to job redesign experiments. As in Japan, a uniquely German approach to quality of work life is developing in a way that is consistent with the cultural, economic, and political heritage of the country.

I do not think we can ignore the traits present in Japanese and German systems. There is much for us to learn from what is occurring in both countries. In this country we have been overly loyal to organizational tradition. But today we cannot afford not to take new risks. In time of war we did not hesitate to form coalitions that gave us strength and fixed our hearts and minds on a common objective. The joint efforts of business, government, and labor are essential if we are to respond to the needs of a changing work force and resolve our economic problems.

OBSTACLES TO QUALITY OF WORK LIFE

As we push forward the frontiers of quality of work life in this country there are some formidable obstacles to be overcome. One of the questions we must answer is the issue of control. Should control be viewed as external to the individual, as provided for through a supervisor and shop rules? Or should it lie within the individual's self-regulating ability and value system, based upon mutual influence and interest that leads to "win–win" rather than "win–lose" relationships? Moving from external to self-regulating sources of control would seem to be consistent with the quality-of-work-life viewpoint.

Related to the issue of control, how much training and how much information is management willing to provide if employees are to be self-regulating? Many organizations in the past have been cautious about sharing information, particularly financial information, for fear employees will use this knowledge to make "unfair" claims on the enterprise.

Another obstacle in the way of quality of work life is the traditional role of the first-line supervisor. In innovative new plants where there is a high degree of employee involvement, supervisors may function as advisers to the teams of hourly employees. As quality of work life develops in established plants, the role of the supervisor will have to change to keep pace with changes in the total work system. Such change may be rejected by some supervisors.

A few General Motors locations have introduced quality control circles, but we have found that first-line supervisors are not always prepared to function as leaders in problem-solving meetings with employees. Sometimes supervisors do not see circle activities as dovetailing with their own supervisory responsibilities. In other cases supervisors are reluctant to start a circle because they feel out of place in the facilitating mode. Our experience has shown that with the proper education, experience, and support from above, supervisors can take on facilitating and coordinating roles that are consistent with quality of work life. The transition, however, is not always easy and will continue to be a significant challenge in the decade ahead.

Other organizational roles will have to undergo change as quality of work life progresses. One of them is the role of the union steward. The steward's role today has evolved out of decades of adversary relationships. But in our new plants we are finding that systems can be created in which organizational objectives are compatible with human needs and goals—systems in which harmony and cooperation are in the best interests of everyone. While any redefinition of the role of the steward is first the responsibility of the union, management must provide assistance and cooperation in the development of an appropriate alternative.

Related to the role of the union steward is another challenge for quality of work life—the labor contract. The first labor contracts were written with union and management at war, and they have been amended over decades of distrust. I think that as we implement quality of work life more fully, and as union and management search for ways to cooperate, we will find that some provisions of the labor contract may impede the growth of quality of work life. Aspects of the labor contract should be examined on the basis of whether they contribute to, or detract from, the development of quality of work life. Both sides have to be willing to reevaluate the contract and develop modifications that provide far greater latitude for implementing quality-of-work-life practices and are, at the same time, in keeping with the spirit of the contract.

If the obstacles to the development of quality of work life are to be overcome, three important conditions must be in place. First, the integrity of the union and management must be assured. Quality of work life cannot be perceived to be a plot by management to keep the union out or to diminish the union's strength. By the same token, management must be confident that the union will not use quality of work life as a bargaining lever.

Second, employees must have a high degree of economic security. Unless employees feel they are economically secure, quality of work life has little chance of developing its full potential. In Japan, for example, which has a strong quality-of-work-life program, employees are not laid off when there is a downturn in business. I think we in this country too must find innovative ways of utilizing people during economic downturns. This is critically important because we cannot expect people to immerse themselves in the organization if the threat of layoff hangs over their heads.

Third, we must develop managers and union leaders who can and will practice quality of work life. If our American brand of quality of work life is to prosper, then we must develop a new breed of manager who will be responsive to the new breed of employee. In our selection, development, and evaluation of managers we must make it clear that there is no room in the organization for managers who are not committed to quality-of-work-life principles.

The quality of union leadership in the future will be just as important in determining the success of quality of work life. Union leaders who are willing to take risks and to express their commitment and support can significantly help in the diffusion of workplace innovation. One such individual is Irving Bluestone, former vice-president of the UAW and former head of the union's GM department. By his support at the top echelon of the UAW, Mr. Bluestone, now retired, made a valuable contribution to the quality-of-work-life movement in General Motors and in other companies.

Now is the time to take new risks. Now is the time to be innovative and to form new coalitions. The great problems being experienced in this turbulent period demand a change in the nature of existing relationships. The collaborative relationship among government, unions, and employers in many societies demonstrates the great potential for resolving issues that affect the working lives of people.

Our generation has begun to explore new territory. Today we are at the threshold of a revolution that holds great promise for our organizations and for people. America's quality-of-work-life movement, with the partnership of government, unions, and employers, can bring to our country renewed strength and the promise of a more secure future.

Management will not solve these problems alone. Labor will not solve them alone. Only through a team effort of management and labor, linked together by common interest and mutual respect, will these obstacles be conquered and quality of work life given the freedom to advance to new horizons.

We have the resources and the opportunity. Do we have the courage to ascend to new heights of human excellence?

NOTES

1. W. F. Dowling, "System 4 Builds Performance and Profits," *Organization Dynamics,* Winter 1975.
2. Daniel Yankelovich, "Work, Values, and the New Breed," in *Work in America: The Decade Ahead,* edited by Clark Kerr and Jerome M. Rosow (New York: Van Nostrand Reinhold, 1979).
3. G. William Miller. Remarks at a productivity conference sponsored by the American Productivity Center, New York City, October 3, 1978.
4. United States Department of Labor, Bureau of Labor Statistics.
5. Joji Arai, "Productivity—the Japanese Approach," *Production Engineering,* September 1979.

15.

Employee Participation for Productivity: A Labor View

Douglas A. Fraser
President, United Automobile Workers of America

Productivity trends are of great concern to workers and unions. We recognize that growing productivity is the only reliable basis for real progress in living standards: it provides access to increased and improved services, such as health, education, and recreation, as well as to more and better material comforts. Accordingly, we in the United Automobile Workers (UAW) have long acknowledged the importance of continual improvements in productivity, that is, increases in the output associated with an hour of human labor. American workers can enjoy greater purchasing power, greater leisure, or both, as the economy increases its capacity to convert a given amount of intensity of work into ever more output.

This truth has been painfully brought home to us in the seventies, as wage and salary earners have experienced real declines in their incomes throughout the decade at the hands of the "stagflation" that is partially rooted in the widely discussed productivity slowdown.

For workers, however, higher productivity is not without its penalties in the form of job downgrading or, more frequently, outright job loss. Hence, workers cannot be enlisted in wholehearted efforts to increase productivity unless protection against unemployment is assured. In industries where demand for the product is not expected to increase enough to provide this assurance, other remedies, such as reduced work time, adjustment assistance, and training and relocation benefits must be forthcoming. For example, in the auto industry in 1980, the combination of the business cycle, the increase in gasoline prices plus the fear of gas shortages, the onslaught of imports, and high productivity growth decimated the ranks of auto workers. The impact on employment would have been far worse, of course, had the union not negotiated many arrangements to reduce scheduled work time: holidays, vacations, retirement programs, paid absence allowance, paid personal holidays, and other programs.

One cannot overemphasize the connection between job security and increasing productivity. Workers can reasonably be expected to cooperate with management's attempts to substitute new machinery and new processes for direct labor only if they perceive that they will not be the victims. An intriguing international study found that job security was critical in influencing what industrial workers in 15 countries thought about technological innovations and the effects of automation. The authors assert that

> The important question here was not the spectre of being unemployed, but whether the worker felt secure in his own job, or could count on an acceptable alternative if necessary. This consideration was evident in all countries, even those socialist states which had guaranteed full employment. What bothered many workers was that they might be displaced from a position they liked and have to move to a less agreeable job or location. Assurance that this would not happen stimulated confidence that automation had benefited workers and support for introducing new machinery and equipment.[1]

THE INVESTMENT SHORTFALL

In recent years we have been told, with no little alarmism, that our economy is threatened by a decline in the trend rate of productivity increase. That rate, according to government statistics, plunged from about 3 percent per year in the 1950s and 1960s to just 1.4 percent in the 1970s. Dark insinuations are drawn from these official data: American workers are getting lazy; our mature economy is becoming soft; we have lost the "work ethic."

Only one of these statements has any possible merit. It is true, I think, that the economy is getting soft, losing its postwar dynamism:

American business has, since the late 1960s, been guilty of what amounts to a "capital strike." In a word, business has been deindustrializing America by failing to invest fast enough and creatively enough. The annual growth rate of real nonresidential fixed investment declined from 6.6 percent in 1945–66 to 2.6 percent in 1966–79. That is a substantial decline, and all the more worrisome because—for at least two reasons—there must be an increasing rate of investment just to maintain constant productivity growth. First, as much as 10 percent of recent new investment has gone to meet government standards; much of this spending is treated as unproductive, since safety, health, and environmental preservation are not counted as output. As stated later on, we believe this is a shortcoming in the measurement of output. Second, new investment is occurring "on top of" an existing capital stock whose efficiency is being undermined by changes in the relative price of energy. A significant proportion of current investment thus has to be devoted to restoring past efficiency.

In any case, one result of business's sagging investment commitments is the declining rate of increase in capital per worker, and hence in productivity growth. Table 15.1 shows clearly the close connection between the investment slowdown and the downturn in the rate of productivity advance.

Note that the rate of productivity growth was between a narrow range of 45 percent to 55 percent of the rate of real investment growth for both periods.

Given a work force with a certain level of education, training, and health, the key to productivity growth is innovative technology resulting from research and development, the gains from which are embodied in investment in plants and equipment. In our society,

Table 15.1.

Compound Annual Growth Rate of Real Nonresidential Fixed Investment		Average Annual Growth Rate of Productivity, Private Business Sector*	
1945–66	6.6%	1948–69	3.0%
1966–79	2.6	1969–79	1.4

* The effect of increased investment on productivity is assumed to affect productivity with a lag averaging three years. Hence, investments made in 1945–62 affected productivity in 1948–65.

Source: *Economic Report of the President*, 1980; Bureau of Labor Statistics.

management has practically full control over the decisions leading to expanded investment; workers thus have little or no power to thrust productivity forward. This lack of power leads to a "no-win" situation: while a high rate of productivity growth may lead to job insecurity, the productivity slowdown is largely responsible for the slackening course of real wage and salary increases during the last decade, as table 15.2 below makes clear.

Between 1948 and 1966, output per labor hour grew at an average of 3.0 percent per year. American workers captured much of that productivity progress in the form of rising incomes, as their real (corrected for inflation) average hourly wages increased 2.5 percent a year. (The rest of the productivity advance was spent in nonwage compensation and in profits.) With Vietnam spending competing for resources with domestic civilian investment, productivity increases began to slow after 1966. Despite a strong, war-driven economy characterized by nearly full employment, real earnings started advancing more slowly. Finally, the 1974–79 investment slowdown, noted earlier, pulled down productivity gains, and that, along with record inflation by the end of the period, pulled down real wage growth. In fact, from 1966 through 1979, the total real average hourly earnings increase was less than 8 percent, as compared with almost 31 percent from 1953 to 1966.

ON THE SHOP FLOOR

Management has traditionally held the key to the state of working conditions in the American shop. Making the shop a more suitable environment for human beings leads to a more productive work force. Sometimes, however, productivity—defined in a narrow

Table 15.2.

Years	Average Annual Growth Rate of Productivity, Private Business Sector	Compounded Annual Rate of Growth of Real Nonagricultural Hourly Earnings*
1948–66	3.0%	2.5%
1966–79	1.5	0.6

* Mostly wages; no fringe benefit costs such as health insurance, pensions, and so on, are included.

Source: Bureau of Labor Statistics.

sense—declines rather than grows as a result of changes that common sense tells us should increase workers' productive capacities in the longer haul.

When I worked in the old DeSoto stamping plant (a now defunct division of Chrysler Corporation), a press on the oil-pan line was running all the time. The men had a certain rhythm: The worker on the one side would put the metal in, and the one on the other side would take the oil-pan out. It was very efficient as long as the rhythm kept going, but hands were severed when something suddenly interrupted that rhythm. The union thus insisted on two-hand controls, to make it impossible to have hands under the dies when the press came around: that is, we fought for safety over apparent efficiency.

In the UAW's attempts to win improvements in physical working conditions, we have often found that even elementary remedial steps, such as placing safety guards on dangerous machinery, providing adequate protective clothing, or scouring slippery floors, are usually taken only when they can be shown to coincide with higher profits and measured productivity. Many times, conditions become unsafe or unhealthy because maintenance is reduced in an effort to cut back on indirect labor. Where there is a conflict between productivity and improved conditions, gains must be wrested away from management inch by inch. The matter of relief time is a good example: In 1961, the UAW had to strike General Motors Corporation to win the first 24 minutes of relief time as a matter of right.

Health and safety personnel is another good example: It was not until 1973 that we obtained the right for workers in the big companies to have health and safety representatives. This was one big step in the right direction, but the battle for a healthful and safe work environment was far from over. The average blue-collar worker faces 20 times the chance of injury faced by the desk worker. The injury hazard is indeed so great that blue-collar workers must expect to be hurt at some time during their work lives.

Moreover, occupational disease and illness dwarf injuries as a cause of lost work time; and the blue-collar/white-collar disparity in these areas is just as great. Exposure to heat and noise are among the hazards rampant—if not the rule—in plants throughout industry. In the auto industry, many well-documented hazardous exposures to chemicals and severe safety-standard violations can be found in any major facility. The brutality of the working environment is bound to lower productivity by fostering alienation from the job and compounding the absenteeism problem.

Nothing underscores the insensitivity of management to safety issues more plainly than one company's appeal, all the way to the Supreme Court, of a worker's option to refuse work under life-threatening conditions. The Court's ruling[2] was a victory for labor—employers can no longer force workers to choose between their jobs and their lives—but the point is that management still refuses worker safety as a right.

The excessive overtime periodically forced upon workers is not only hard and disruptive for those working the overtime, it is unfair to the jobless, especially if they are laid off from the same plants that are running overtime. The relevance to the productivity issue is that, as a rule, tired workers turn out a poorer product; both scrappage and the need to rework defects increase. Absenteeism is used by some workers as a defense against having their entire lives controlled by the shop. The UAW first signed agreements on voluntary overtime with the auto companies in 1973, but the struggle remains to be won for the absolute right to a 40-hour week, and ultimately for a shorter workweek, as a standard.

Production standards—the speed at which people are required to work—is a pivotal element of working conditions as well as of productivity. Our contracts recognize management's right to enforce production standards, which are negotiated between management and union locals. Once the work pace is agreed upon, it must remain constant unless the operation is changed or the "normal rate" renegotiated.

In spite of these clearly spelled-out provisions, grievances related to speedup are not uncommon. Perhaps the most bizarre instance took place at a truck plant north of Detroit, where union members discovered a hidden control system. This was used by management to speed up the line by overriding the main speed control, which was in full view of the workers. The company's trickery was exposed and a strike was averted only after management agreed to compensate the workers for the excess production. Events such as this create suspicion and ill will among workers and interfere with the relationship between management and the union.

To summarize, workers' lives in the shop remain under authoritarian domination. Workers are presumed guilty and are subject to punishment until proven innocent. There is only limited opportunity for them to participate meaningfully and creatively in the decision-making process, either relative to their specific jobs or to the actual realm of corporate power, investment decisions.

These conditions indicate a contradiction between the democratic principles on which society as a whole is anchored and the autocracy prevailing at the workplace. Since the early 1970s, this contradiction has been receiving increasing attention. Whatever their motivation—higher rates of absenteeism, the dissatisfaction of a younger, better-educated work force against oppressive authority, and so on—more managements have realized that life at work must change. In the words of a former chairman of General Motors: "We must improve working conditions and take boredom out of routine jobs. We must increase an employe's satisfaction with his job, heighten pride of workmanship and, as far as feasible, involve the employe personally in decisions that relate directly to his job."[3]

Many experiments and projects have been carried out in the United States from this perspective; the UAW has been involved in several of them. The most successful approach so far appears to be the program first adopted between the UAW and the General Motors Corporation in 1973.

During that round of negotiations the union submitted a proposal under which the development and implementation of programs directed at "job enrichment," "humanizing the workplace," or "improving the quality of worklife," as they are variously called, would be a joint union–management effort. A National Joint Committee to Improve the Quality of Worklife was established there, and later in Ford Motor Company. The parties agreed to some general principles on the subject and pledged to urge their respective local managements and local unions to cooperate in these programs. The approach necessarily varies in each situation since, in order to work, the program cannot be imposed from the top down but must be cooperatively and voluntarily developed and implemented from the bottom up.

At the General Motors Corporation, the first phase in setting up a program is to achieve and consolidate a mutually respectful relationship between local union and management. The next step is to set up pilot projects in which workers, on a volunteer basis, become involved in problem solving and participate in making decisions regarding the workplace that had hitherto been denied them. By then, the parties generally have learned to work together more cooperatively, and can jointly analyze conditions that trouble the workers and hence create the opportunity for workers to help resolve them. Whatever is decided is by mutual desire and consent at the local level. The corporation central office and the international union merely advise and consult when called upon.

In a speech at a Work in America Institute conference in Washington, D.C., in December 1979, my friend and colleague Irving Bluestone described the accomplishments of the QWL effort at the General Motors Corporation.[4] The concept had caught on at a number of plants: In early 1980 there were approximately fifty QWL programs at one stage or another of development in UAW–GM bargaining units. Most were still in the early stages—an indication that QWL programs are not "instant utopias" but, rather, follow definite lines or stages of development. He went on to report on the positive findings detected in QWL workplaces (although, admittedly, they may not be attributable solely to the QWL program):

- A more constructive collective bargaining relationship.
- A more satisfied work force.
- Improved product quality, less scrap, fewer repairs.
- Reduction in grievance handling, since problems are more frequently resolved directly as they arise on the shop floor.
- Reduction in absenteeism.
- Reduction in labor turnover—and as a corollary—
- Reduction in the number of disciplinary layoffs and discharges.

These are all mutually desirable objectives. In and of themselves, they represent benefits for the workers and advantages for both the union and management, and they certainly result in a more productive operation. Above all, from the workers' point of view, they add up to one of the most fundamental objectives of unionism: the enhancement of human dignity and self-fulfillment at work.

We recognize, however, that making cars is never going to be the most pleasant of activities. It will, in a word, remain a job rather than a career, a means to an end rather than an end in itself. Therefore, the UAW places great emphasis on reducing the proportion of auto workers' lives spent on the job. Our latest success at this came in 1976 when we developed the new concept of individually scheduled days off, in order to achieve the joint goals of increasing workers' paid leisure time, allowing for utilization of company capacity, and adding to employment. Under that plan, which was expanded in 1979, each worker will have a total of 26 Paid Personal Holidays during the 1980–82 contract. These days occur at approximately one-month intervals, so that about 5 percent of the work force is scheduled off each workday. For the worker who gets the days off, the plan means a periodic break in the 40-hour week. For the company, the plan means that, unlike a holiday on which the entire work force is off, full capacity can continue to be utilized. In particular, while it is expected that the plan will require more workers on the payroll than would otherwise be the case, the number on the job each day is stable. Thus, the company does not need additional plant, equipment, parking facilities, and so on, and is free to direct that capital into investments to improve productivity.

CORPORATE DECISIONS

At the same time that management has kept a tight grip on conditions in the shop, it has decided, practically unchallenged by the rest of society, on levels and composition of investment and on the amount of resources devoted to research and development. These decisions overwhelmingly determine the pace of productivity growth for the corporation.

This lack of challenge is typical of most U.S. unions; they have seldom taken management on over the question of the production process, the mix of people and machines, and the ways they are teamed up. The UAW, for example, has explicitly pledged not to oppose the introduction of productivity-enhancing, labor-saving technological advances. As stated in the UAW contracts with the auto companies as early as 1950:

> The improvement factor (an annual wage increase equal to 3 percent since 1968) provided herein recognizes that a continuing improvement in the standard of living of employees depends upon technological progress; better tools, methods, processes, and equipment; and a cooperative attitude on the part of all parties in

> such progress. It further recognizes the principle that to produce more with the same amount of human effort is a sound economic and social objective.

While that language may be unique to UAW contracts, the American union movement as a whole has, with few exceptions, put up little resistance to productivity-increasing technology. One study showed that the most common response of unions to the introduction of new technology was acceptance.[5] Another study found that by increasing job security and hence reducing turnover, unionization is associated with 20 percent to 25 percent greater productivity than is found in otherwise identical, unorganized workplaces.[6]

The dynamic push to productivity gains is increasingly coming from the electronic controls/semiconductor/microprocessor sector, technologies which can be expected to diffuse throughout industry. There is good reason to believe that the growth emanating from this sector will be qualitatively more displacing of direct labor than economic progress has been in the past. For example, the company that builds the Unimate robots (which first operated in the General Motors Corporation's Lordstown plant), although steadily increasing its output, cannot be considered a "mass production" operation. Even at that scale, the cost of robots has dropped each year. Critical to this argument, Lordstown was able to produce, by the late 1970s, 20 percent more cars per hour using 10 percent fewer workers. Knowing the cost of Unimates and hence the upper limit of the amount of labor they embody, we can be certain that the effect of their introduction is an absolute decline in total labor time. In other words, this is not merely a shift from auto industry labor to steel and robot industry labor—unless car prices fall far enough to increase sales volume, which is unlikely.

In response to this new wave of wafer technology, the UAW has sought new ways to protect its members from displacement. For example, the Statement on Technological Progress, first signed by General Motors and the union in 1967, was amended in the 1979 contract to provide that:

> Advances in technology may alter, modify, or otherwise change the job responsibilities of represented employes at plant locations and that a change in the means, method, or process of performing

a work function, including the introduction of computers or other new or advanced technology, will not serve to shift the work function from represented to nonrepresented employes.

Advance notification provisions were also agreed upon:

Where the initial introduction of new or advanced technology at a plant location may cause a shift of work from represented to nonrepresented employes or otherwise impact the scope of the bargaining unit, Local Management will discuss the matter with the Shop Committee. Such discussion will take place as far in advance of implementation of such a technological change as is practicable. The Local Management will at that time describe for the Shop Committee the extent to which such technological changes may affect the work performed by represented employes at the plant location involved. The Chairman of the Shop Committee and the International Union will be provided a written description of the technology involved, the equipment being introduced, its intended use, and the anticipated installation date(s). Comments by the Shop Committee concerning the information provided will be carefully evaluated by the Local Management in accordance with the Corporation's policy relative to the assignment of work which comes within the scope and content of the work normally assigned to represented employes at the plant location.

Settlements in the assignment of work functions are thus considered within the GM–UAW National Committee on Technological Progress; the tasks of this committee also include discussion of the development of new technology at the corporation level and its impact upon the scope of the bargaining unit. In addition, the committee members discuss technology matters referred to it by local unions or local managements and assess claims of erosion of the bargaining unit.

The advent of this "new" technology presents particular problems going beyond the elimination of jobs. Its inherent flexibility means that management will be capable of continuous, tight control (for example, by systematic recording of production and breakdowns, uninterrupted time studies, and so on) over certain sectors of the work force heretofore subjected only to general monitoring. This trend is objectionable in that it could extend the "big brother" mentality and a lack of freedom to units in the shop where workers have enjoyed the least restraint. The quality of their work life is bound to suffer as a result. Additionally, while some of the jobs performed by computers are hazardous and undesirable, many others are skilled and highly skilled, learned through years of education and experience. Many workers find that, from one day to the next, their jobs are degraded or they are prevented from using their skills.

These problems were addressed in our 1979 negotiations with Ford Motor Company, where the UAW presented a far-reaching document underscoring the concept that new technology must not only improve productivity, but enhance the quality of the work environment as well. The guidelines proposed would disallow the use of computer technology to monitor, time study, or discipline workers; they would bar the use of technology to destroy skills or remove work from the bargaining unit. To ensure that technology be used as a force to benefit rather than victimize workers, meaningful workers' input in the design, development, and use of all technological systems must be assured by notifying and involving the union at the time that the pertinent investment decision is made. Although these demands did not become part of the UAW–Ford agreement, a tone was set for the future.

I foresee workers becoming more and more cognizant of the direct connection between top-level managerial decisions and their immediate welfare. Increasing demands from unions for a role in the process leading to decisions that vitally affect the work force will inevitably follow. These demands stem from setbacks suffered by the rank and file in many areas: labor-saving technological innovations is one of them; the rising tide of plant closings or relocations is another. Countless workers have seen their plants close down and their jobs, income, and other benefits vanish; they have been subjected to lengthy or permanent layoffs due to management's lack of foresight or excess of greed; they have borne the brunt of economic policies that, while sometimes benefiting society as a whole, too often disregard the welfare of those directly affected.

Often, not even society is served well by these decisions. Although supposedly taken in the name of greater efficiency, many times these dislocations reduce rather than increase productivity. Investment funds are wasted in relocating productive facilities in response to relatively small interregional cost differentials, rather than made available to improve output-to-input ratios. The workers thrown out of their jobs are prevented from employing their skills in products or services and instead see them depreciate in forced idleness.

THE UNION RESPONSE

In an effort to alleviate the victimization unleashed on workers by plant closings and relocations, unions have bargained for severance pay, early retirement, and the right to receive a moving allowance and to transfer with the job. Along those lines, in 1979 the General Motors Corporation agreed under the UAW–GM National Agreement to negotiate provisions for the transfer of unionized workers with seniority to all new GM plants manufacturing similar products; this, in effect, means automatic recognition of the union as the bargaining agent for workers in all such new plants.

Other unions have been gaining some protections as well. In the 1979 round of bargaining between the United Rubber Workers and B.F. Goodrich and Uniroyal, pioneering plant-shutdown provisions were negotiated. Those corporations are now contractually required to give the union six months' notice of an intended shutdown. There was also an agreement that the company must now give good faith consideration to union proposals to avert the shutdown or, failing that, the terms on which the closing is to be carried out.

These are still largely reactions to the results of a process, not involvement within the process itself. I predict that in the future merely reacting will be seen as increasingly insufficient to protect and further workers' interests.

The UAW was made painfully aware of these facts in 1979 when the Chrysler Corporation gave the union just one hour's advance notice that it would close one of its largest assembly plants—Dodge Main, in Hamtramck, Michigan—permanently laying off 3,000 workers. The possibility that some different course of action might have been chosen had the union been involved in making the decision convinced us of the wisdom of, and the need to seek, workers' representation on the company's board of directors in the round of negotiations that same year.

My election to that board marked the first time that a major private corporation in the United States proposed and voted in a labor-union official as a director. It did not mark, however, the end of the adversary relationship between ourselves and management: it was never my intention to participate in board deliberations on the corporation's collective bargaining strategy. Incidentally, there is a double standard in the argument that my presence on the board results in a conflict of interest: to my knowledge, there has never been any suggestion that bankers should not sit on the boards of their client corporations.

My intention has been to use my position as a director to be a vigorous advocate for the workers and their needs, and to be a lever for democratizing the workplace. This includes raising and addressing any and all issues which may affect the corporation's workers, including but not limited to those of worker health and safety; plant closings, relocations, asset disposals, and other major investment decisions; product planning and quality; new technology; and affirmative-action employment practices. In this task, I have enjoyed continued access to a unique resource: Chrysler workers, whose ideas and perceptions I am able to transmit.

Despite the many problems, hazards, and disappointments that auto workers have encountered in the workplace, their productivity has grown tremendously. From 1957 to 1978, the average annual rate of change of output per labor hour in the motor vehicle and parts industry was 3.5 percent, substantially higher than the 2.7 percent registered for the entire manufacturing sector.[7] This impressive performance stemmed from an increase in output (number of vehicles adjusted for qualitative and quantitative changes) of 183 percent, accomplished with a 37.5 percent rise in hours.

Still, these official figures undercount—at least in one respect—the productivity gains achieved by auto workers. Official statistics measure the industry's productivity as output per compensated labor hour. The more useful and more correct definition—the one that remains true to our concern with the fruits of a given amount of human effort—would be output per hour worked. Since 1957, when the figures were first published, the increase in hours worked has clearly lagged with respect to compensated hours, as the UAW has won different provisions which translate into more paid time away from the job. The lag has lengthened since 1977: as the paid personal holiday plan described earlier went fully into effect, there was a jump in the relationship between hours compensated and hours worked.

This shortcoming of the official figures is, incidentally, also present in the productivity statistics for the entire private-business sector. A 1978 study shows that a good share of the reported decline in productivity growth up to 1975 "could be explained by a tendency . . . to understate the decline in the workweek" from about forty actual weekly hours in the early 1960s to about 36.8 actual hours in 1975.[8]

THE LEGISLATIVE ARENA

Past experience and future prospects lead me to believe that government has a crucial role to play in ensuring and enhancing productivity growth. However, it must do that by undertaking a more activist role in our economy, rather than—as some suggest—by pulling back and letting private-sector decisions extend the roller-coaster performance of the past.

First and foremost, the administration and Congress can promote a healthy, expanding economy through an adequate mix of fiscal and monetary policies, including "targeted" measures. Economic slowdowns and outright recessions as means to curb inflation must be firmly discarded from the bag of economic policy tools. The recessions of 1969–70 and 1973–75, especially the latter, brought about long spells of low utilization of both industrial capacity and human resources; this in turn acted to significantly depress productivity growth.

The effect of economic conditions on workers' response to technological innovation is documented in a study cited earlier.[9] The author concluded that:

> The state of the economy—in the country as a whole or in the particular segment of it in which the union operates—is the single most important factor underlying a union's response to the introduction of new technology. Normally, if the economy is expanding and alternate work is available as a consequence, technological innovation poses no threat and is readily accepted.

In a contracting economy, in contrast, the opposite is true. Even if the economy in a particular industry is contracting, if like jobs are available in other segments there is likely to be less resistance to change on the part of affected union members.

Second, the government must expand and complement its employment and training programs with investment in the capital equipment needed to improve the productivity of public-service workers. Productivity would thus rise as a consequence of a higher capital/worker ratio; and, if a broader concept of output were used, a topic on which I will comment later, it would also rise as it measured the improvement in the quality of our lives.

Third, the government can undertake public activities which will improve the performance of the entire economy. For example, energy, housing, and railroads are natural targets of a public-investment program. Similarly, the government can contribute to the deceleration in the cost of raw materials, which stands in the way of higher investment, by directing more R&D funds and involving itself more actively in resource extraction and in efforts at substituting renewable for depletable energy sources. This should not always result in the private sector profiting from publicly financed technological breakthroughs. Instead, those technologies should be used in publicly owned industry.

Fourth, government can set tax policy so as to cut unnecessary, inefficient subsidies and privileges to the very rich in the vain hope that they will "trickle down" to productive investment. It also can redirect current special-interest, misallocated subsidies to business toward industries and sectors which can be expected to provide jobs in areas of chronically high unemployment, invest in ventures which will eventually cut input costs, allow the United States to compete more advantageously in world markets, and achieve further advances in technological knowledge. Increased federal support for quality education is instrumental to the latter.

Due to its broad impact and its ramifications, the fight for a workers' role in decisions leading to economic dislocation and for workers' protection must be waged in the legislative rather than in the collective bargaining arena. Moreover, only one U.S. worker in four is protected by a union contract and, given the industrial distribution of unionization, those who need plant-closing protection the most are the least likely to have it. Accordingly, the labor movement, and in particular our own union, has been in vigorous support of protective legislation in Congress.

Federal regulations have often been cited as both inflationary and detrimental to productivity growth. While the UAW would look favorably upon several instances of deregulation, regulations such as OSHA, those having to do with environmental quality, and others, should not be tampered with on the grounds that their loss would exacerbate inflation and would be too costly to society. Most of those regulations enhance the quality and the length of human life and most unavoidably—and in a broad sense—lead to a better, more productive society.

WHO WANTS WHAT?

In spite of this, business continues to steadfastly resist protective legislation, as events of the past several years must convince even the most confirmed skeptic. In 1978, the business community blocked the Labor Law Reform Bill, even though the law would not have organized a single worker. Why then? Because it would have limited the freedom of employers to deny workers the opportunity to decide whether or not to be represented by unions.

Nor has this been an isolated incident. The same principle—human rights in work—is at issue in the serious attack on OSHA mounted by business in 1980, after an endless stream of skirmishes against that landmark piece of legislation. We are confident that any crippling assault on OSHA will be beaten back; however, we cannot ignore the fact that business would jeopardize the health and safety of million of workers in a misguided effort to improve efficiency and reduce costs. How can business expect cooperation from workers in the drive for greater productivity if it offers only confrontation in return?

This, of course, raises the question, "Is business interested in the same kind of social progress as labor?" Are both business and labor committed to more and more socially useful output from less and less work per person? I believe that they are not and that, as a result, workers and their unions need to redefine "productivity" so that its pursuit will mean genuine human progress rather than just intensified exploitation.

Consider the inadequacy of current definitions of productivity, particularly the systematic undercounting of output:

- Productivity figures tell us nothing about whether life is made easier, richer, or longer for most individuals. Accordingly, it has been proposed that output measures should include increases in quality of life: literacy, life expectancy, and infant mortality, to name a few. While these measures would not be sufficient as an overall productivity indicator, they are important evidence that productivity data undercount human progress.
- Productivity data do not show the social costs of many activities. When a factory pollutes air and water, when strip mining defaces the earth, when poor education leaves a student unable to get and hold a job, there is no attempt to adjust the output of these activities for their negative byproducts, nor, consequently, to adjust productivity statistics.
- Productivity generally doesn't measure the benefits of any activity that isn't paid for. When a family member takes better, faster care of the home and children, for example, productivity data remain unchanged even though more is being done in the same amount of time.
- When safer working conditions prevent accidents or illness, there may be no increase in physical output, and therefore no change will show up in productivity data.
- Productivity data count all outputs the same. The increase is the same whether output is of things that are really needed—housing, transportation, medical care—or of fad, luxury, or war-related items. Increases in social-service spending and, until 1977, decreases in the military share of GNP, suggest that useful output probably grew faster in the last decade than before; yet productivity figures fail to reflect this.
- Output doesn't reflect the distribution of income; therefore, productivity data do not measure progress toward increased equality. Imagine a country with a few people who are very rich and many who are very poor. If, without changing the total volume of goods and services produced, output is shared more

equitably, no change would show up in output or productivity data, despite the fact that the poor would gain more "satisfaction" than the rich would lose from redistribution.

In fact, productivity is so unreliable a measure of how an economy is advancing that the data may indicate exactly the opposite of what is really happening. For example, when cancer dangers in a workplace are reduced through a new manufacturing process that slightly reduces output per hour, productivity is measured as declining. Yet, productivity should be tending upward due to the increased welfare and life expectancy of the workers being spared.

CONCLUSION

Workers remain prey to many problems: overtime, hazardous and unpleasant working conditions, job security, unequal or unsatisfactory pay. These problems carry consequences for productivity, including high absenteeism, high turnover, and low motivation.

The UAW posture toward these problems is well known. We favor productivity growth, but feel that workers and consumers must share in the benefits of that growth. We do what we can to shorten hours and work careers, and we carefully monitor work pace in order to be certain that our members are not made the victims of illegitimate ways to raise productivity. We look closely, on a case-by-case basis, at many alleged problems and alleged solutions. In several instances, we are working with management to look at what can be done to improve attendance and reduce absenteeism. The UAW also participates in employee involvement programs at several companies, and our members have, in a few cases, taken part in Scanlon Plans, profit-sharing programs, employee stock option plans, and the like. The bottom line, however, is not productivity as it is traditionally measured but the kind of lives that a highly productive economy allows its citizens. If the road to that kind of economy—humane, safe, equitable, and fully employed—also raises the government productivity figures, so much the better.

But there are many things that are far more important to society's productiveness than the motivational factors that labor is always asked to comment upon: the uneven quality of education, the lack of access to adequate health care—all of these are part of a national economy policy content with having millions of people unemployed and many more millions of people living in poverty, a policy whose victims must find it hard to reconcile with rhetorical concern for "productivity."

Workers know that higher productivity without higher output means unemployment. Until a full-employment economy becomes a reality, society cannot expect nor demand unambiguous employee participation for productivity improvement. The solution to the problem of the displaced and the jobless requires a far greater measure of public economic planning—for people's needs rather than for private profit—backed up both by substantial public control over private investment and disinvestment decisions, and by direct public investment.

NOTES

1. Betty M. Jacob, and Philip E. Jacob, "Automation and Humanization," (draft) Research Corporation of the University of Hawaii, August 20, 1979, p. 91.
2. Decision of the United States Supreme Court in Whirlpool Corporation vs. Marshall, February 26, 1980.
3. Richard M. Gerstenberg. Speech at a Tax Foundation dinner, New York City, December 6, 1979.
4. Irving Bluestone. Speech at a conference on "Critical Economic and Work Force Issues Facing Western Countries," sponsored by Work in America Institute, Inc., Washington, D.C., December 6, 1979.
5. Doris McLaughlin, *The Impact of Labor Unions on the Rate and Direction of Technological Innovation* (Ann Arbor, Mich.: Institute of Labor and Industrial Relations, University of Michigan, 1978), p. 100.
6. Charles Brown, and James Medoff, "Trade Unions in the Production Process," *Journal of Political Economy* 86 (June 1978): 355–378.
7. Bureau of Labor Statistics, U.S. Department of Labor.
8. Frank Stafford, and Greg Duncan, "Market Hours, Real Hours, and Labor Productivity," *Economic Outlook U.S.A.*, Survey Research Center, University of Michigan 5 (Autumn 1978).
9. Doris McLaughlin, op. cit., p. 103.

Index

Index